SWAGGER

SWAGGER

10 URGENT RULES for raising boys in an era of failing schools, mass joblessness, and thug culture

LISA BLOOM

A THINK PUBLICATION
in association with

Vantage Point Books and the Vantage Point Books colophon
are registered trademarks of Vantage Press, Inc.
FIRST EDITION: May 2012

Published by Vantage Point Books
Vantage Press, Inc.
419 Park Avenue South
New York, NY 10016
www.vantagepointbooks.com

Manufactured in the United States of America
ISBN: 978-1-936467-69-3

Library of Congress Cataloging-in-Publication data are on file.

0   9   8   7   6   5   4   3   2   1

Cover design by Victor Mingovits

*To my son, Sam,
and my daughter, Sarah—
my best work*

CONTENTS

PART ONE
THE FORCES ALIGNED AGAINST YOUR BOY

PART TWO
TEN RULES FOR RAISING BOYS RIGHT NOW

INTRODUCTION

THE URGENCY OF FIGHTING FOR OUR BOYS' BRAINS

AT THIS very moment, through no fault of their own, our boys are caught in the vortex of four powerful, insidious, often invisible forces that conspire to rob them of their future.

First, our heartbreakingly subpar schools. To say that twenty-first-century America doesn't value education is like saying Donald Trump doesn't prioritize humility. Class sizes grow, as kids sit on the floor or are crammed into "temporary" classrooms in hallways or bathrooms. School buildings crumble, leak, and emit toxic fumes. Junk-food school lunches make our kids sick and fat (while bloating the profits of giant food processing companies), dropping their test scores.[1] Teachers are reduced to begging on charity websites for books for first graders. At even the best schools our kids graduate without knowing the basics of US history or the rudiments of science. Our kids already enjoy some of the shortest school days and school years in the developed world. And now we are witnessing a new sickening trend: in over one hundred counties in America, state budget cuts have pared the school week down to only four days. *Hooray! An extra day every week to watch* Fear Factor *and play* Xbox!

The minds of our children matter so little that we barely notice how many of them are now checking out of school. Only one in three Baltimore kids graduates from high school.[2] For those who stay in, the news isn't much better: one in five American high school seniors graduates illiterate. And every miserable bit of education news skews worse for boys. Boys underperform compared to girls in every grade and subject. They're medicated, disciplined, suspended, and expelled far more often than girls are. In what should be in screaming, fist-sized headlines daily, nationwide the *majority* of our African American and Hispanic boys drop out of high school. Some of our schools are little more than holding pens, releasing antsy, angry, unskilled young men into our communities.

There, young men are pounded by the second force: the harshest economy facing graduates and dropouts since the Great Depression. Economists may debate whether or not we are officially in a recession, but there's no doubt that our economy falters, as thirteen million are unemployed, nine million are underemployed, and millions more "discouraged" workers have given up on looking for a job altogether. For young men the numbers are even worse than the painful national averages. For them, the jobless rate hovers at *18 percent*—four million young American men who want to contribute and earn an income and support themselves and their families, but who just can't find a job. Like the rest of America's jobless, they'll likely resort to relying on public assistance. An astonishing forty-six million Americans today need food stamps (now issued on debit cards), a huge jump in the last two years.[3] So many people run out of food at the end of the month that Walmart now opens many stores at 12:01 a.m. on the days the cards are loaded, to allow for the midnight rush of hungry Americans.[4]

One hundred million Americans are now poor or near poor.[5]

Traditionally "male" jobs? They are mostly gone, and they are not coming back. Most of the jobs lost since the Great Recession commenced in 2008 disappeared from the predominately male sectors such as manufacturing. In 1992 presidential candidate Ross Perot warned of the giant sucking sound we'd hear if the North American Free Trade Agreement passed, sending American jobs to Mexico, but even Perot could not have imagined the gargantuan vacuum created when millions of American manufacturing jobs were siphoned off to China, India, and elsewhere. Those jobs are now extinct in America. The giant sucking sound turned out to be a muted, steady bleed-out of the blue-collar male work force.

As they are negotiating their way through our miserable schools and jobless economy, our popular culture—the third soul-leeching, invisible force—seduces our boys with flashy, loud messages that manhood equals macho bravado, emotional numbness, ignorance, and thugdom. "Man enough to pull a gun, be man enough to squeeze it," raps NBA star Allan Iverson. "I'm a leader, not a reader," said a once-leading presidential candidate in 2011, as if the two are mutually exclusive.[6] As our sons turn away from books and school and knowledge and critical thinking, the alarming new idea that "reading is girly" has caught on among them. Glamorization of drug use has increased six-fold in rap and hip-hop music, a genre that once warned "don't do it!"; now a full 69 percent of songs in these genres contain positive references to illegal drugs.[7] "I got mushrooms, I got acid, I got tabs," raps Eminem, idol to many boys, *"I'm your brother when you need some new weed...I'm your friend."* [8]

There is one road for boys who don't overcome their failing schools, who aren't exceptional enough to find a job where there is none, who absorb the message that real men express anger via gun violence or who use or sell drugs to escape or to make a few bucks, and that road has one dead-end terminus: our ever-expanding, bursting-to-the-seams prisons. Our prison population has skyrocketed to its highest level in US history, *more than any other country on earth now or in human history,* more than anyone could have imagined a generation ago, more than we have ever had by any measure—raw numbers, percentage of our population, you name it. Largely casualties of our misguided War on Drugs, which has caused the number of incarcerated Americans to quadruple since 1980, over two million of our people are locked up, 93 percent of them men and boys, with another nearly five million under an increasingly restrictive system of correctional control in lieu of or after incarceration. This fourth potent force, mass incarceration, deprives its subjects of a future by literally locking them in cages. Criminalizing human behavior like never before, our judges are required by law to mete out increasingly punitive, long sentences, even for children. Even after inmates are released, they remain under the heavy-handed control of the criminal justice system for years or for life, often unable to vote, get a job, secure housing, or support a family.

In the United States, one man out of eighteen is incarcerated or on probation or parole, and more are locked up every day. We may be the last country on the planet to lock up juveniles—overwhelmingly boys—for life-without-parole sentences for crimes committed when they were minors.

New prisons are under construction as you read this, waiting to house the next generation of American boys.

———

BORN INTO this user-unfriendly world, one not of their choosing and entirely beyond their control, our sons need us now more than ever. Ensnared by these four powerful forces—failing schools, an unwelcoming economy, thug culture, and a harshly punitive justice system—more boys and young men than ever are on the sidelines, cut out of a middle-class life, scratching their heads as to how that happened. Although women and girls suffer under these conditions too, there's no question that, on the whole, these forces disproportionately hammer our boys.

To help them, we need to understand deeply the waters in which our boys swim. Parents, family members, teachers—all of us who care about boys—need to know. Closing our eyes and hoping for the best won't cut it, not when our boys live in the real world. And so the first half of this book is an unvarnished, clear-eyed look at what our sons are facing, day in and day out, right now, as they navigate through boyhood and emerge as young men, yearning for a decent life.

Knowing matters. Without an awareness of each of these conditions and how they whipsaw our boys, we as parents may apply obsolete attitudes that unintentionally harm them. For example, we may think that although we didn't finish school, we've still done all right, and although we'd all like our sons to graduate, if they don't, they'll probably get by. Wrong. The job market for young men has changed dramatically in the last decade. Or we may think that the older generation has always objected to kids' music, and we'd sound like fuddy-duddies if we complained. Wrong. We're not talking about a little racy innuendo; some of the biggest artists today advocate joining the Crips, punching your girlfriend, or murdering gay men. You need to know. You need to stare down the reality and critically discuss media messages with your boy. In these and so many other areas, knowledge is power when raising your son to manhood.

———

THESE ARE challenging times not only for boys but also for parents and nearly everyone in the bottom 99 percent of American families. Layoffs and foreclosures slam us directly or, if we still have jobs and homes, threaten us like dark clouds overhead that never seem to dissipate. Discouraged but soldiering on, we adapt and endure. Resigned, many adults grudgingly accept less for ourselves: a harder life than we expected, a less fulfilling job, living in a depressed neighborhood. We muddle through. We postpone our dreams. We adjust.

But when we become parents, something stirs. Mothers and fathers look at their sleeping babies, and they awaken. Although we'll put up with doors closing in our own lives, we will *not* accept bleak futures for our children. Not a single one of us. It is deeply encoded in our parenting DNA to want—*to clamor for*—more for them, to sacrifice our time and effort and dollars to give them that better life. Immigrant parents leap across rivers and oceans and borders like Superman to give their children opportunities they never had. A party girl brings a life into being and suddenly she's Wonder Woman, casting off her old ways, assuming the mantle of protector, insisting on the best for her son. A one-time slacker-dad internalizes Spiderman's credo: *with great power comes great responsibility.* We rise to the occasion.

Singlehandedly, we may not be able to turn around our failing schools, our dumbed-down and punitive culture, or our stagnant economy. (Though we can and should push back at every opportunity.) But there is a great deal we as parents can do at little or no cost to give our boys the advantages they need right now to jack up their odds of finishing high school, going to college, and leading a decent, free life in which they can not only support a family but also contribute to their communities. Because parenting can't wait. Our boys are growing up *now*, in conditions they did not create, and they deserve more than an adulthood defined by illiteracy, poverty, and reporting to a parole officer.

This book will show you how. There is much good news: research-proven, parent-tested, teacher-approved solutions. These steps are mostly free or cheap, can be done anywhere by nearly any caring adult, and will significantly boost your boy's chances of surviving and thriving notwithstanding all the hurdles our culture throws in his path. Powerful forces may be aligned against him, but his number-one role model has always been and always will be you: Mom, Dad, or the grown-up who has the guts to step up to the plate for him.

Give your boy a hug, don your superhero cape, and let's begin.

A Preliminary Note: Why Boys?

WHY IS this book about boys rather than all our kids—boys *and* girls? Shouldn't we be concerned about *girls'* literacy, for example, and making sure that they too stay in school, fend off negative cultural messages, and become adults who find productive work so that they can support their families too?

Hell, yes, we should!

In fact, I didn't intend to write about the dumbing down of our guys, at least not initially. I figured that would go over about as well as a Jane Austen reading in a strip club. I wrote my first book about my own team, we of the XX chromosomes, *Think: Straight Talk for Women to Stay Smart in a Dumbed-Down World.* There, I blast away at a culture that persistently rewards girls for looks over brains; detail our out-of-control female obsession with reality shows, celebrities, tabloids, and the beauty industry; and outline the real-world harms this causes to our psyches, families, neighborhoods, and world. For females in twenty-first-century America, it's the best of times (we are killing it in education, for example) and the worst of times (25 percent of young women would rather win *America's Next Top Model* than the Nobel Peace Prize...*are you kidding me?*).

As I said all along, the problem of American ignorance applies equally to both genders. The distractions may be different (girls: *Real Housewives*, TMZ; guys: ESPN, *Call of Duty*), but the lack of focus, the disconnection, is the same or, perhaps, even worse for guys.

At my speaking events around the country, parents would talk to me about the challenges of raising girls, but they would also tell me about the problems they were having with their sons: falling behind in school; addiction to video games; inability to communicate socially; music, TV, and films that encourage boys to become macho jerks; how hard it was for them to get their son to pick up a book.

I wrote an article, "How to Talk to Little Girls," exhorting us to refrain from talking to young girls about how they look and instead encouraging us to engage their minds.[9] To my surprise and delight, "How to Talk to Little Girls" went viral and became Facebook's twelfth-most-shared article of 2011. Millions of people read it all over the globe. I did interviews in Ireland, Australia, and all over the English-speaking world about how to speak intelligently to our daughters. And during these interviews, and in the subsequent e-mails, tweets, and Facebook messages came: *what about boys?*

As the mother of both a daughter and a son, I could hardly ignore half the population. I began to research what's going on with the male side of our country. And what I found shocked me and upended some of what I thought I knew.

I gloated a little in *Think* about how much better girls are now doing in school compared to boys, for instance. But now I see the error in that. Because the more I read the studies, the more I spoke to parents and teachers, the more I came to see that this educational achievement gap and especially our boys' stunningly low reading proficiency is a painful, festering problem that follows boys as they grow into men, affecting nearly every aspect of their lives. I now saw problems for boys everywhere, and I saw how dismal the future is for boys who aren't thriving. I myself was guilty of a great deal of thinking that is now outdated in our new economic order. I realized that the information I was discovering wasn't being reported much. (Don't get me started on how idiotic most of our media is—*oh look! breaking news about Snooki's latest drunken arrest!*) I'd poured myself into my first book about how girls and women have gone off track. Now, I realized, I had to scrutinize the gritty problems facing our boys. And thus, this book was born.

Does some of *Think* apply to boys? Sure. Does some of this book apply to girls? Yes. Is everything a bright-line gender issue? Of course not. But there is no getting around facts like the beauty industry markets almost entirely to women (and its incessant ads make us feel ugly and flawed), and *Grand Theft Auto* is overwhelmingly played by boys (and depicts for them a manhood defined by fighting, guns, and violence). The research is clear that boys are much harder hit in certain areas, such as illiteracy and juvenile detention. Often, children's role models differ by gender: few girls model themselves on hard-core rappers or display the unhealthy swagger that infects our boys.

Gender still marks so much of how the world approaches us. (To those who break out of traditional gender molds, I salute you.) So a quick note about generalizations: as a lifelong feminist (my dad used to say I needed "consciousness lowering"), I bristle at gender stereotypes—false claims made about an entire group. "Women are lousy drivers." "Men are better with money." Uh, no. Statistically speaking, the reverse of each of those statements is true, as we shall see. Sadly, every day assumptions are still made about individual women and men based on sexist stereotypes, ignoring individual talents and merit. A woman is perceived as "softer," less promotable, and less of a leader simply because of her gender. A man is told he wouldn't be as good at caring for children because "women are naturally better caregivers." Pernicious biases restrict individuals from demonstrating their own unique gifts, training, and skills.

I do not traffic in gender stereotypes, I assure you. I simply follow the research to see what it tells us about girls and boys, women and men, and report it to you straight. When I found a small but statistically insignificant bit of information, I left it out. We have enough silly stereotypes percolating around our culture without me adding to it. Instead, this book brings you clear trends about what's happening for our boys. I aim to open a window into their world, supported by interviews, facts, and data, and to provide workable, boy-tested solutions.

And naturally, every child is different. Even in our thuggish, hypermacho culture, there are boys who are gentle, who love art and theater and dance, who are kind and compassionate.

In our failing schools there are boys who read Shakespeare on their own and check out ten library books at a time. Despite the drumbeat of bad news for minorities, I met Latino and African American boys in East Harlem who are beating the private school kids in advanced robotics competitions. Although particular cultural pressures are at play for boys generally, your son—every boy—is unique and deserves to be loved and approached as he is.

He's not a statistic; he's one-of-a-kind. Of course. I get that. I have a son too.

PART ONE

THE FORCES ALIGNED AGAINST YOUR BOY

CHAPTER ONE

EDUCATION: NO LONGER A NATIONAL PRIORITY

"I think by far the most important bill in our whole code is that for the diffusion of knowledge among the people. No other sure foundation can be devised for the preservation of freedom, and happiness.... Crusade against ignorance; establish and improve the law for educating the common people." [10]

—THOMAS JEFFERSON, 1786

How bad are our schools?

LET'S BEGIN at the end, with results—or lack thereof. One in five American adults can't read a simple storybook to their children, according to President Obama. Only one in twelve white seventeen-year-olds can pick up a local newspaper and understand the science section. For Hispanics the number drops to one in fifty; for African Americans it's one in one hundred.[11] To state the painfully obvious, the science section of a newspaper (or news site) is written for a *lay audience*, without the expectation of any specialized knowledge or training in biology, chemistry, or physics. And virtually none of our teenagers is capable of reading it.

Europeans and East Asians consistently, mercilessly, slaughter our high school and college students of both genders in international academic competitions. Compared to young people in thirty developed countries, American students rank twenty-first in science and twenty-fifth in math. Even our crème de la crème are at the bottom of the heap in international competitions. If we skim off our best performers, the top 10 percent of American students, they still rank a dismal twenty-fourth out of thirty developed countries in numeracy (math literacy).[12] (Shanghai, China, is number one in every category, and education-focused South Korea, Singapore, and Hong Kong are all in the top ten, dramatically trouncing US kids.[13])

Only a third of our fourth graders are proficient in reading at their grade level. Two-thirds of American fourth graders can't read these sentences: "What do bees do? Bees make honey and they sting."[14]

I asked college students in the spring of 2011 to name an issue currently before the US Congress. Any issue. Anyone? (*Bueller...? Bueller...?*) Most could not name a single one. One young man came up with only "NFL work stoppage?"

At that time we were in the midst of three wars and the worst economic crisis since the Great Depression.

"Where are our troops actively engaged in combat operations?" I asked.

Crickets. Most common answer: "I don't know."

Other students guessed wildly.

"Morocco?"

"China?"

"Japan?"

"Mexico?"

This, as their peers flew warplanes over Libya or came home in coffins from Iraq and Afghanistan.

The lack of knowledge and skills isn't limited to our children. *What is the Taliban?* Forty-two percent of Americans don't know, though nearly two thousand Americans have perished in the longest war in US history—the conflict in Afghanistan—in large part fighting that extremist sect. (But, hey, over 90 percent of us can correctly identify actor Mel Gibson, who made headlines for anti-Semitic rants and a domestic violence conviction, and Britney Spears, who for a time dominated the "news" for erratic behavior that caused her to lose custody of her young children.)

One sad example: almost half the adults in Detroit today are functionally illiterate. That's right. In a major American city one in two cannot read or write in any meaningful way—not a book, not a magazine, not a warning sign, not a prescription bottle. It gets worse. Only 10 percent of those who are unable to read have made attempts to learn how.[15] Why not? Despair, maybe. Or simply the fact that we live in an anti-intellectual culture in which knowledge and learning and even literacy are not particularly valued.

And perhaps worst of all, I learned about this only from a tiny news story buried in a little-read newsweekly, *The Week.* There's no outcry. No politicians slamming their fists, declaring—our favorite American metaphor—"war on illiteracy." Thomas Jefferson exhorted us to "crusade against ignorance," but that's not happening, even as we are drowning in it. Twenty-seven million illiterate Americans can't read a job application.[16] Yet no talk show hosts vituperate on the subject, no groundswell of concern percolates, no candidates pound the podium, demanding swift action as crowds roar approval. No screaming yellow headlines blare:

WE CAN'T READ OR WRITE! HELP! SOMEBODY HELP!

If our schools were factories, we'd shut them down for producing defective products.

It's not the fault of our kids or even our teachers or administrators, many of whom, as we shall see, struggle valiantly in the trenches against all odds. Our failing schools are a direct result of our culture's deprioritization of education. Outside of academic journals and an occasional mention, our mainstream media and our country yawn over the entire topic of our slipping intellectual abilities.

We don't know what we don't know, and mostly, we don't care.

When in Doubt, Cut Education!

INDIVIDUALLY, OF course, many of us—especially parents—value education. We move to a better public school district; beg, borrow, and steal to send our kids to private school; drive them to enrichment activities; volunteer in the classroom; oversee homework. The problem is that parents who do these and other laudable activities are swimming against the powerful current of our country's lackadaisical attitude about the importance of schools.

How do we know for sure that we don't prioritize education? A look at how little time we set aside for our kids to learn will swiftly answer that question. Our kids have one of the shortest school *days* (six and a half hours) and shortest school *years* (180 days of instruction, on average) in the first world.[17] Though our kids start strong, the longer they stay in American schools, the worse they do relative to kids in other developed countries. By twelfth grade American kids—both male and female—have lost an *entire year* of school compared to other first-world students. And there's no political will to change this shortfall, no rising up of the masses to demand better for our kids and our country's future.

The trend is not to remedy this by giving our kids additional school hours and days but rather to keep our kids out of school *more*. When budget cuts come, class time goes—over and over again. Where can we cut further? Hmm, let's see. When it comes to schools, we've already cut so much. Hey, how about…

school *weeks*? Hawaii and then a bunch of rural counties in New Mexico and Idaho recently cut their kids' regular school weeks to just four days.[18] They decided that when it came to spending priorities, a five-day school week was fat that could be trimmed. And so, quietly, with little public discussion, 120 school districts nationwide now give their schoolchildren a three-day weekend, week in and week out of their pitifully short school year.

Proponents of the four-day school week cite improved student "morale" as a benefit.[19] Hey, if we canceled school altogether and served kids candy for breakfast, lunch, and dinner, kids' spirits would go through the roof! But this isn't about smiley faces; it's about slashing a service our culture now deems nonessential: educating our kids.

The question is framed not as "How can we improve our kids' schools?" but instead "Where else can we cut?" Summer school has long been an important place to give kids the remedial instruction they need when they have fallen behind during the school year. Students who go are better able to retain what they learn during the school year and do significantly better when they return in the fall, especially in math. No matter. My hometown, Los Angeles, slashed summer learning programs three years in a row, most recently from their 2010 level of $18 million to just $3 million in 2011.[20]

The message: *Having trouble in school, kid? You're on your own.*

Oregon's public schoolchildren go to school only 165 days per year.[21] This means that for the majority of their days—200 per year—those kids sit at home, watching television and playing video games. We need to get over our fantasies that kids are building tree forts or swinging from tires during their days off. In their free time American kids are staring at screens. Our children pack in an average of eight to eleven hours a day watching TV, playing computer games, surfing the web, texting, or talking on their cell phones. They're either in class or they're playing *Angry Birds* (or both). Down time is screen time, period.[22] Winter, spring, summer, and fall—and on every single one of those generous vacation days we give them.

Slashing education is all the rage, and it's getting worse. Coast to coast, 2011 was a banner year for cutting anything and everything related to schools, as lawmakers nationwide hacked away at programs that had already been cut to the bone, dramatically increasing class sizes, lowering academic standards, and eliminating textbooks, tutors, art, music, and bilingual programs. Enrichment programs for gifted students, help for struggling readers, advanced math and science courses, drama, sports programs—gone.[23] Show me your neighborhood public school and I will show you despairing administrators, teachers facing jam-packed classrooms, and kids who miss out on what for many of us were the best parts of school: music, theater, or the track team.

When Public Education Is Not Free

WE'VE BECOME so accepting of slashing education that we've contorted ourselves into some odd "solutions." For example, for decades schools have accepted free "educational" materials from private companies. Let's call that what it is: direct-to-child advertising, circumventing the messiness of parental involvement. Two-thirds of the five hundred largest US industrial corporations pony up for these handouts and videos on nutrition, energy, the environment, and economics. Think corporate America is providing unbiased information in the public interest, unrelated to their goal of increasing their profits? Then I have some oceanfront land in Kansas I can sell you. These materials are designed to prime young people to become lifelong consumers of their products.[24]

For example, children are bombarded with dairy industry advertising in the classroom, in the form of pamphlets and other teaching aids, encouraging them to drink up to six glasses of milk a day, notwithstanding the large number of kids suffering from lactose intolerance or milk allergies or the whopping quantities of fat and cholesterol whole-milk products deliver to our children, who are already beset by an obesity epidemic. Dairy industry executives are open about the fact that these materials are a marketing tool for them, intended to "lay a foundation for industry promotion efforts...to motivate Americans to take the action we want them to take even more frequently—consuming milk and other dairy foods."[25] There's a growing body of scientific evidence that dairy products cause myriad health problems.[26] Health classes could center on reading the scientific literature on the subject, analyzing the studies, and discussing them pro and con. That they don't—instead teaching only from the multibillion-dollar industry's one-sided advertising materials on the subject—is a travesty.

Another foolhardy response to these school budget cuts is the imposition of fees on public school students. No longer free across the board, public schools around the country are now billing families for basic and advanced classes as well as extracurricular activities. The bill for Spanish I, Earth Science, band, and after-school sports totaled over $4,446.50 for one family with four children in Medina, Ohio, public schools. Fees like $235 for registration, $350 to join chess club, $200 to participate in Students Against Drunk Driving, $85 to write for the literary magazine, and $50 to clean up beaches with the Environmental Club are not uncommon, according to the *Wall Street Journal*.[27] (In my day we were allowed to pick up trash for free!) After-school clubs are not only fun, team-building, leadership-training experiences for our kids, often granting them some sorely needed exercise and fresh air; colleges also want to see extracurricular activities on student's applications. Yet students in families on fixed incomes—which are most students—are now, in effect, fined for getting involved on their own time to improve themselves and their communities. In Medina, for example, more than half the 192-member high school track team quit after $660 school sports fees were imposed.

Worse, some kids are forced to skip expensive Advanced Placement classes or advanced science classes that have high lab or technology fees. *We are pricing kids out of higher-level thinking classes.*

It's not all bad, the Medina Superintendent told the *Journal.* "Students have to realize, as our country is realizing, that you can't have everything. We all have to make tough choices." What—hello? How is that an upside? Education didn't used to be considered a "tough choice," and those young people who opted for math, science, and language instruction as well as sports and arts programs weren't accused of greedily "wanting everything." They were considered admirable, well-rounded, hardworking students. In my high school we had an award for the kid who had the most breadth of academic achievement and extracurricular involvement: Best All-Around. American families in public schools didn't used to have to choose between a daughter taking AP English and a son playing a musical instrument in the band. Now they do.

How do school districts get away with this? Isn't there a law somewhere that public school activities are supposed to be free and open to all, regardless of income? Sometimes. Beyond Medina, when over fifty California districts required students to purchase required textbooks and workbooks for academic courses, charged lab fees for science classes and material fees for fine arts classes, and required students to purchase school-issued P.E. uniforms, the American Civil Liberties Union sued. After all, the California Constitution states unambiguously that all students shall receive a "free and equal education." The ACLU alleges that charging students hundreds—and in some cases thousands—of dollars to participate in school-sponsored extracurricular activities, violates the "free and equal" Constitution clause. A little boy with the pseudonym Jason Roe had to go to class without a chemistry manual or Spanish workbook because his family could not afford those materials. Other kids, the ACLU alleges, were humiliated by teachers, having their names written on the board or docked with a lower grade when they failed to show up with required purchases or when their families were unable to pay as much as $440 in fees.[28]

Shortly after the ACLU filed its suit, the California Department of Education put a stop to those fees statewide. Apparently in California, "free" really does mean "free." It helped that a 1984 California Supreme Court had made things pretty clear: "In guaranteeing free public schools, article IX section 5 [of the state constitution] fixes the precise extent of the financial burden which may be imposed on the right to an education—none."[29] Unable to get around that, school districts were ordered to stop charging kids like Jason. (This ruling applies only in California. Other states are able to continue imposing fees on public school families due to differing state laws.)

Good news? Yes, in the short run. Schools had to stop charging families for educational necessities; Jason was issued his books. But the shortfall remained. Where would the money come from now, as the state had cut so much education funding? Once those fees were eliminated, music, cooking, arts, and speech and debate teachers worried they wouldn't be able to cover class expenses and would either have to cancel classes or resort to what teachers across America have been doing for years: dipping into their own pocket to pay for class materials. In a phenomenon called "teacher-funded classrooms," 92 percent of public school teachers purchase pencils, markers, notebooks, scissors, bulletin boards, books, computers, and other necessary classroom supplies, averaging $450 per year per teacher.[30]

Teacher-funded classrooms are a particularly unfair "solution" to our slashed school budgets. The average starting teacher salary is $39,000 per year—considered "poor" or "near poor" by the US Census, depending on region, especially if that teacher is supporting a family, as many are.[31] These good folks are the closest adults to the problem of school budget deficits, acutely aware on a daily basis of what their classrooms lack. They know state funding isn't there for them or their classrooms full of kids. So they shrug and dig into their own pocketbooks to provide for our kids.

Is there *anyone* who thinks this is right?

―――――

I OBSERVED California's 2006 Charter Teacher of the Year, Brad Koepenick, a lively, gangly former actor (*ER, Scrubs*) grab the attention of a diverse group of public high school juniors in his performance art class. "'Dear Bully,'" he told a class of rapt teenagers. "That's your project for the next five minutes. Paper out! Get ready!" Paper and pens zipped out of backpacks in a mass display of responsiveness that would make any teacher proud. "Everyone in this class has been bullied at some time, by someone, someone who made you feel afraid or abused or humiliated." The students' eyes registered this acknowledgement of their pain. Several nodded quietly. "Write a letter to that bully, and be prepared to deliver it," Koepenick continued. "'Dear Bully,' your essay begins. You do the rest. Go!" They considered, soberly. Girls twirled their hair. Boys twirled earrings. Then, they wrote. Everyone scribbled diligently in their notebooks.

When time was up, eager students stood to deliver heartfelt prose, standing up to long-ago tormentors or yesterday's oppressor. Next, "Dear Bullied." What? The students were baffled. "That's right," Koepenick said, "each of you has been on the other side of this. Think of cyberbullying. That picture you posted, that mean status update. What do you want to say to your victim now? 'Dear Bullied,' your essay begins. Go!" Once again, students sweated and grieved and cogitated, then put pen to page, and stood and delivered their impromptu confessional apologies, some deeply moving.

Koepenick is the kind of teacher whose classes fill up quickly, who inspires and energizes his students. In less than an hour his kids advanced their writing and public speaking skills as well as discussed an important topic in their lives: bullying. But like every other public school teacher in America today, Koepenick can't just focus on teaching. Money, or, more specifically, the lack of funding for his basic classroom needs looms large in his mind.

Actually, I use the term "classroom" euphemistically. Teacher of the Year or not, Koepenick *has no classroom.* His classes meet outside, at lunch tables, competing with city noises and weather for students' attention. Kids wrote their essays with coats zipped up, woolen hats on their heads. A little embarrassed when he first told me to meet him at the lunch tables for his class, later Koepenick said, "Oh, no, it's fine having class outside!" putting a brave face on it.

For an upcoming media project for the class, Koepenick casually told the kids he needed some film projectors. "I went on DonorsChoose.org today to ask an angel for help," he casually mentioned to the kids, most from low-income families. "If we get them, we can make our documentaries." Unable to pull together a few film projectors at a performing arts high school, he had to go to the Internet, hat in hand, asking for charity from strangers. No further explanation was necessary for his students, who were well aware that their teachers often had to shoulder the burden of finding someone to pay for school supplies.

But I wasn't familiar with the site, so I thought I'd investigate.

Making Beggars of Our Teachers

DONORSCHOOSE.ORG, BEGUN in 2000, is a charitable website connecting public schoolteachers seeking classroom supplies with "angels," or donors, who are willing to purchase them. As the name implies, the donors select which type of class they want to help: science, reading, history, or health—much as one might sort results shopping online for a dress: by size, color, or label. Except that in education, our children need *all of the above*. Or angels can select by age: prekindergartners? Grades three through five? Finally, donors can select the type of materials they'd like to supply to underfunded American classrooms.

Many teachers beg for books. Ms. Gonzalez in Multnomah Elementary School in Los Angeles, California, says many of her first graders have already read the limited number of classroom books she has available for them. Her plea: "If I had read and reread every book available several times, I'd probably get bored of reading. I can't allow this to happen to my students. More books will give them more reading materials to choose from. More choices means more reading!"

It was only September, and an American teacher in my hometown had to plead with the public to send money for books to stimulate her young readers because the school wasn't providing them and she'd already run through her very limited supply.

First-grade teacher Ms. Casucci in Flint, Michigan, lacks children's literature books needed to engage her students during reading time at their "leveled library"—a rug on the floor. "With thirty minutes of independent reading time built into the daily schedule, students will benefit greatly from high-interest books by their favorite authors. I have seen firsthand how even the youngest children seek out literature as reading becomes a favorite activity for them," she says.

Make it stop. Do we really need teachers to explain to us that getting intriguing books into the hands of kids will encourage them to read? If that's a given, when did we decide that we cared so little about education that we left our public school teachers on their own to plead on the Internet for supplies as basic as *books for first graders*?

I can guarantee you this isn't happening in Shanghai or Singapore.

When small donations of, say, ten or twenty dollars trickle in to DonorsChoose, teachers write polite, chipper thank-you notes that are then publicly displayed on the site. "Caitlin, We appreciate your generous donation very much," says Ms. Casucci. "School days are so busy, children can find time to read whenever possible. Having books available to them at their own level allows them not only to choose books that interest them but also to improve their skills while they read. Thank you for helping us in our efforts to expand our leveled library! Sincerely, Beth C."[32]

With everything else teachers have to worry about—how to devise lively lesson plans, handle the acting-out boy smacking the kid in front of him, challenge the class brainiac sufficiently, figure out what to do about the depressed daughter of absent parents, do more with smaller budgets and larger class sizes—teachers now have to draft perky, succinct financial appeals and promptly follow up with cheerful thank-you notes to the online strangers who found it in their hearts to help.

Why? Because teachers' appreciation and responsiveness is graded on DonorsChoose. "'Thank-you punctuality' captures the teacher's track record of submitting photos and thank-you letters on time," the site announces. Woe to the busy teacher who neglects to upload immediately a smiling photo of a child reading a donated book and draft a "complete and compelling" personalized thank-you note! Her online score will so reflect, and perhaps her six–year-old charges will suffer with fewer book donations in the future.[33]

Ridiculous. Obscene. Teachers, I apologize that we are doing this to you.

Don't get me wrong. DonorsChoose.org is a brilliant stopgap effort to get books and pencils and lab supplies to cash-strapped schools, and I salute the site for supporting education. Anyone with fond memories of childhood classics would *want* to give an armload of requested books to Ms. Johnson's class in Shiprock, New Mexico, for example. On DonorsChoose she requests *Pearl, The Call of the Wild, Fahrenheit 451, Huckleberry Finn,* and *The Borrowers.* I fervently hope that the site gets those books into the hands of her kids. Certainly, better that Ms. Couture's

K-2 students in Modesto, California, get her sought-after *Magic Tree House* books and workbooks through this well-meaning, clever website than not at all.

But when did we relinquish our obligation *as a nation* to provide our kids with the basics they in order need to learn how to read, write, create art and media, or use computers?

When did we lapse into blasé acceptance of making beggars of our teachers and administrators? One public high school principal told me he spent more of his time and energy on fundraising than on anything else. As a result, his other duties got short shrift: overseeing faculty, updating the curriculum, interacting with students and parents, keeping up with education trends. This year, though, he told me brightly, in the ever-optimistic tone I found common among educators—bless them—that a famous musician's daughter was starting at his school. Perhaps they could entreat the singer to do a concert to raise funds for the school! He was working on that! Putting on a full-scale professional concert would, of course, be an enormously labor-intensive project. He'd need to figure out how to do the whole thing from square one because, naturally, his graduate degree was in education, not event planning. But he had to pursue his concert idea. It was a glimmer of hope that allowed him to fantasize about having classrooms with walls and textbooks for every student.

A generation ago a popular counterculture poster read, "It will be a great day when our schools have all the money they need and the Air Force has to have a bake sale to buy a bomber." And that was written back in the day of the occasional *bake sale.* No one could have imagined then that we'd cut so many school hours and school days, let so many private industries advertise in the classroom, hack art and music and sports programs, bombard private and public school parents with never-ending fundraising appeals, or charge extra for advanced classes, telling kids who can't afford them: *too bad, you can't have it all.*

We could never have imagined that we'd go from selling a

few cupcakes at the football game to requiring teachers to perform the online version of standing on a street corner, hat out to the public, pleading for each $4 book needed to teach our children to read.

Where Did We Go Wrong?

I HAVE to digress briefly to explain why requiring families to pay for public education services is misguided, a deviation from our history, and harmful to us all. After all, in 2012, after a major presidential candidate criticized government-run public schools as "anachronistic," there was little public outcry even though 90 percent of Americans send their kids to public schools.[34]

Our commitment to providing a quality, public education to every child is clearly slipping. Maybe that's because we have taken free neighborhood schools for granted. For as long as any living American can remember, this was a basic entitlement we expected our communities to provide, as noncontroversial as our expectation of government-provided clean drinking water. But it wasn't always so.

In fact, the concept of a free, public education for every American child was a subversive notion from its inception, a century into our young republic's history. In the nineteenth century poet Ralph Waldo Emerson called it "the most radical of revolutions," the idea that "the poor man, whom the law does not allow to take an ear of corn when starving, nor a pair of shoes for his freezing feet, is allowed to put his hand into the pocket of the rich, and say, You shall educate me."[35] The gall!

Sure, the poor taking from the rich via entitlement programs—including education—met with resistance in the nineteenth century, and it still does. Thus, childless taxpayers today sometimes push back against funding schools. "Why should I have to pay for someone else's kids' education?" the argument goes. "I have a hard enough time supporting myself.

They chose to have kids. I didn't. Let them educate them."
And so those burgeoning school fees, it is argued, are only fair.
Some say that "direct users"—families of school-aged kids—
should bear all or most of the burden for cash-strapped public
schools because they're the immediate beneficiaries.

This argument misses the point of providing a no-cost, public education to all our children: we are *all* direct beneficiaries.
Our nation, now and henceforth, is the direct beneficiary. This
isn't a vague or sentimental "children are our future" appeal;
rather, ignorant citizens are too easily swayed by duplicitous
leaders—that's harmful to us all. In a democracy we're voting on leaders and issues, and if many of us are ill informed,
we'll all suffer with lousy outcomes…like, say, spending more
on prisons than on schools, getting into wars we have no business being in, ignoring pressing environmental issues, failing
to fund preventative programs and, as a result, lurching from
crisis to expensive crisis, wondering how it all happened. These
outcomes hurt all of us, even if we are educated, knowledgeable,
connected, and take care that our kids are too. The majority
rules in our democracy, and so we need our neighbors, citizens
of distant states—*everyone*—to know which way is up.

When Adlai Stevenson was running for president in 1952, a
supporter called out, "Governor Stevenson, all thinking people
are for you!" "That's not enough," he answered. "I need a majority."[36] Adlai wasn't the only one; *our country* needs that educated
majority, and patriots as early as Thomas Jefferson understood
how vital it was that all children be educated. "Without high
quality education," the US Supreme Court has said, "the populace will lack the knowledge, self-confidence, and critical skills
to evaluate independently the pronouncements of pundits and
political leaders." Uneducated, we'll fall for anything: corrupt
politicians, loud commentators unmoored to the facts, slick
corporate advertising.

Most of us are in favor of education to some extent. Few
argue that we should stop sending kids to school. The more
controversial question is, who pays? And, why not have families

chip in, because although we all benefit, don't they benefit more? If poor kids can apply for fee waivers, aren't we then fulfilling our promise to provide an affordable education for all if we ask some parents to cough up some fees?

No, we're not. First, we don't want to humiliate poor kids with applications for fee waivers to, say, get a chemistry book or play basketball. We don't want to single them out. "The primary aim of education is to serve as an equalizing instrument for society," says Dr. Pasi Sahlberg, a respected Finnish educator and author. (Finland's kids routinely rank at the top of world reading and math tests.) In America public schools should be leveling the playing field, not highlighting whose mom got laid off or whose dad is in prison.

But more pressingly, we don't want to leave it to families to decide which parts of their kid's education to fund and which to sacrifice. California's free-school advocate, John Swett, memorably said in 1863, "If left to their own unaided efforts, a great majority of the people will fail through want of means to properly educate their children; another class, with means at command, will fail through want of interest. The people then, can be educated only by a system of Free Schools, supported by taxation, and controlled directly by the people."[37]

Sure, we want every family to place the highest value on their children's education. But we live in the real world, not utopia, so we can't be sure that every family, even those with money, will. Some parents will decide Junior must skip AP Chemistry so they can pay their heating bills. Others will choose booze or skiing in Aspen over their kids' music lessons. Many kids, knowing their family's tight finances, won't even ask to join the Environmental Club or soccer team. So we as a nation must continue to take that choice out of parents' hands. Thus all aspects of public schools—science labs, the chess club, the hockey team, AP classes—must be free to all students so no one is barred from learning at the level of their merit.

But instead, we've done the opposite: slashed programs and ratcheted up fees.

As public schools continue to impose fees on their kids, however, this point of view is becoming anachronistic. If you have a child in public school, you may already be aware of the cuts, the limits, the lack of a gifted program—or art class, or music, or theater. You may have noticed how few books there are in the classroom, and how dog-eared and sad those worn books are. You may be getting billed monthly for fees and field trips and "extras," and you're probably constantly hounded to participate in money-raising events. (I used to silently wish that I could pay a flat fee at the beginning of each school year to block all fundraising calls and e-mails to come to meetings, silent auctions, lunches, dinners, and, yes, those dreaded bake sales. *How much do I have to pay to end these appeals?*) Perhaps your child's teacher can be found online, seeking markers or whiteboards or other basic items on their wish list.

I've got just one item on my education wish list: I wish my country valued education.

––––––

ONE MORE depressing piece of evidence to show how little we value education: the shameful food and housing we provide to our kids during their school day.

School Food and Facilities: *This* Is What We Give Our Kids?

THIRTY-TWO MILLION American kids eat school lunches each day provided by the National School Lunch Program—twenty-one million of those for free or reduced price, a number that's been rising by about a million per year due to the financial hardships so many are suffering in our flagging economy. Anyone who's eaten a big, fatty, sugary lunch and then tried to work in the afternoon knows the effects, how sluggish and sleepy and...zzz...*what? Huh?* Exactly. And anyone who's read a newspaper in the last decade knows that the American junk-food diet is larding us up with diabetes, heart disease, cancer, and obesity. So why on earth would we feed this crap to our kids at school?

Because dollars and cents, not our kids' health, is the bottom line. The National School Lunch Program was devised to support American farmers' prices when demand dipped sharply after World War II and, only secondarily, to feed children. Increasingly, that food is delivered by super-sized "food management" companies who, according to the *New York Times*, get kickbacks from big food-processing companies for turning apples, sweet potatoes, chicken, and turkey into unhealthy fried chicken nuggets, sugary fruit pastries, and pizza—junk food that lowers our kids' test scores and contributes to skyrocketing rates of childhood obesity and related illnesses.[38] Here and there, schools try to provide healthier food, but they quickly give up, allowing kids to call three bags of Flamin' Hot Cheetos and Coke lunch.[39]

Big profits for corporate America. Planting the seed for lifelong unhealthy food consumption and weakened school performance for our kids. Are we *trying* to make it as difficult as possible for our kids to learn?

We know that healthy food measurably raises kids' test scores and lowers absenteeism.[40] For that reason alone schools should be insisting on higher nutrition standards. Instead, the National School Lunch Program (NSLP) feeds our kids meat that has been rejected by Burger King and McDonald's and chicken rejected by Kentucky Fried Chicken and the Campbell Soup Company for poor quality, according to a *USA Today* investigation.[41] An American College of Cardiology study found that students who ate NSLP food were more likely to be obese compared to students who brought lunch from home, and NSLP eaters were more likely to eat fatty meals, drink sugary beverages, and eat fewer fruits and vegetables than their counterparts.[42]

Even the air our students breathe at school can be toxic. While teachers like Brad Koepenick have no classroom, lecturing outdoors at the picnic tables, that's actually an improvement over those who teach in crumbling, polluted facilities. The National Clearinghouse for Educational Facilities estimates it would take over $300 *billion* of work to perform essential building and grounds maintenance in our nations' elementary, middle, and high schools, excluding administrative facilities.[43] Of course, it's not happening.

The effects on the health of those who inhabit those buildings daily are disturbing. Teachers in Chicago and Washington, DC miss at least four days of school annually because of health problems caused by adverse building conditions, with poor indoor air quality being the biggest problem. A national survey of school nurses found over 40 percent of the nurses *knew* that avoidable indoor pollutants adversely impacted children and staff.[44]

Crumbling walls, leaking roofs, schools lacking heat in the winter and air conditioning in the sweltering warm months.[45] Thousands of California schools cannot pass an earthquake certification. School safety inspectors have been laid off.[46] This is the sorry state of American schools today.

The Old Testament exhorts, "Do not put a stumbling block before the blind" (Leviticus 19:14). Our children come to us blind, and we must teach them to see by educating them about the world. Instead, we erect barriers and stumbling blocks, making learning more challenging for them every step of the way.

College: Increasingly Out of Reach for Ordinary Americans

AS WE put more stumbling blocks before our children, fewer students are able to achieve the holy grail of education: a college diploma. This could not come at a worse time, as a bachelor's degree is now virtually a required ticket for entry into a middle-class future.

In just ten years more than 60 percent of all new jobs will require a college education, according to Complete College America, a nonprofit committed to raising awareness about college dropout rates and supported by the Bill and Melinda Gates Foundation.[47] President Obama said in 2009 that he wanted America to lead the world in college graduation rates. Notwithstanding that worthy goal, we are going in the wrong direction, because we are making college attendance and graduation increasingly available only to children of wealthy families. We have slipped to tenth place among nations for college completion rates—we were once number one.[48]

How bad is it? Young people today are the first generation in US history slated to be less educated than their parents—another shocking piece of information that should be leading newscasts but isn't.[49] Fewer will enter universities, and fewer will receive college or other advanced degrees. And the problem will mount for the next generation, because those students who do earn college diplomas will graduate with substantially more debt, making saving for *their* children's education even more unattainable. And so on. The United States already has the least social mobility among thirty-four developed countries, as indicated by our highest correlation of education levels between parents and children.[50] Translation: if your parents went to college, you probably did too. If they didn't, you probably didn't, and neither will your children. In a land that prides itself on equality of opportunity, this is one of the more depressing facts I've read. And unless action is taken quickly to address this decline, the lack of social mobility will only worsen.

Let's take a look at the cold reality for most of our college students today—it's quite different from our popular image. Many of us imagine college as a place where young people go to live away from their parents for four years as they study, go to ball games and student theater projects, and maybe work in the summers or on winter break, and this is mostly paid for by dear old Mom and Dad—like in the movies! In fact, however, only one in four college students today fits that profile. College students' lives have changed radically over the last generation as tuition has skyrocketed.

The older generation always believes the younger one is goofing off, unable to put their noses to the grindstone as we did when we walked barefoot uphill through the snow both ways to and from our Dickensian schools. In fact, today's typical American college student toughs out long hours at school and at work. Almost half of American students attending four-year institutions as well as the majority of community college students now work twenty or more hours per week.[51]

Working and going to school at the same time is grueling. Studying, reading, and keeping up with school work become sacrificed. Forget about doing any extra credit or spending idle hours in extracurricular discussion with professors or other students. I met a flight attendant with her nose in a textbook on her break at the back of a plane. She worked twelve-hour days flying on Friday, Saturdays, and Sundays as she shouldered a full-time load at her state college Mondays through Thursdays. When was the last time she'd had a day off? "It's been years," she told me, wearily.

More college students live this way, working and going to school, sleep deprived and exhausted. Ultimately, the challenge becomes too overwhelming, and so *the majority of our college students drop out before they obtain a degree.* The number-one reason so many drop out? "The need to work and make money" became too stressful. Only one in ten leaves because he didn't like college, studying, or sitting in a classroom. Most want to stay, learn, and get a degree, but the financial pressures just become too oppressive. The number-two reason for leaving college is similar: "I just couldn't afford the tuition and fees." [52]

They couldn't get past the stumbling blocks we have erected.

Attending college part time may be most difficult of all. As one study found:

> [Part-time college students] had to have a paying job to make ends meet. Far from being slackers, as some people imagine, they were often assuming responsibilities and financial burdens that traditional full-time college students do not have to shoulder. It is a test of maturity and perseverance that more affluent students are usually not required to face.[53]

Young people who drop out of school are often going it alone financially, with little help from grants, scholarships, financial aid, or family money. College costs have risen 400 percent over the last twenty-five years, while median income has risen only 150 percent. Because of these heavy financial burdens, there is no question that going to college today is more challenging than it was a generation ago, and if present trends continue, it will be even more of a hardship for the next generation.

Today's students are the ones who are walking uphill barefoot in the snow.

Far from being slackers, dropouts yearn to return to higher education, still longing for that college degree. Two-thirds say they give returning to school "a lot of thought." Yet overwhelmingly they say, "I really need to work full-time, and I don't think I could work and go to school at the same time." As a group, dropouts know that a college degree would provide access to better jobs and a brighter future, and most dream of returning for the knowledge, the skills, the degree. And if not for them, then for their children. Poignantly, 97 percent say that they want their own children to go to college—to complete what they were unable to finish themselves.[54]

If we wanted our young people to learn, we'd make higher education accessible. If we wanted to compete with Singapore, Finland, Korea, and other high-performing, educated nations, we'd remove the stumbling blocks and make college affordable for all our young people who have the brains and work ethic to get in and get through.

Instead, we've allowed tuition to rise dramatically, often at rates double or triple the rate of inflation, year after year. Private schools like Harvard University boast staggering endowments greater than the GDP of many nations (Harvard's exceeds $34 billion) while also jacking up tuition and fees at double the rate of inflation. Because donations to those bloated endowments and the earnings on those endowments are tax-exempt, Congress has the power to regulate private colleges. Though they conduct an occasional hearing, our lawmakers largely sit on their hands, as the schools become richer and students are bled dry.[55]

Even public college education, once a haven for low- or middle-income students, is now out of reach for many. Florida, for example, has increased its state college tuition by 15 percent for each of the last four years. The sticker price for a year of studying and living on campus at an American public university is now over $21,000. Many public colleges openly favor affluent students in admissions, an act that would have been heresy a generation ago.[56] At a private college the average price of one year of on-campus life and classes exceeds $42,000. Federal aid to college students is now limited to $23,000—total. That doesn't help much toward a four-year degree with these tuition rates, especially in the more prestigious—and more expensive—private schools.

This, as real American income declines and young people have a harder time finding part-time jobs during school and in the summer to help defray costs. The median American income is $33,000 per year.[57] There is no way that even the most frugal average American family can save enough to cover four years of college expenses, even for one child. The system feels rigged against the middle class.

And that's just tuition and living expenses. One little-noticed phenomenon that's symptomatic of the gouging that college students endure, with the complicity of universities and with no public discussion or outcry is exorbitant textbook fees. Every three years textbook publishers reprint their books, jacking up the price a whopping 45 percent, apparently for no other reason except they *can*. The standard political science textbook, *Understanding American Government*, today typically costs $169.70. The biology book used by California State University undergraduates is now $202.50. For Algebra II, it's $166.70. Over four years public college students in California can expect to pay $5,000 simply for textbooks.[58] That's double the cost from just a few years ago—and a screaming outrage. Why should a textbook that a group of students are all required to buy—a fact that should drive *down* the price, giving them a group rate—cost hundreds of dollars?

The majority of college dropouts say that the cost of textbooks and other fees besides tuition affected them financially.[59] Of course it did—how many of us can afford $200 books? Other than coffee table art books, what other publishers dare to charge these kinds of prices?

MORE STUMBLING blocks currently proposed in the California legislature is a plan for open-sourced electronic textbooks. At a cost of $25 million, publishers would be paid to create digital textbooks for the most popular classes that students could then download onto e-readers, like Kindles or iPads, for free from school libraries. Saves trees, fuel from transporting paper books, students' backs from lugging around all those heavy tomes in their backpacks, and *one billion dollars every year* for struggling students. A state that valued education would snap up this deal in a hurry, right?

No one doubts that digital textbooks are the way of the future. A group called the 20 Million Minds Foundation, led by former California Senate Majority Leader Dean Florez,[60] labors valiantly to get the ball rolling on this. However, the bill is stalled in committee, unlikely to pass.[61]

We've left families on their own with these offensive education costs. Even with scholarships or grants that lop off a chunk of the tuition and fees, students must choose (a) to graduate with a heavy debt burden that they will likely be paying off for the next twenty years (two-thirds of our young people graduate in debt, averaging over $23,000), making it difficult to buy a home, save for retirement, or pay for their own children's educations;[62] (b) to pare down their college aspirations (four-year college enrollment has dropped for middle-income students, while cheaper two-year community colleges are now so crowded with students that they offer classes at midnight[63]); or (c) skip higher education altogether.

Cynically advocating for the latter approach, one popular media topic in the last few years has been: "Is college worth it?"[64] Mainstream media outlets such as *Reuters* and *Time* earnestly analyze college costs and graduates' income levels to calculate a numeric answer. But the discussion assumes that outrageous college tuition and fees are a given, and that the benefit of higher education is only to a student's bottom-line net worth. Entirely lost in the debate is the fact that our deprioritization of education has *allowed* skyrocketing costs to spiral out of control and that an educated citizenry is key to our country's future.

The answer is a loud YES, it is still worth it, without a doubt, as we shall see when we get to the rules section below (Rule Two). When 60 percent of new jobs require a college degree, when the vast majority of jobs supporting a middle-class lifestyle require a diploma, when the average college grad's increased earnings outpaces his debt within a year or two, when life in the twenty-first century requires the ability to separate fact from hype, critical reasoning skills, knowledge, and intellectual curiosity, how could we even ask this question?

We can ask it because we live in a culture that doesn't value education.

All the Bad News about Education Is Even Worse for Boys

ALTHOUGH BOTH girls and boys emerge undereducated after their time in our deteriorating, failing schools, and although both genders struggle to attain college degrees, the results are worse for boys and young men. Girls are now outperforming boys at every level of school, graduating in significantly greater numbers and with better grades and test scores. This is true in every demographic subgroup: rich, middle class, poor, white, African American, Latino, Asian American.[65]

And after thousands of years of being told we were intellectually inferior, our smaller brains unfit for logic, being barred from many schools and universities and professions, girls and women deserve a victory lap for this historic triumph. But the other side of this story emerges when we look closely at what's going on with boys—the sting of their underachievement. This educational achievement gap—and especially our boys' stunningly low reading proficiency—is a painful, festering problem that follows boys as they grow into men, affecting nearly every aspect of their lives.

Our Boy Problem

LITTLE BOYS now start to lag behind girls when they're still in diapers, and the gap only widens with time. In fact, many boys withdraw early from education and learning, never to return.

What's going on here?

Let's start at the beginning. Boys get expelled from preschool at almost five times the rate of girls.[66] Who knew anyone got expelled from preschool? The parents of the little guys who

got cut, that's who, who often feel it's just *their* son, *their* humili-
ating individual problem. But it's not. Too many young boys,
who tend to be fidgety and have a harder time sitting still and
listening for long stretches, experience the confines of school
as a punishment, zoning out until recess or sports time. As days
go by and their usually female teachers label them as "bad" in
a setting where boisterousness is considered disruptive, these
boys go home and complain that they *hate* school and don't
want to return. Forced back each morning, they rebel and act
out further, until finally the teacher has had it and they're out
of there, learning their first lesson about school: their type isn't
welcome there.

Often we overreact to the normal wiggliness and mischie-
vousness of boys. "Hot sauce mom" captured headlines in 2011
for punishing her seven-year-old son by pouring hot sauce into
his mouth, forcing him into a cold shower, and videotaping the
punishment for a television show. Cable news spent hundreds
of hours on the case, analyzing whether her choice of discipline
crossed the line into child abuse. (It did. An Anchorage jury
convicted her of misdemeanor child abuse.[67]) Almost never
discussed was the boy's "crime" that preceded the punishment:
fidgeting in his seat and having a pencil "swordfight" with
another boy in school. Hot sauce mom's reaction was extreme
and cruel, to be sure, but differed only in degree from what
many boys face at school and at home: punishment for their
energy and childhood playfulness. If we continue to react puni-
tively to this typical boy behavior, they will continue to hate
school and disconnect from it. Especially as recess and play time
has been cut from schools to make room for more rote memori-
zation and "teaching to the test," young boys in particular have
an increasingly difficult time sitting still for hours on end.

Certainly there are restless little girls too. (I was one of them;
to this day sitting still for more than a few minutes feels like con-
finement for me.) And there are boys who are more sedentary,
who *can* remain quiet for long stretches and concentrate with
ease. But there's no getting around the fact that in elementary

school boys are diagnosed with attention disorders four times as often as girls are. More kinetic and with shorter attention spans, boys struggle through preschool, kindergarten, and the early grades, where they are held back twice as often as girls.[68]

Girls and boys are now neck and neck in math and science, fields until recently considered to be boys' natural strengths. Girls are far and away better readers than boys (more on this critical issue in a moment). Overall, girls get better grades, spend more time on homework, and crowd the top of class rankings. Many more girls are in the top 10 percent of their class by middle school, whereas many boys sink to the bottom. Boys dominate in one area: remedial and special education classes.[69]

In high school the divide widens. In the classroom girls rule in every subject. They take harder classes, do better in them, and dominate all extracurricular activities except sports. Girls take more algebra, geometry, trigonometry, precalculus, biology, honors biology, and chemistry. On the whole, girls get better grades.[70]

Many more girls take Advanced Placement classes (sometimes girls outnumber boys two to one in AP English and AP foreign languages), and they compose 64 percent of the National Honor Roll,[71] participate in more after-school activities, and receive more school and district-wide awards. Seventy-two percent of girls compared to only 65 percent of boys graduate from high school, and the gap widens for students of color. Recently, in one North Carolina county twenty-six of the thirty-one valedictorians were female.[72]

This girls-kicking-ass-in-school phenomenon has seeped into our consciousness to become a new expectation of gendered educational excellence. At my daughter's 2011 Ivy League college graduation, all five top awards in her department went to girls. All around me parents rustled their programs, smiled, and clapped politely as the winners all smiled for their award photos in dresses and heels. Ho hum. When's lunch?

A few weeks later I was to deliver a commencement address myself at a local college. The night before the speech I was struck by laryngitis. Considering my options, I said to my daughter, "If my voice gives out, I'll just hand my speech to the valedictorian and have her finish it."

"How do you know it'll be a 'she'?" Sarah asked.

"Oh, right," I said. "Just assuming." I had no idea who the valedictorian was, but I was confident she would be a she.

And she was.

Significantly more boys than girls drop out of high school. And when they stay in school, boys engage in riskier behaviors. They drink, smoke marijuana, and abuse prescription drugs (their own or others') in greater numbers than girls. And this should come as no surprise because boys are medicated far more often than girls in nearly every age group.[73] (Is boyhood itself now a disease fit for Big Pharma's exploitation?) Considering that 25 percent of our children and teenagers now take medication regularly—drugs that, for the most part, have not been tested on children[74]—this is a particularly gripping statistic. Boys are suspended and expelled far more frequently than girls are.[75]

Is it any wonder, then, that boys report liking school less or complain that "school is stupid"?[76] I hear that as, "I don't fit in there."

For college admissions officers, the new, agonizing challenge is how to avoid having an entering class that is two-thirds or even three-quarters female, which is how it would break down if kids were accepted based on merit alone. Although girls who worked hard for those high GPAs and SAT numbers bristle at affirmative action for boys, many also don't want to go to "girls' schools," which they loosely define as tipping more than 55 percent female. My own daughter pored over those gender breakdowns in her college guidebooks a few years ago, drawing thick black Xs through school names that weren't sufficiently coed.[77] The solution: many prestigious colleges now favor boys over girls in admissions, requiring lower grades and test scores for boys so they can reach deeper into the applicant pool for male students. They do this, in part— irony of ironies—to attract and retain the high-performing girls, who want a pool of guys to date in college.

The US Commission on Civil Rights even launched an investigation, subpoenaing nineteen public and private colleges to determine whether they were discriminating against qualified female applicants. As legal analyst Dan Abrams says, "Accusations of affirmative action policies—*for men*. That kind of says it all."[78]

Despite colleges' efforts to bring in more male applicants and come up with innovative programs to keep boys in college through completion, girls dominate college campuses and graduation ceremonies. Fifty-seven percent of all undergrads in the United States are female, and the same number of bachelor's degrees go to women.[79]

Many college guys just seem to check out. In college, men are more likely to be slackers.

> According to the 2005 National Survey of Student Engagement, which reported results from 90,000 students at 530 postsecondary institutions, male university students are significantly more inclined to relax or socialize (eleven hours weekly, to be precise)…college men are more likely to skip class, turn assignments in late, or just drop out than collegiate women.[80]

And so here we are. For the first time in history young American women are better educated than young men. A young woman in her late twenties is significantly more likely to have a college degree than a young man in that age group.[81] There are more female than male college grads in the next oldest age cohort too—thirty- to forty-four-year-olds.[82] If present trends remain, that gap will only continue to widen. The educated class will be majority female; the uneducated, majority male.

Where does this all leave us? As it turns out, it's not a *neener-neener* moment for females. Women having more degrees than men, or girls outperforming boys: no problem. Boys who can't or won't read, boys tuning out in school, young men dropping out of high school and college: big problem.

Real Boys Don't Read?

WHY ARE so many boys performing poorly in school? The nub of the issue is the new idea that seems to have landed in many boys' heads at an early age that *reading is for girls*—only girls. A generation ago no one thought this way. As boys, the dads of today competed squarely with the girls in their classrooms. But this new, twenty-first-century attitude means that boys now do worse on national reading tests than boys did thirty years ago.[83] Their proficiency is down, and their approach to reading is often negative. Most kids don't like activities they're not good at, and so boys' difficulty with reading dampens their enthusiasm for school generally. In one study of nine-year-olds, more girls were reading enthusiasts, whereas more boys said they liked reading "not at all."[84]

The eerie, haunting parable of the rebellious boy, *Where the Wild Things Are*? The goofy, fun *Diary of a Wimpy Kid*? The glorious, awe-inspiring *Harry Potter* books or *The Lord of the Rings* trilogy? Are you kidding me? *What's not to like?*

Whether boys innately have more difficulty with verbal skills compared to girls or whether school is structured in such a way as to make life more challenging for little boys—as many believe—or a combination of the two, regardless, boys lag behind girls in reading skills in the early grades and afterward. Take a guess on this one: in how many of our fifty states do girls outperform boys in reading in elementary, middle, *and* high school?

Answer: all fifty.[85] And the gap continues to widen.

Nine out of ten boys do not read for pleasure—at all.[86] According to a major study by the National Endowment for the Arts, reading is now a marker of gender identity: girls read, boys don't.[87] As one boy put it: "I'd rather be BURNED AT THE STAKE than read a book!"[88] (Get that boy a book about someone who was burned at the stake!)

Remarkably, it's a worldwide phenomenon, or, at least, where girls and boys have equal access to education, it is. UNESCO recently surveyed girls' and boys' reading scores in forty-three developed countries. In how many of those countries did the girls have higher reading proficiency?

All of them.[89]

Boys are turning away from books because they're not cool in their world. Of course, boys have always enjoyed clobbering each other, chucking balls, and, for the last few decades, exploding aliens on screens. But where do boys get this new, crazy idea that reading is "girly"?

From us. After all, Mom is usually the one who reads for pleasure at home, not Dad. (Women read almost twice as many books as men.[90]) That role modeling alone goes a very long way. "Do as I say, not as I do, kid" has never worked, and it still doesn't. Boys love their moms, but they emulate their dads. Typically, Mom reads the kids their bedtime story. Mom takes the children to the library or the bookstore. Dad throws a ball with them. At school they are read to or encouraged to read on their own by their (usually) female teachers, while their team coaches are (generally) male. Children's book publishers reinforce this by portraying girls more often as readers and boys more often in action roles in illustrations in children's books. (Think Hermione Granger, the prodigious reader, in the *Harry Potter* books.) As blogger Margot Magawan recently noted in her survey of popular children's films, *all* the title characters— the active protagonists who make it all happen—were male, even the animated ones. Females are nonexistent or, at best, sidekicks.[91] For birthdays, holidays, or "just because," we give books as gifts more often to girls and sporting equipment to boys. Kids get the message early, despite our best intentions: girls read, boys do not.

I asked my twelve-year-old friend Oliver about this recently.[92] Whenever I see him, I always encourage him to read, but he drags his feet, reading only when absolutely required to. You'd never find Oliver sneaking a book under the blankets with a flashlight, as I did when I was growing up.

"Do you like reading, Oliver?" I asked him on a sunny summer day out by a pool as we popped watermelon chunks in our mouths.

"Sure," he said, unconvincingly, in that way kids tell you the answer they know you want to hear.

"Really?"

"Well, like, if there's nothing else to do, it's okay," he allowed. "Like if you can't play sports or watch video games or play with your friends."

There's a ringing endorsement.

"Do you think reading is *girly*?" I asked, keeping my face as flat as possible.

"No," he said, possibly giving me the answer he believed I wanted, adding, "but a lot of my friends do."

"Why do you suppose they think that?"

"Because we'd rather *do* stuff," he said, gaining steam now on behalf of his "friends." "When you're reading you're just *sitting* there. Girls don't mind sitting around,[93] but we'd rather be skateboarding or something where we're *doing* something."

Pressed by me, Oliver could name only one book series he likes, *39 Clues*. I suggested *The Hunger Games* (which may be a bit violent for a twelve-year-old, Lord help me, but no more so than his video games), and his eyes shone. "I heard about that one! I heard there are games and kids fight to the death!" Indeed they do, which is why I was of two minds in recommending it to him. But if it will get him reading…

"Did you know that reading used to be considered more of a boy thing?" I continued.

He looked out at the horizon, enduring my questions. "No. Can we go swimming now?"

————

SO WHAT? you may say. Some people are bookworms; some have other interests. If the girls are getting better grades, good for them. They work hard and deserve the recognition. Sports

is good for kids. If that's what they're into, let it go. They're not
hurting anyone. Let boys be boys. Right?

No. Not right. Not at all. Because this attitude has dangerous
consequences. Devastating repercussions follow nonreading boys as they grow into men. Because José and Jamal and
James aren't just missing out on *Captain Underpants*; less reading means less proficiency in reading comprehension as well
as poor writing and communications skills, requirements for
many subjects. It means they are less likely to get through the
assigned text, less likely to read the extra credit, less likely to
explore topics and conduct research on their own.

Weak readers struggle through school generally and for the
rest of their lives. Reading is the foundation for nearly all other
subjects. Children who lag in reading fall behind not only in
English, language skills, and foreign languages but also in
social sciences, history, health, and science, struggling to inter-
pret the pages and grasp the assignments.

Educators know that if a boy isn't reading proficiently by the
fourth grade, he's highly likely to be a high school dropout—
a perilous status in today's economy. Having lost interest and
motivation, by the time he starts high school a nonreading boy
already has one foot out the door.[94] Thus, low reading scores
are one of the most reliable predictors of whether a student
will finish school. (Though finishing school is no guarantee of
reading skills. In what's been called "education malpractice,"
20 percent of our high school graduates are illiterate.[95])

And the life of a high school dropout or a young man with
only a high school degree isn't what it used to be. In fact, it's
almost a surefire road to a life of poverty at best and incarceration at worse, as we shall see.

Thus, we cannot shrug off nonreading boys as simply fun-
loving, school-hating imps. Real peril lies ahead for those who
lack literacy skills.

Black and Hispanic Boys: Where the Need Is Greatest

FOR BLACK and Hispanic boys the situation is dire, starting young. Only 12 percent of African American fourth-grade boys read at grade level (compared with 38 percent of white boys). Only 12 percent of African American eighth-grade boys are proficient in math (compared with 44 percent of white boys). In high school African American boys drop out at nearly twice the rate of white boys, and their SAT critical reasoning scores are on average a whopping 104 points lower.[96]

A great deal of this is because of poverty. Because our public schools are, for the most part, funded by a local property tax base, schools in wealthier neighborhoods are better by nearly every measure. Inner-city schools crumble even more than the average public school, have classrooms jammed with too many kids, and lack the computers, books, and field trips that afflu-ent schools take for granted. Poor kids have worse nutrition, more health problems, and have more economic motivation to drop out and find work. As depicted in the heartbreaking documentary *Waiting for Superman*, desperate parents in poor neighborhoods enter their kids in school lotteries, hoping against hope they'll pull the golden ticket that will get their kid into a decent charter or magnet school. As with all lotteries, nearly everyone's a loser. So kids born into poverty are stuck in America's worst schools.

But poverty alone can't fully explain these painful numbers, because black and Hispanic girls are growing up in the same homes and neighborhoods, going to the same depressing, dilapidated schools—and succeeding. At least they are signifi-cantly better at staying in school and graduating than the boys they grow up with. The majority of black and Hispanic girls (59 percent and 58 percent, respectively) graduate from high school. The majority of black and Hispanic boys (52 percent and 51 percent, respectively) do not. Over the past decades the college graduation rates for black women have shown strong and steady gains. African American college women have improved their completion rate, so nearly one in two who start college get their degree, whereas nearly two out of three of their male counterparts who start college drop out—a rate that seems to be holding steady.[97]

Black and Hispanic young men are falling further behind not only their female counterparts but other males as well. The disparities are significant: only 28 percent of young African American men and 16 percent of young Latino men have obtained an associate's (two-year) degree or higher, compared with 44 percent of white men and—wow—*70 percent of Asian American men.*[98]

A crystallization of everything that's wrong for young minority men in America today: 3 times as many black men and 2.7 times as many Hispanic men live in prison cells than college dorms.[99]

To be blunt: if you're an African American boy today, you're more likely to drop out of high school than graduate. If you're an African American male who didn't finish high school, you're more likely to be unemployed than have a job, and by your midthirties you're more likely than not to have served time in prison.[100] If you're an African American male high school dropout in your late twenties, you're more likely to be in prison on a given day—34 percent—than working—30 percent. And if you're a black man in your late twenties or early thirties without a college education, you're just about as likely as not to be the noncustodial father of children.[101]

Few governmental bodies have taken any real notice of this problem. One notable exception is New York City, which has roughly the same numbers of young white, African American, and Latino males. Yet 84 percent of those incarcerated and nearly *all* of those admitted to children's and family services facilities are black and Latino youth. "The magnitude of the disparities is stunning," said Linda I. Gibbs, the deputy mayor for health and human services. "It's tragic."[102]

The situation is so dire that in the midst of budget shortfalls New York City recently launched an ambitious, far-reaching $130 million campaign to improve education and job training for sixteen- to twenty-four-year-old black and Hispanic males, $30 million of which will be funded by New York City Mayor Michael Bloomberg's private charitable foundation.[103]

Even a decade ago a program like this specifically targeting minority males would have evoked a hue and a cry from women's rights advocates like me, complaining about discrimination against women of color. But for the most part feminists aren't objecting, and the program has been generally well received. Because the facts are the facts: illiteracy, dropout rates, joblessness, and incarceration rates are at crisis levels for black and Hispanic men, and this is not the case for black and Hispanic women. We must change with the times and target our funds where the need is greatest.

One can only wish the program success. By one estimate, if our male graduation rate were increased by only 5 percent, the United States would see an annual savings of $4.9 billion in crime-related costs.[104]

What We Don't Know Does Hurt Us

EVEN IF boys who don't read somehow beat the odds, graduate from high school, find steady employment, stay out of prison, and enjoy life, liberty, and the pursuit of happiness, we all lose when our populace is ignorant about key facts about our country. Boys struggling in school join underperforming girls to comprise sad statistics like this one: overall, only 20 percent of fourth graders, 17 percent of eighth graders, and 12 percent of high school seniors demonstrated proficiency—competency—on a recent history exam, according to the National Assessment of Educational Progress. In fact, our students are less proficient in US history than any other subject.[105] (Among other reasons, this is disconcerting considering that US history only goes back a few hundred years. The Chinese, Greeks, and Persians, for example, have more or less ten times as much history in their history. The basics of ours, comparatively speaking, are far quicker to learn—our grandparents lived through a good chunk of it.)

Oh, history! some say. *Boring!*

Dusty, old meaningless tomes? Irrelevant to modern life?

If only. I hope you're sitting down when you read what they didn't know.

Don't Know Much about History

IN 2010 more than twelve thousand American high school seniors were given this quote from a well-known US Supreme Court decision, which they were told occurred in 1954:

> To separate them from others of similar age and qualifications solely because of their race generates a feeling of inferiority…that may affect their hearts and minds in a way unlikely ever to be undone…. We conclude that in the field of public education separate but equal has no place. Separate educational facilities are inherently unequal.

The question: The quotation is from which Supreme Court decision?

a. *Miranda v. Arizona*
b. *Gideon v. Wainwright*
c. *Mapp v. Ohio*
d. *Brown v. Board of Education of Topeka*

The National Assessment of Educational Progress, which devised the test questions, ranked this question "easy."[106] Nevertheless, only 2 percent of high school seniors correctly picked (d) as the answer.[107]

Had monkeys taken this test, and stabbed randomly at the four answers, roughly 25 percent of them would have gotten the right answer; only 2 percent of our kids got it right, though—to me, a horror scarier than any *Saw* film.

Americans sacrificed, suffered, and died to end the shameful Jim Crow period between *Plessy v. Ferguson* (1896), which held that "separate but equal" facilities were constitutional, and *Brown v. Board* (1954), which reversed that decision. *Brown v. Board* was such a cataclysmic event in our history that some Virginia schools closed altogether rather than accept black kids. For years after the decision the South was rocked in violent turmoil. In 1957 Arkansas Governor Orval Faubus called out his state's National Guard to block black students' entry to Little Rock Central High School. President Dwight Eisenhower responded to Faubus by deploying elements of the 101st Airborne Division. *Brown v. Board* catalyzed the civil rights movement, which within a decade saw the enactment of sweeping, historic legislation banning discrimination in housing and employment. Not only one of the most important Supreme Court decisions in the US history, *Brown v. Board* was also one of the most monumental events in twentieth-century America, reshaping classrooms, reordering communities, triggering debates, sit-ins, fire-hosed mass rallies, violence, and chaos, and it ultimately re-ordered our country into a more tolerant, just nation, all because nine white justices unanimously decreed that African American kids deserved not to be demeaned as second-class citizens. It was the beginning of the end of legalized racism in America and, nearly a century after the Civil War, the final chapter of the liberation of the descendants of American slaves.

And our kids don't know this.

One other problem: our kids have such poor logical reasoning skills that even if they had no clue as to the answer, they could not correctly *guess* that a quote about "public education" might come from the only choice offered that was against a *school board: Brown v. Board of Education of Topeka, Kansas.*

When I posted my own personal alarm at the fact that only one in fifty of our high school seniors could correctly identify the Supreme Court's monumental desegregation decision, a Facebook friend was motivated to write this on my wall:

> If it's only a matter of skin color or gender preferences, some people fit in better with others like them and some fit in better segregated. Everyone is different.... If people want to be segregated, let them.

Translation: the problem isn't school kids' ignorance about *Brown v. Board.* No! The problem is all this ruckus about integrated schools! This "friend" (someone I've never met; I accept all comers on Facebook and Twitter unless they turn psycho) is not at all convinced that people *shouldn't* just go to school only with "others like them." In other words, this American is still arguing the prosegregation position, which apparently did not die with former Alabama Governor George Wallace, who proclaimed famously, "Segregation now, segregation tomorrow, segregation forever!" and stood on the steps of the University of Alabama to block the brave young African American man and woman who had the temerity to want to be educated at their own public university alongside white folks (the "people who want to be segregated").

If people want to be segregated, let them.

Without a knowledge of our past, there may be some internal logic in advocating for allowing people to go to school with their own kind. This is but one disturbing example of the price we pay for our lack of knowledge about key events of our own nation's recent history. Candidates and politicians often misstate our country's history as well, unchecked. A nation that does not know its own history is doomed to repeat mistakes of the past.

Don't Know Much about the World Outside Our Borders

*"His ignorance covered the whole earth like a blanket,
and there was hardly a hole in it anywhere."*

—MARK TWAIN, *Eruption*

WE'RE NOT only strikingly uninformed about our own country's history; we're dangerously unaware of what's happening *right now* on our planet. When it comes to what's happening in our communities, our nation, and our world—present tense—we seem to be sleepwalking. The most likely reason: entertainment- and profit-driven American media covers international news significantly less than the media does in Europe and East Asia.[108]

The most urgent example: climate change. As I outlined more fully in *Think*, every reputable mainstream scientific organization is now sounding the alarm that climate change is real, it is upon us, it is human caused, and it is shaping up to be the worst humanitarian and ecological disaster in human history. Our official scientific agencies—the National Aeronautic and Space Administration (NASA), the Environmental Protection Agency (EPA), and the National Oceanic and Atmospheric Administration (NOAA)—regularly issue clarion calls on the subject. The greatest convergence of top scientific minds in human history, the United Nations' Intergovernmental Panel on Climate Change (IPCC), has four times warned that the warming of our planet is clear and unequivocal and that urgent action must be taken immediately. Over one hundred world governments, including ours, endorsed these findings.

Ice caps melt *now*, extreme weather is the new normal *now*, coastal towns are submerged *now*, droughts cause famines *now*, and this is only a cruel taste of the devastation that lies ahead if we fail to act. Yet in the latest Pew poll only 28 percent of Americans feel that climate should be a top priority for our leaders. The American public has ranked climate change dead last on a list of legislative priorities for each of the last three years.[109]

We don't know much about history, and we don't know much about science either. As we've seen, only a tiny minority of us are capable of understanding the science section of our local paper.[110] When only a few elites understand basic science, we're vulnerable to exploitation by religious extremists who maintain that the sun revolves around the earth,[111] pandering presidential candidates who claim that evolution is as scientifically valid as creationism,[112] or enormous corporations who'd like us to believe that climate change is a back-burner issue so that they can continue to profit while destroying our planet's climate.

We're also unaware of issues that require no special historic or scientific learning. Preventable genocides rage. Three million women and girls are held as slaves in brothels—literally, *slaves*, many of whom were kidnapped as children, who are drugged, raped, and threatened frequently, who are beaten and killed if they try to escape, who never see a penny of the money their "owners" make off them. Eight thousand children die every day, many from curable or preventable diseases like diarrhea and malaria. The ambitious and worthy UN Millennium Development Goals, to which the United States is a signatory, are designed to halve that and other suffering of the world's bottom billion, the extreme poor. Eighty-nine percent of us have never heard of the program.[113]

Here's another enormously important world issue that most of us know little about: overpopulation.

In 1999 world population hit six billion, an alarming number that strains the world's resources, causes the razing of rainforests and polluting of air, water, and land at an alarming rate. Just a dozen years later we hit seven billion in 2011.[114] Current projections forecast over nine billion by 2020 and over ten billion by 2100.

As triple Pulitzer Prize–winner Thomas Friedman points out in *Hot, Flat and Crowded*, from the planet's point of view, worse than those numbers alone is the fact that "we will go from a world population in which maybe one billion people were living an 'American' lifestyle to a world in which two or three billion people are living an American lifestyle or aspiring to do so."[115] As the world's emerging middle class copies our high-consumption, high-waste, deep-carbon-footprint, unsustainable lifestyle, the planet warms more quickly, our air and water become dirtier, forests continue to be razed. Overpopulation speeds up climate change, and climate change is creating harsher conditions for the world's extra billions of citizens.

The growth is enormous, just in one generation. In 1975 the world had just five megacities—cities with populations over ten million. We'll see *twenty-six* megacities by 2015. These exploding population numbers are "driving loss of arable land, deforestation, overfishing, water shortages, and air and water pollution."[116]

Worse, the countries that are growing by leaps and bounds are those that can least afford growth. If the projections are accurate, Yemen, a country whose population has quintupled since 1950 to twenty-five million, will see its numbers grow to one hundred million by century's end.[117] This Arabian Peninsula country already depends on food imports and faces critical water shortages, and it's one of the most repressive countries on earth for the female half of its population.

In Nigeria, the most populous country in Africa, population is expected to rise from today's 162 million to 730 million by 2100. Nigeria is seeing increased terrorist attacks on civilians, including the summer 2011 bombing of the UN headquarters in its capital, Abuja, that killed eighteen people.[118] Malawi, a tiny, land-locked, crowded, desperately poor African country of 14 million today—including 1.4 million orphaned children— could grow to 129 million.[119]

The tripling of the populations in places like Afghanistan,

Liberia, Niger, and the Democratic Republic of the Congo by midcentury is *the single-most worrying trend in the world,* according to Michael Hayden, former CIA director. "If their basic freedoms and basic needs—food, housing, education, employment—are not met, they could be easily attracted to violence, civil unrest, and extremism."[120] Many already are.

Given these disturbing reports about where we are headed, distributing contraceptives in countries with out-of-control population growth seems like a no-brainer. Whereas about three-quarters of married American women use a modern contraceptive, the comparable proportions are a quarter of women in East Africa, one in ten in West Africa, and a mere 7 percent in Central Africa, according to UN statistics. The 2011 famine in Somalia and neighboring Horn of Africa countries, with 3.7 million hungry and 12 million people in need of aid, is a lethal combination of drought (thanks to climate change) and a burgeoning population, most of whom have little or no access to birth control. The land, even in better times, simply cannot support the population, which has doubled in a generation.[121] We will only see more mass tragedies like this if we allow overpopulation to skyrocket as predicted.

Half the women in the developing world *want* to avoid pregnancy; two-thirds of those want no more children and one-third want to delay the next child.[122] The unmet need for contraceptives is concentrated most heavily in the poorest countries.

And yet in 1984 America adopted the "Global Gag Rule," denying any family planning assistance to any foreign organization that "promotes or performs abortion," even with their own private funds. If a clinic's work was 99 percent birth control and 1 percent abortions, they were defunded. If their work was 100 percent birth control and they simply gave referrals to others who performed abortions, they were defunded. The Gag Rule shook the world of third-world family planning, forcing clinics to close, eliminating outreach efforts, and denying access to simple birth control to many women around the world.[123]

In 2001 we cut all US funding to the UN Family Planning

Agency, the primary international body that focuses on reducing overpopulation.[124] Little attention was paid to this policy change, as world population continued to skyrocket. It took 120 years, from 1800 to 1920, for the world to grow from one billion to two billion people. *We are now adding a billion roughly every dozen years.*[125]

And this issue is almost entirely off our radar.

At the root of the overpopulation problem is our inattention to *preventative* programs. We are more accustomed to reacting to crises like terrorism then to nipping emerging problems in the bud with preventative measures like birth control, education, or jobs programs. Prevention is not sexy. Prevention requires critical thinking, long-range planning, the ability to understand how pennies spent today will save dollars tomorrow, and the patience to wait out long-range results. Yet instead, we cut prevention programs today and hope that tomorrow never comes.

Abroad, we'd rather cut family planning services (considered a "best buy" by global health initiatives for cost-effectiveness[126]) and leave to our children the problems of a crowded, unsustainable planet. Similarly, at home we fail to educate our kids adequately about reproduction and contraception. One-fourth of American children get abstinence-only sex education—they're told not to have sex, period, without any instruction in birth control or disease prevention. As a direct result we have one of the highest rates of teen pregnancy in the first world. (As the sad joke goes, what do you call kids who get abstinence-only education? Parents.)

We'd rather cut drug and alcohol treatment programs ($1,433 per course of outpatient treatment[127]) and then incarcerate addicts ($47,000 per year per inmate in California[128]). We'd rather cut school days, summer school, and after-school programs and then unleash bored juveniles onto the streets, later locking them up for adult sentences when they commit crimes. As former Harvard University President Derek Bok said, "If you think education is expensive, try ignorance." To paraphrase: if you think birth control in the third world is expensive, try another three billion hungry, desperate, angry people on a hot, crowded planet plagued by droughts, floods, and Category 5 hurricanes. Will this be the legacy we leave to our children?

———————

WE BEGAN this section with the sad results of our failing schools: millions of illiterate Americans, many unaware of what the Taliban is or where our troops are engaged in active military operations. Schools aren't the national priority they were a generation ago. We've seen the now-annual ritual of hacking away at school programs, as though education is just another government program to be minimized as much as possible. Teachers are reduced to beggars, food and facilities that make people sick, arts and sports are cut, and everyone is forced to make do with less. Is it any wonder so many boys report hating school?

It all boils down to this: as we become increasingly illiterate and uneducated, will we continue to turn away from preventive programs and lurch from crisis to crisis, bewildered at how they came about, or will we require rigorous synthesis of the facts and a stomach for long-term planning to stop problems from taking root? Will we ignore the lessons of history and repeat its mistakes, or will we synthesize and build upon the lessons of our past? Will we mock our thinkers as elitists, as ivory-tower nerds, or will we respect their expertise and embrace the complex analysis we so vitally need to move forward? Will we value education and give our young people the skills and tools they need to compete with countries that are currently graduating millions of thinkers each spring, or will we allow our children— and our boys in particular, who are falling further behind both girls at home and students of both genders in other developed nations—simply to fall off the grid?

CHAPTER TWO

OUR ECONOMY: THE DE-INDUSTRIAL REVOLUTION

"To him that hath, more shall be given; and from him that hath not, the little that he hath shall be taken away."

—PERCY BYSSHE SHELLEY
(PARAPHRASING JESUS CHRIST),
"A DEFENCE OF POETRY"

OUR SCHOOLS fail our boys, but the condition is temporary. Eventually they release them to the larger world. There, many are in for a rude awakening: the most challenging economic conditions for young men in living memory.

How bad is our economy for working Americans?

There's a lot of talk about our dismal economy, but most of what we get from our media are a morass of unemployment statistics that go up and down monthly, reported breathlessly but without context; politicians running on "jobs" platforms but then failing to produce them; and, more recently, some discussion of income inequality and the rise of the top 1 percent of income earners. These stories are only a piece of what's going on. The weightier, more profound underlying story is rarely told: regardless of this month's job numbers, our economy will likely remain entrenched in its current malaise for years because we're not just in a temporary down cycle; instead, many of the fundamentals have changed. And because deep budget cuts have taken many of our communities in the wrong direction for the last few years, it will take us considerable time and effort just to get back to the starting line before we can move ahead. Yes, the gap between rich and poor in the United States has widened to levels comparable to banana republics. In 2010 income disparity in the United States was greater than any other Western industrialized nation.[129] Between 1992 and 2007 the four hundred wealthiest Americans saw their incomes quadruple while their tax rates plummeted by 37 percent over the same period.[130] But it's not just that the 1 percent has pulled so far ahead; the real news is that today's 99 percent is losing so much ground compared to yesterday's middle class and poor.

We think of ourselves as a nation always moving inexorably forward. As scientific progress enriches our lives, technology improves, enabling each generation to surpass the next with better toys (computers, gadgets, TVs, cars, homes) and longer, healthier lives. Prices on flat-screen televisions, cell phones, and air travel have, in real dollars, fallen enough that many working families enjoy some of these previously only-for-the-rich luxuries. The Internet in particular has been a revolutionary force for progress, dramatically improving efficiencies and allowing us all to communicate quickly and easily with one another. But in many other areas our quality of life has slipped away unnoticed, without even giving us the chance to say goodbye. A look away from the statistics and into our cities, suburbs, and rural counties reveals our gritty decline.

Just a generation ago, a young man with a high school diploma could land a blue-collar job in a city like Philadelphia, with its then-strong industrial base, and raise a middle-class family. His children would be educated in reasonably competent public schools, and he could own a home in a neighborhood like Germantown, whose main thoroughfare, Chelten Avenue, boasted department stores, restaurants, and theaters. Today, Philadelphia's manufacturing jobs have vanished, and Chelten Street features boarded-up store windows, "For Rent" signs, and check-cashing shops. It's the same story in Detroit, Michigan; Oklahoma City, Oklahoma; Toledo, Ohio; Greensboro, North Carolina; and city after city across America, as factories disappear and previously middle-class communities are reduced to pockets of poverty.[131]

In many places we are going *backward*. Cities and counties with dried-up budgets are taking deep breaths and then instituting previously unthinkable policies. Paved roads are being torn up, for example. Ever driven on a smooth road that edged out into the countryside and then turned to gravel? Recall the teeth-jangling, windshield-busting, car-damaging transition, especially if you weren't in a Jeep or SUV? It's tough to endure for more than a few minutes. Then remember when you turned around and got back to the interstate—what a relief that was? Paved highways are a sign that we are a viable first-world country with modern infrastructure. Goods and commerce flow quickly and, therefore, relatively cheaply across the asphalt, family members can visit one another smoothly, ambulances can speed the sick to the specialty hospital, and so forth. Well-maintained highways are the kind of municipal service we all take for granted—until they're gone.

Forced to make difficult choices, budget-strapped rural communities are now *ripping up* asphalt roads in states like Michigan, South Dakota, and Alabama, leaving their residents to the slow, jarring, pinging gravel and dirt roads from what most of us thought were a bygone era. No longer able to afford the maintenance of their tar roads, counties are quietly removing them. A local professor in one such newly depaved community calls it "Back to the Stone Age."[132]

A return to gravel and dirt roads in some places is matched

by a return to darkness in others. Street lights are being turned off in city neighborhoods. In Highland Park, Michigan, two-thirds of the streetlights that had helped reduce crime and improve traffic safety were not only turned off; in 2011 they were *pulled up and hauled away*. Parents are now concerned about young children going to school in the early-morning darkness. Evening church services have been rescheduled. "Long stretches of blocks are dark, silhouettes of people are barely visible and potholes appear suddenly beneath tires," reports the *New York Times*. Dozens of towns and cities nation-wide have done the same.[133]

Our commitment to public parks and green spaces, another sign of a developed, modern country, is withering. My fiancé, Braden, and I went hiking recently in a state park called the Santa Susana Pass in Chatsworth, California, a perennially sunny southern suburb in the San Fernando Valley. As we walked along the street on the way in, Braden pointed to some large, ugly gray asphalt squares set into the edge of sidewalk we passed every five or six steps. What the...? Then it dawned on us—*trees*. There were once trees lining this suburban road. Foliage costs money to maintain, so they'd been torn up and removed, like the paved roads in Alabama and the streetlights in Michigan.

We paused for a moment of silence for the lost greenery. The traffic noisily rushed by, seeming louder now. I would have loved to ask a park ranger about this, but there weren't any on duty—budget cuts. California has the nation's largest system of state parks, beautiful showpieces of my state's diverse deserts, mountains, and beaches. But perhaps not for long, because almost half of the state's parks department funding has been cut since 2006, forcing closures of *seventy* state parks in 2012.[134] Many that remain "open" are closed unofficially as well, as they have no one to maintain them. We had to climb through low holes in spiky chain-link fences to get inside Santa Susana Park and out again, though it's a historic area where stagecoaches rumbled through a century and a half ago and would be an inspiring place to take the kids in the surrounding suburbs for some fresh air and to discuss our pioneer past. Nope. Closed, for now—and maybe indefinitely.

We're regressing in city services as well. At the end of 2011, to take just one example, four Detroit libraries closed amidst community protests. Lack of funding was the reason, of course, not lack of use.[135] The libraries had, in fact, been heavily used. Local elementary school children, whose school had no usable library—*we have entire schools in our country without libraries*—had used the computers at their local Lincoln Branch as well as the books for, say, science research. Fifth-grader Benny Trubel wrote this letter to his library commissioner (I cleaned up his spelling):

> Hey my name is Benny. Please don't shut down our library that's the best library ever. I go to Mason Elementary. I have to do my science project at home. But I can't because I don't have no computer so I have to do my project somewhere else 'n that's at Lincoln Branch. Also I like to read books because my S.F.A. teacher said I have to pull my reading level up. I'm in 2nd grade level 'n I'm in 5th grade. Lincoln Brand was helping me very good! *Please.* Sincerely, Benny."[136]

Benny's letter fell on deaf ears. He lost his library.

Charlotte-Mecklenburg, North Carolina, shuttered twelve public libraries in 2010 despite resident outcry and offers to fundraise to save them.[137] Half the libraries in Denver, Colorado, were on the chopping block in 2011.[138] The same year hours and services have been cut in all the libraries in Greenwood, Indiana, and two libraries there were closed forever.[139]

Everything that libraries countrywide can cut, they already have, such as hours of operation, staffing, and their magazine and journal subscriptions. What might seem like a reasonable efficiency in the Internet age—the *New York Times* can be read online, after all, much more cheaply—has been a disaster for academic journals, especially higher-priced science publications that rely on library subscriptions for their research budgets.[140] Library cuts and closures have ripple effects on scholarship and research, and they prevent computerless local residents from educating themselves or searching for jobs online.

Fifth-grader Benny, who wrote the note above, knows he needs to read a lot of books to bring his reading up from a second-grade level. Benny highlighted the word "please" as he pleaded for access to a library.

We are making an American child beg us for the chance to read.

Our bridges, roads, public buildings, dams, and other necessities are crumbling, leaking, and deteriorating. In 2009 the American Society of Civil Engineers issued a comprehensive report on America's infrastructure. Overall grade: D. Transit and aviation: an unnerving D. Roads: a dangerous D minus. Dams, hazardous waste, and school buildings: another unsettling D. Drinking and wastewater: D minus. Over videos of cars falling off unsafe bridges, tankers stuck in sinkholes, and Americans drinking contaminated water, civil engineers remind us on their website that we spend far less of our GDP on infrastructure than do Europeans and the Chinese.[141]

Many trains in America now take longer to move from one major city to another than they did sixty years ago. Chicago to Minneapolis? Four and a half hours via the Olympian Hiawatha in the 1950s, Tom Vanderbilt of Slate.com discovered. Today, that trip takes more than eight hours.[142] I love riding trains from city to city, but in my experience at least half the time US trains are significantly delayed, often due to "track work," whatever that means. In Shanghai, China, I rode the high-speed "maglev" train, short for "magnetic levitation" because somehow, miraculously, the maglev hovers above the track as it averages 267 miles per hour, whizzing its occupants from downtown to the airport in eight minutes flat. There's not a city in the United States that even has plans to build the kind of efficient airport-to-city train that is taken for granted in most European cities and that, as you read these words, are being built throughout China's rapidly modernizing cities.

Ripped up streetlights in the suburbs, highways in the country, trees and libraries in our cities, disintegrated bridges and levees and sewers nationwide, our antiquated transportation system—these are the signs of our decline, telling symptoms of the overall increase in poverty in and around those dirt roads, dark streets, and libraryless, parkless neighborhoods. In fact, our suburbs, once a bastion of middle-class prosperity, the place most families wanted to raise their children, are now home to the country's biggest and most rapidly expanding segment of the poor. Between 2000 and 2008, the poverty rate in the suburbs of the largest metro areas in the United States jumped 25 percent.[143] And the even bigger fiscal picture reflects this.

What's the best economic indicator for how the nation's economy is doing overall? Let's see. How about the stock market? Sure, television, radio, and news websites love to track its gyrations as a barometer of our economic health. *The Dow is down! The S & P is up! Nikkei averages*…yada yada. But the majority of Americans in the bottom 80 percent don't own a single share of stock.[144] The top 20 percent own 91 percent of shares. And, of course, the much-ballyhooed top 1 percent owns the most, by far. Those busy graphics running along the bottom of our television screens with the daily NASDAQ numbers keep us all posted, second by second, on how the rich's investments are doing.

Spare me. To most of us this is as relevant to our lives as yacht racing. A big stock drop today? Tragically, a billionaire may not be able to scoop up that private island. Shares rally? The rich get richer, but there is little or no impact on the ability of teachers or nurses or firefighters to provide for their families. In fact, there are disturbing indications that layoffs *improve* Wall Street's bottom line. While publicly traded corporate profits jumped 720 percent between 2007 and 2009, the unemployment rate climbed by 102 percent during the same period.[145] This is because higher unemployment rates can provide a large pool of cheap (read: desperate) labor for industry, thereby further enhancing its bottom line and shareholder profits. Perhaps when markets rally, working Americans should duck for cover. Perhaps news reports of Dow Jones numbers should carry a disclaimer:

Warning: stock market gains are probably losses for you!

A more meaningful flashing number at the bottom of news screens would be the "misery index"—the sum of the country's inflation and unemployment rates, used by economists to measure the pain middle- and working-class Americans feel. In October 2011 the misery index reached its highest level in thirty years, as joblessness remained high and prices rose, making life painful for millions.[146]

Seeking to improve on the misery index, the *Huffington Post* developed the Real Misery Index, incorporating additional information that matters to middle- and working-class Americans: unemployment numbers; inflation rates for essentials such as food, gas, and medical costs; and data on credit card delinquencies, housing prices, home loan defaults, and food stamp participation. By mid-2010 the Real Misery Index was at its highest level on record (data had been charted since 1984).

Or we could choose to judge ourselves by how the least among us are faring. More than seven hundred thousand people are currently homeless in the United States—a number that grew 20 percent from 2007 to 2010.[147] How different our focus and our policies would be if hourly updates of those numbers flashed along the bottom of our news screens:

4,000 more of our neighbors are sleeping on the street tonight...4,001...4,012...5,187...

The income stagnation of the middle class, the working class's misery indexes, and the rise in the homeless population don't—and probably never will—get the breathless coverage the rich's investments do. And at the root of all this pain for ordinary Americans is one overarching, megaproblem:

joblessness. In December 2007 the US economy employed 146 million people. Four years later it employed only 140 million. During the same time period our population rose by more than 10 million. So we're not only losing jobs, but we're also gaining people—a double whammy.

Unemployment in and of itself is hell. Myriad studies have long documented the increases in depression, domestic violence and other crime, and even suicides among those who are disconnected from their communities and have lost the sense of contribution and, of course, money, that work provides.[148]

Add to that the fact that since most Americans have no cushion, no nest egg, a layoff can quickly become a calamitous event. Living payday to payday, millions of people are just one eliminated paycheck away from economic disaster in their personal finances. That's because the lowest two quintiles (the bottom 40 percent) control only 0.3 percent of the wealth in the United States. That is, many of us have no rainy day fund squirreled away. None at all. A rainy day becomes a no-end-in-sight hurricane for many, who have nowhere to run for shelter. And thus a job loss can become a long-term, life-changing catastrophe. Even after finding a new job, the misery continues. According to Pew's Economic Mobility Project, one-third of adults who experience a one-year income loss of more than 25 percent fail to recover even after ten years.[149]

For those who have managed a little savings, the balance is shrinking. The average American's already-low net worth dropped another 8 percent between 2005 and 2011.[150] And so we increasingly turn to borrowing to get by, sinking ever deeper into a financial hole. The bottom 80 percent of America spends 110 percent of its income, going deeper into debt each month to pay for housing, transportation, food, and other expenses of life.[151] Our credit card debt is truly staggering, a number so big it's difficult to comprehend, really: a total of $793 billion as of May 2011, according to a Federal Reserve report, divided among 50 million Americans. Of those of us who have at least one credit card, the average debt is $15,799.[152]

What does all this add up to? Not only a staggering level of suffering but also real fear for the future. When asked in late 2011 which catastrophic event they feared most—such as terrorist attack, natural disaster, outbreak of disease—Americans' number one answer was "economic collapse."[153]

Why the Bad Economic News Is Worse for Boys and Young Men

FOR YOUNG men entering the work force now or boys who will be entering in a decade or so, the economic news is particularly disturbing. Largely unheralded, a dramatic change has occurred in what used to be a rock-solid portion of our economy: traditional blue-collar male jobs.

Fifty years ago about a third of all jobs in the United States were in the manufacturing or agricultural sectors, which skewed 70 percent male and for which a high school degree was sufficient.[154] Those jobs, many unionized with good health and retirement benefits, used to support a decent middle-class lifestyle, and many of our fathers and grandfathers (and some of our mothers and grandmothers) worked in our industrial plants. Their families owned homes and cars, took vacations, and enjoyed the trappings of American life. With astonishing speed, however, those industries have disappeared. In 2003 only 17 percent of our jobs were in those sectors, and by 2014 the US Bureau of Labor estimates that the number will dip to only *5 percent*, as US companies continue to ship jobs overseas and automate. In the Great Recession of 2007–2009, three-quarters of those who lost their jobs were men in traditionally male sectors like construction and finance, and many of those jobs just aren't coming back, no matter if our economy rebounds. These jobs have been outsourced or eliminated, and employers are enjoying those efficiencies and cost savings, thank you very much.

America is undergoing a De-Industrial Revolution, as entire formerly robust industries are relocating abroad, taking millions of jobs with them. According to a 2011 study by the Economic Policy Institute, in the last decade since China entered the World Trade Organization, the United States has lost 2.8 million jobs, 70 percent of which have been in manufacturing. The biggest hit was in computer and electronic parts (909,400 jobs), then apparel and accessories (178,700 jobs), textile fabrics and products (92,300 jobs), fabricated metal products (123,900 jobs), plastic and rubber products (62,000 jobs), motor vehicles and parts (49,300 jobs), with miscellaneous manufactured goods losing another 119,700 jobs. And these are only the trade losses: all the satellite businesses that existed to serve these industries, such as marketing, advertising, and legal, have also laid off workers.

Vermont Senator Bernie Sanders tweeted recently that America has lost an average of fifteen manufacturing facilities *a day* over the last ten years.[155] The last spoons and forks made in America were in a Sherrill, New York, plant that closed in 2010. (Recall that Revolutionary War hero Paul Revere was a flatware craftsman.) Stainless steel rebars, the sturdy rods that reinforce concrete in construction—outsourced. Vending machines—outsourced. Light bulbs, cell phones, laptop computers—all outsourced.[156] Amazing American-designed technology like the iPad or iPhone? Made in Asia—not here.[157]

Since World War II men (and women) without higher education have worked in factory jobs, supporting families and the broad prosperity of the American middle class that for sixty years was the envy of the world. The disappearance of these industries seems to have snuck up on many communities, which are now baffled as to what has happened. *Where did all the jobs go? When will they come back?*

In 1950 roughly one in twenty American men of prime working age was not working; today that ratio is about one in five, the highest ever recorded.[158] As unemployment hovers at around 9 percent overall, for young men, as the jobs they once poured into have vanished, the numbers are far worse than these painful national averages. Eighteen percent of young men are actively seeking work but can't find any—that's four million guys whose lives are stalled, as they are unable to get a foot in the door.[159]

Men today fare worse than men did a decade or a generation ago, and they also fare poorly compared to today's women at the lower rungs of the economic ladder. Over the past decade, as men lost more than three million jobs, the total number of jobs for women went up by close to a million. From 1960 to 2008 the average unemployment rate for men twenty-five years and older was 4.2 percent. From 2008 to 2010 that number more than doubled, shooting up to 8.9 percent. By contrast, unemployment for women of the same age and for the same period of time went from 4.7 percent to 7.2 percent, a disturbing increase to be sure, but only half of the men's increase. Today working men are more likely to be unemployed than are working women, and as the educational gap widens and more women earn college degrees, so will this employment gap.[160]

As jobs in traditionally "male" industries evaporate, jobs in "women's" fields increase. In construction, where men fill 87 percent of positions, more than 1.4 million jobs were eliminated between 2008 and 2010. Approximately 4.4 million jobs have been added in the education and health care sectors—where women dominate, comprising 77 percent of the work force. Men continue to do well in senior management and at the top of the corporate hierarchy—only eighteen of Fortune 500's CEOs were women by the end of 2011—but at the entry-level, just-out-of-school level your boy will face in his early adulthood, expect he'll have a more challenging time landing a job than his girlfriend will.[161]

In some minority communities men lag even further behind their female counterparts in the work force. Ten years ago both African American men and women had the same unemployment rate of 8.2 percent. Since then, however, the men's rate has more than doubled and now is almost four points higher than the unemployment rate for women. Similarly, Hispanic men now have a 1.7 percent higher unemployment rate than Hispanic women, whom historically they have outperformed.[162]

Unemployment statistics like these are important to watch, but they don't tell the full story, because some people get temporary jobs now and then, thereby getting counted as "employed" when they are really only barely scraping by—for now. Those who have given up looking entirely—"discouraged workers"—aren't even counted in the numbers. Thus, because unemployment numbers are imprecise, tracking only those who are actively seeking work (not your brother-in-law who stopped looking and is now living off his wife's income, or your uncle who's working an inferior job because it's better than nothing, or your buddy who's doing odd jobs part time), another way to approach the issue is to look at how few men now have jobs. Only 66 percent of American men were working in 2010—*the lowest number in US history.*[163] Until the 1960s more than 80 percent of men worked consistently. Since then, the number has been dropping steadily. For those men who do have jobs, they're just not making enough money. The median take-home pay of male full-time workers, adjusted for inflation, has stagnated since its peak in 1973.[164]

Of the fifteen growth job categories today, women dominate thirteen. They're relatively low-paying jobs, like nursing, home health assistance, child care, or food preparation.[165] But at least it's paying work. Even men desperate for work rarely apply for traditionally "female" jobs like teaching or nursing, despite programs trying to recruit them.

It's not a matter of waiting out this slump. The world has restructured itself, and there is no viable scenario in which any significant quantity of traditionally male jobs are coming back. The nearly three million US manufacturing jobs we lost to China in the last decade are now entrenched in China's increasingly sophisticated, rapidly growing economy. Unskilled work goes to places like Indonesia, where workers are paid as little as $2 a day.[166] What can we dream up that will bring those jobs back to the United States? Are Americans going to stop wanting cheap toys for their kids, or inexpensive shoes? Are employers going to wake up one morning and say, "I'd like to triple the amount I pay to fabricate my clothing line?" Are shareholders going to occupy Wall Street, holding placards demanding lower dividends?

And even skilled, white-collar jobs are beginning to slip away to places like India, whose low-wage labor pool speaks English, is becoming increasingly educated and skilled, and now controls not only many manufacturing industries but also sectors of white-collar employment, such as back office accounting, human resources, and customer service jobs. Knowing this, I suppose I should not have been surprised—but I was—in December of 2011 when I received this unsolicited e-mail to my law firm:

Ms. Bloom,

I am a lawyer (Mass. Bar member; JD, University of Chicago) and wanted to make an introduction. I have a business which focuses on reducing the cost of litigation for personal injury law firms.

At a significant discount to alternatives, we provide a range of work including medical records review, demand letters, bill itemization, deposition summaries and indexing. We are based in India and I am an American. We have experience in auto accidents, nursing home negligence, workplace accidents, various spinal injuries, medical malpractice, trucking accidents, etc.

We typically increase client profitability by tens of thousands per year. Our client references from personal injury litigators are available and convenient.

I look forward to making an introduction and discussing how we might be of value.

Thank you and best regards,
Suhrud —, Esq.

I certainly can't blame Suhrud for coming up with a business plan and marketing it: that's the American way. But outsourcing American *lawyer and paralegal work*—at a fraction of the price, naturally—well, that hits close to home for me. I can only assume this e-mail was sent to every attorney on some online list that attorney Suhrud obtained. What small business (the vast majority of lawyers work solo or with just a few others) could resist the appeal of getting the work done at, say, $10 an hour instead of $150? What client, seeking redress for an injury, would think to ask her lawyer whether her medical records will be reviewed in house or in Bangalore?

And this is why, no matter how well intentioned our political leaders may be, stopping this flood of jobs from leaving the United States is next to impossible. The economic incentives to American business owners to farm out their work to bright, hardworking foreigners at low, low prices are too powerful.

Our Staggering Youth Unemployment Rates

MANY OF us think that *young people*, at least, can always get a job. Perhaps it will be an entry-level, thankless, starter job, but so be it; they can start small, get their foot in the door, work hard, and rise up the corporate ladder as the years go by. That's the vision most of us have for teens and twenty-somethings once they're out of school. But even that depleted vision for our young people is out of step with reality. As Roosevelt Institute fellow Mike Konczal points out, American youth unemployment (again, people who are actively looking for work but can't find it—this *excludes* students) is in line with Arab Spring countries. As pundits criticize Middle Eastern and Northern African countries for high youth unemployment rates ranging from 12 to 30 percent, here in the United States youth unemployment in late 2011 was 25.3 percent for sixteen- to nineteen-year-olds, and

18 percent for sixteen- to twenty-four-year-olds. Factoring in all the young people not counted as unemployed—the disabled, those who are incarcerated, and those who have given up and are living off mom and dad, for example—the picture is even more disturbing. For the first time in fifty years the *majority* of our young people—55 percent—are not working.[167] Yes, some have stayed in school or gone back to school to wait out the job market, but many students would like to work while going to school so as to support themselves and defray their tuition debt, but they're unable to.

I met eighteen-year-old Giuseppe,[168] a hulking young man with long, bushy hair, engulfed in dark, loose clothing, meeting the world with a fierce, intense gaze. He banged his backpack down on the picnic table in his school's outdoor lunch area and agreed to answer a few of my questions, warily. I wanted to know: why was he eighteen and only beginning his junior year of high school? "It's a long story," he said, looking away. "I'm just here for the classes. I'm not like these other kids," he said, glowering first at the stream of girls in miniskirts and leggings, boys noisily jostling each other, then back at me.

I changed the subject to the one I'd come to discuss. "Do you read for pleasure?" I asked. "Oh, yeah," he said, brightening. "My mom's boyfriend gave me this." He pulled from his backpack a surprise: a worn book of Buddhist philosophy. "Have you read this?" he asked me. He pushed it across the table into my hands. "It's amazing. You should. *Everything* is in here." His screw-you mask lifted; he now waxed on about the beauty of Buddhism. I told him about Buddhist countries I'd visited, like Nepal, and recommended books by the Dalai Lama. *Now* we had something to talk about. Buoyed by his change in mood, I went for a big, open-ended question, asking Giuseppe, "If you could have one thing in the world, what would it be?"

I was expecting an iPhone, the coolest new sneakers, or, maybe, given our philosophical discussion, world peace.

Instead, the mask returned. Anger shadowed across his face. "A job!" he said. "I've filled out like a hundred applications.

Haven't even gotten one call. Do you know of any jobs?"

Boys like Giuseppe have not been prepared for the lack of opportunities, the rejection of so many doors slammed in their faces, the discouragement of joblessness. It's a new world order that few young people fully grasp, one that often leaves them behind. Coupled with boys' relatively poor school performance, the job market young men encounter delays their independence and self-sufficiency for years. The message they get is: *there's no place for you here.*

And as they struggle to find meaningful or, for many, *any* work, they do so steeped in treacherous cultural messages about what it is to be a man.

CHAPTER THREE

THUG CULTURE: BIG MONEY IN UNDERMINING OUR VALUES

UNDEREDUCATED BY our schools and battered by a tough economy, boys, like the rest of us, need an escape. And just like us, they turn to entertainment. Through their earbuds and Xboxes and iPhones come the driving beats and irresistible rhythms of today's biggest artists as well as dazzling, slickly produced TV, films, games, and YouTube videos. Who can turn away? Billions of dollars for enormous entertainment companies ride on capturing and holding our boys' attention. Five media conglomerates (Disney, Time Warner, Viacom, GE/NBC, and News Corp) control the vast majority of American entertainment programming.[169] Each of these companies is, in fact, among the 325 largest corporations in the world. Decades of market research have now solidified what works and what sells, and the megacorporations are pumping it out at a fast and furious pace, reaping enormous profits from the social and political world they choose to depict.

Calling music, film, television, and Internet "entertainment" really underplays its current role in young people's lives. More accurately, our children live simultaneously in two worlds: the physical world of school, home, and what adults call "real life," and the digital world, which, to young people, is equally if not more "real." As a harrowing example, so many young people have committed suicide after reading devastating online posts about themselves that Facebook recently created a special program to connect users to crisis counselors via its chat feature.[170] It doesn't get any more real than that.

Young Americans between the ages of eight and eighteen on average spend more than seven and a half hours a day receiving images, text, and sound on a smart phone, computer, television, or other electronic device. During much of that time they are multitasking, such as watching TV while chatting online, thereby doubling or tripling their media exposure.[171] And whenever possible—on the school bus, walking anywhere, doing homework—they are listening to their favorite songs and watching free YouTube music videos over and over again until the words and moves are memorized.

The problem is that most parents are blithely oblivious to the messages being delivered during this nonstop feed into our kids' brains. Let's take a close look at the music industry's most popular genres for boys today: rap and hip-hop.

If a violent criminal knocked on your front door and said he'd like some time alone with your son to sing some catchy and slickly packaged songs he'd written about life on the streets and behind bars, would you give him ten bucks, show him to your son's room, and leave the two of them alone for hours, unmonitored? Allowing our minor children to absorb these communications while we ignore them—and while we're even *funding* this stuff—is functionally the same as this scenario.

Bad boys have always had some allure, from Butch Cassidy and the Sundance Kid to Al Capone. To some extent every generation celebrates outlaws with a wink, a biopic, and even fashion: baggy zoot suits were first popular among thieves to hide their takes and then became hip in the 1940s among law-abiding citizens in the same way "pants on the ground" baggy jeans are today. (When belts were taken in jail, inmates' trousers drooped, and thus a fashion was born on the outside as well.)

And as surely as night follows the day, each generation laments the decline in quality of the younger generation's music. Elvis Presley, the Beatles, Madonna, and Britney Spears all had parents shaking their heads over the alleged moral decline they heard in the music. As a result many parents now feel that one entitlement of youth is a certain level of social subversion in their music, to be tsk-tsked at in adult disapproval. Listening to songs your parents hate is part of growing up, right? A rite of passage? And some parents are loathe to complain for fear of being uncool. Even parents who hear the occasional obnoxious lyrics figure that there are more important things to worry about, and we have to pick our battles. And surely it's just a random song or two, by some alternative indie artists? So it really doesn't matter much, right?

I wish.

The difference between today's music industry and that of a generation ago is astonishing. Twenty-first-century superstars are not just shaking up sexual conventions or making music that's loud and jangling to the older generation's sensibilities—the objections of prior years. Rather, today's artists are selling brutality, misogyny, and homophobia on an audacious scale. Never before have hate messages like these been so popular and widespread in our country, reaching down to even the youngest children who listen to and imitate their favorite artists' words and moves. Never before has advocating violence on a mass scale been so profitable, as the enormous global media companies peddle American rap and hip-hop music worldwide, reaping billions. To be clear: the ugly messages are coming *not* from fringe, no-one-buys-them indie artists. The *top-selling* artists of our day peddle this evil, multibillion-dollar companies back them, bypassing you, selling directly to your boy. They have created—and daily reinforce and perpetuate— thug culture.

Oh, it's not all bad, you say. *You can't broad-brush an entire musical genre.* And that's true. Not all rap music today is thuggish—Common and the Black Eyed Peas are notable exceptions. But get this—*most* of the top songs from the biggest artists spew anger, hate, and criminality. According to one comprehensive study, two out of three top-selling rap songs glorify brutality and violence. That's a survey of *all* popular rap music, not just its more thuggish subgenre, gangsta rap, which is all felony, all the time. Nihilism—the rejection of morality and religion and the belief that human values are worthless and life is pointless—shows up in one out of four platinum-selling rap songs. The reliable old standby, objectification and degradation of women, is present in "only" 22 percent of the top-selling songs, according to the study.[172] ("Only" one out of five songs insults our sisters and mothers? Would we have the same blasé reaction if "only" 22 percent of the lyrics were overtly racist or anti-Semitic?)

Many parents take a look at what their kids are reading in school or restrict their kids to PG or PG-13 movies, but they never listen to the words of their children's favorite songs. So let's tune in now. Warning: what you are about to read is not appropriate for kids (which is exactly my point). It's not appropriate for adults, either. It's unfit for any human being with a soul. Some of it is downright repulsive.

Our boys are jamming to music that constantly glorifies the indefensible, like, say, gang membership. Multimillionaire artist Snoop Dogg, backed by Universal Music Group (UMG), rapped in his top-selling song, "Drop It Like It's Hot":

> *I keep a blue flag hanging out my backside,*
> *But only on the left side, yeah that's the Crip side.*

Really, Snoop? You're proud of your *gang affiliation*?

The bloody violence between the Crips and the Bloods is reported to have killed more than fifteen thousand people, ripping apart families, devastating neighborhoods—almost entirely young male African Americans from Snoop Dogg's own community. More deaths have resulted from the Crips-Bloods street battles than in all the violence in Northern Ireland in the last few decades.[173] Grieving mothers and other community activists in Los Angeles, where the Crips and Bloods have been shooting each other and innocent bystanders for a generation, have worked long and hard to turn young people away from the perceived allure of gang membership. Yet Snoop and UMG, *the largest music company in the world*, display no moral qualms whatsoever about glorifying his affiliation with the Crips in this multiplatinum song, one of the most popular in the last decade.[174]

"Drop It Like It's Hot" is just one example from a mountain of music celebrating thug culture. If love songs and teenage angst were the major themes in popular music in the 1970s, 1980s, and 1990s, today the *dominant theme* is violence and gore. Rappers, who boys look up to for their machismo, wealth, and fame, almost universally portray themselves as macho, hair-trigger crazies, liable to shoot anyone who looks at them sideways. They are the worst possible role models your boy could follow—the male counterparts of the brainless, catty women on reality shows that girls now emulate. Rappers defiantly call themselves "assassins," "hustlers," "gangstas," "madmen," and "killas." "Some rappers are even more colorful in their depictions," says George Washington University Professor Charis Kubrin, calling themselves

> "untamed guerillas" (Hot Boys, "Clear Da Set"),
> "3rd world nigga"(Master P, "Making Moves"),
> "thuggish, ruggish niggas" (BTNH, "2 Glocks"),
> "hellraiser" (2Pac, "Hellrazor"),
> "trigger niggas" (Master P, "Till We Dead and Gone"),
> "the nigga with the big fat trigger" (Ice Cube, "Now I
>   Gotta Wet'Cha"),
> "no limit soldier" (Silkk the Shocker, "I'm a Soldier"),
> "young head busta" (Hot Boys, "'Bout Whatever"),

"wig splitas" (Juvenile, "Welcome 2 the Nolia"),
"cap peelers" (Mystikal, "Mystikal Fever"),
"grave filler" (Juvenile, "Back that Ass Up"),
"gat buster" or "trigger man" (Jay-Z, "It's Hot"),
"raw nigga" (Layzie Bone, "2 Glocks"), and
"Sergeant Slaughter" (Killer Mike, "Snappin' and
      Trappin'").[175]

All this wordplay is euphemism for the ultimate human evil:
murder. And it's not metaphorical. Well beyond attitude or just
portraying a tough-guy image, rappers often boast in graphic
detail about killing other human beings. In his song "How
Many," aptly named C-Murder raps,

> *I was born and raised for this gangsta shit*
> *C-Murder be known for keepin' an extra clip*
> *My pops say look 'em in the eye before I kill 'em*
> *P crank the 'llac [Cadillac] up and let's go get 'em.*

Snoop Dogg had actual murder charges leveled against him
in the 1990s, and in "DP Gangsta" he raps proudly about it:

> *"Here's a little something about a nigga like me*
> *I never should have been let out the penitentiary*
> *Snoop Dogg would like to say*
> *That I'm a crazy motherfucker when I'm play-*
>   *ing with my AK [AK-47 assault rifle].*

Leaving nothing to the listener's imagination, rap music
commonly details the prelude to violence, the beating or
shooting or murder itself, and the bloody aftermath, laying out
exactly how it's done, reveling in the gore. Here's Notorious
B.I.G., "Ready to Die," explaining how he kills:

> *As I grab the glock, put it to your headpiece*
> *One in the chamber, the safety is off release*

Straight at your dome [head] homes, I
 wanna see cabbage [brains]
Biggie Smalls the savage, doin' your brain cells much damage.

The values are so twisted that if a rapper hasn't actually committed a major felony, his best career move may be to pretend he did. In the same way that a guy might exaggerate his education on his résumé or his income on a date, Atlanta-based hip-hop artist Akon wildly exaggerated his criminal history to gain "street cred" as a musician. For years part of the narrative he gave of his life was that he spent three years in prison for running a "notorious car theft operation." In fact, he has apparently never served hard prison time. TheSmokingGun. com exposed Akon as a thug wannabe, a "James Frey with... an American Music Award."[176] Everywhere else in life, those with a criminal record lie to conceal it. In rap music each artist wants to be more criminal, more thuggish, bloodier than all the rest because the genre has redefined manhood as emotionally devoid, callous, and cruel.

There is love in rap and hip-hop, but rarely love for other human beings. Warm feelings, pet names, and admiration are almost entirely devoted to one thing: firearms. The message: *be a man, carry a gun.* Gun worship permeates rap music. Frequently given affectionate nicknames like "heaters," "ovens" or "pumps," guns are highly recommended over old-school street fighting—oh, so twentieth century. Dr. Dre sums up the toxic drug-alcohol-gun combination admired in many songs: "Blunt in my left hand, drink in my right, strap [gun] by my waistline, cause niggas don't fight" ("Ackrite"). The message: no, they don't fight. Tough guys shoot to kill.

Google the lyrics to the music your son is listening to, and you'll likely find gun love like this (*my guns make a bigger noise!*), from rapper Big L:

Aiyyo, you betta flee Hops, or get your head flown three blocks
L keep rapper's hearts pumpin like Reeboks...

I got the wild style, always been a foul child
My guns go boom-boom, and yo' guns go pow-pow.
("Put It On")

NBA star Allen Iverson (doubly cool to kids for being an athlete *and* an artist) raps,

Man enough to pull a gun, be man enough to squeeze it.
("40 Bars")

The song ends with Iverson's words over the sounds of a gun being cocked and fired: *Hey kids! Shooting guns at people you're mad at is cool!*

Academics debate whether thug culture is poignant or ironic. Tupac Shakur coined the phrase "thug life" as an acronym, he said, for "This Hate U Gave Lil' Infants Fuck Everybody," meaning that "existence as a thug is based on the premise and knowledge that you are hated." Internalizing society's hostility toward inner-city ghetto life, rappers throw out an aggressive, in-your-face pose as a form of revolution, or so goes the argument. Others believe that creating a violent identity is a necessary form of self-defense in high-crime communities; in other words, those who are feared are left alone.[177] Some others contend that the words are not meant literally.

The problem with these perspectives is that (1) any irony is entirely lost on *children* listening to the songs, and (2) there's no support in the pro-violence songs themselves for another meaning. As a former English major and a lawyer who's spent nearly three decades analyzing texts, I don't see anything other than straightforward glorification of cruelty and victimization. One searches the lyrics and the performances in vain to find a hint of a double meaning. One may as well believe that *Real Housewives* shows aren't *really* about gossiping and meanness— that's all for show! Really, behind the scenes they're solving quadratic equations and reading Dostoyevsky! Uh huh. Right.

And the bottom line is that rappers' lives have often mirrored the violence and carnage of their music. Yet because many of us have an almost pathological tendency to turn away and insist that this is all just metaphor, hyperbole, and irony, let's stare down a few more examples of that sad reality.

Rapper Big L was shot seven times in the head and chest a few blocks from his Harlem home, dead at age 24. Jam Master J, the DJ and founding member of groundbreaking rap group Run-D.M.C., was murdered at age thirty-seven in his Queens, New York, home in 2002. Detroit MC Proof allegedly shot and killed a man in a bar brawl before being fatally gunned down himself at age thirty-two.[178] Tupac Shakur, one of the most revered artists in the genre, was gunned down in a drive-by shooting in Las Vegas when he was only twenty-five. Six months later Notorious B.I.G. met the same fate at age twenty-four. His debut album, which has sold over four million copies, is ominously titled *Ready to Die*. 50 Cent, one of the top two or three wealthiest rappers today, is a former crack cocaine dealer and convicted felon who somehow managed to survive being shot nine times.

Rappers' gun crimes and deaths are a microcosm of the gun violence that claims tens of thousands of American lives annually in our larger thug culture that reflects back these amoral values. At 270 million guns in our country and growing annually, the United States boasts more guns in private hands than anywhere else on earth. With ninety guns per hundred residents, we are well ahead of the second-most gun-loving country on earth, Yemen (sixty-one per hundred).[179] As such, we cannot afford to be careless with guns, using them as proxies for manhood, foolishly waving them around, loaded. The proliferation of guns in America has not only led to frequent, predictable gun deaths and mass shootings but also to increasingly violent crimes perpetrated by angry young men with easy access to firearms.

The United States is now at epidemic levels of gun violence, which claims over thirty thousand lives annually, according to the US Centers for Disease Control and Prevention. For every person who dies from a gunshot wound, two others are wounded. In the first seven years of the US-Iraq War, over forty-four hundred American soldiers were killed; almost as many civilians are killed with guns in the United States *every seven weeks.*[180] African American males are more likely to be victims of gun violence than are any other group.[181]

In many neighborhoods a teenager can get a gun more easily than a car.[182] In one study *most* young males in ghetto neighborhoods reported carrying a gun; for many, doing so was as common as carrying a wallet or keys.[183] By way of comparison, two-thirds of poor families do not own a book.[184]

Firearms are in Grandma's closet, in Mom's dresser drawer, in a friend's waistband, in the family car's glove compartment, for sale just around the corner. "A gun is power," said seventeen-year-old Lorenzo from South Central Los Angeles. "It makes you feel like somebody." He started shooting at age nine and handled guns frequently as a teen, easily obtaining a gun "whenever he needed one." In his brief life experience, though, he's come to detest them. When Lorenzo was five, his mother was shot and killed. Lorenzo's father's life of petty crime came to an end when he was shot in the leg. His older brother was shot three times. And the uncle who first put a gun in Lorenzo's hands died after he was shot twelve times with an AK-47.[185]

Lorenzo and his family endure the real-life misery that violence and gun crimes produce in communities across America. If the record labels and media conglomerates that profited from glamorizing gun violence were people, we'd call them sociopaths—or accessories to murder.

Another common theme of rap and hip-hop music is degrading women and girls and threatening them with attack. At a time when women and girls are achieving a greater degree of equality than ever before, thug culture teaches that females are nothing more than "bitches" or "hos," designed as sexual receptacles for male gratification, whether they consent to it or not. Indeed, perversely, many artists equate demeaning females with being a man worthy of respect. One of the top-selling songs in any genre on iTunes in early 2012 was the Jay Z-Kanye West duet, "Niggas in Paris," in which Kanye raps that a woman interested in a relationship with him must grovel first and have sex with him in a debased setting in order to demonstrate her worthiness:

She said can we get married at the mall?
I said look you need to crawl 'fore you ball
Come and meet me in the bathroom stall
And show me why you deserve to have it all.[186]

The message—*make the bitch beg!*—courses through the genre.

Kanye's insults to women have been lucrative. His biggest hit to date, "Gold Digger," is an attack on women who have babies with stars like him (did they immaculately conceive?) and then have the gall to seek child support. "Eighteen years, eighteen years / She got one of yo' kids, got you for eighteen years!" he raps, incredulous at the idea that he'd be required to support his own child. "Gold Digger" hit number one on the record charts, was one of the top-ten-selling songs in the 2000s, and at the time of its 2005 release, it broke the record for the most digital downloads in a week.

Merely insulting women—including the mothers of their own children—isn't sufficiently brutal for some artists, who go further to embrace rape. Eminem—another megastar—often revels onstage as his alter ego, "Slim Shady," boasting in "Crack a Bottle,"

Ooww Ladies and gentlemen
The moment you've all been waiting for.
In this corner: weighing 175 pounds,
With a record of seventeen rapes, four hundred assaults,
*   and four murders,*
The undisputed, most diabolical villain in the world:
*   Slim Shady!*

The crowd cheers, including the glittering celebrity crowd at the 2009 American Music Awards, where Eminem rapped these words to roars of approval.

Eminem has based his "rebel" identity and career spewing venom about attacking, raping, and murdering women and gay men. (Would he be admired as a "rebel" or "bad boy" if he promoted KKK-style lynchings? Yet somehow there's widespread shoulder shrugging over misogyny and homophobia—*oh well, boys will be boys.*) Here's Eminem chillingly recounting the method of a rapist on the prowl for his next victim:

> *Fe-fi-fo-fum*
> *I think I smell the scent*
> *of a placenta*
> *I enter Central Park*
> *It's dark*
> *It's winter in December*
> *I see my target*
> *put my car in park*
> *and approach a tender*
> *Young girl*
> *by the name of Brenda*
> *and I pretend to befriend her*
> *Sit down beside her*
> *like a spider*
> *hi there girl you mighta'*
> *Heard of me before see whore you're the kinda'*
> *girl that I'd a-*
> *ssault and rape and*
> *figure why not try to*
> *make your pussy wider*
> *Fuck you with an umbrella and open it*
> *   up while the shit's inside ya.*

If you had a sliver of doubt about whether we live in a culture that winks at sexual violence, consider: Eminem is the

best-selling hip-hop artist of all time. He is the best-selling artist in any genre during the decade of the 2000s. *Rolling Stone*
magazine calls him "one of the greatest one hundred artists of
all time."[187]

Others trying to break into the music scene mimic Eminem's
vile messages as well as those of the thug culture. A *Jersey Shore*
reality TV star decided to make his debut in the rap world with
"Rack City Mix" in late 2011: "Racks racks racks / Ass ass ass,"
Vinny Guadagnino raps inelegantly in the song. "Actin' like
I'm raping it / Fuck her till she fakin' it." He ends the song
with an indignant "It's Vinny, bitch."[188]

One of the most beloved artists in the genre, Jay-Z, threatens
sexual assault of women and even children in the Kanye West
song "Monster" (Jay-Z is featured in the song):

> *Everybody knows I'm a motherfucking monster*
> *Conquer, stomp ya, stop your silly nonsense...*
> *Rape and pillage a village, women and children.*

Jay-Z is one of the most financially successful musicians in
history, with an estimated net worth of $450 million.[189] After
the recent birth of his daughter, a poem supposedly written
by him, in which he promised to stop degrading females, went
viral. Jay-Z promptly announced that the poem was fake and
threw a big party with a song loudly blaring, "What's my favorite word? Bitch!"[190]

Again, reality can reflect this violent misogyny in artists' lives.
Superstar rapper Chris Brown pleaded guilty in 2009 to battering, shoving, and even choking his then-girlfriend Rihanna as,
she told police, she feared for her life. He was ordered into
batterer classes, which he apparently slept through, because he
rapped this on his next song release, "Look at Me Now":

> *Better cuff your chick if you with her*
> *I can get her*
> *And she accidentally slip fall on my dick.*

"Cuff your chick" could mean either to handcuff or strike a woman with an open hand. And his rival's girlfriend would have no choice, Brown brags, once he'd targeted her for sex. For a megastar with a recent domestic violence conviction, it's a defiant middle finger held straight up to the world. The song has sold nearly three million copies.

"Mere" rape is not enough for some artists, who try to compete for ultimate gangster status by pushing themselves to be even more vicious than their rap/thug competitors. DMX, for example, detailed how he would murder his rival's wife and *then rape his enemy's young daughter* while his rival watched:

> *I'm comin' in the house and I'm gunnin' for your spouse*
> *Tryin' to send the bitch back to her maker*
> *And if you got a daughter older than fifteen*
> *I'm a rape her*
> *Take her on the living room floor, right there in front of you*
> *then ask you seriously, what you wanna do?*[191]

Gay men are also constant victims of rappers' scorn and contempt. The uber-macho thug mentality of popular rap and hip-hop music appears unable to tolerate any alternative, such as homosexuality. Bragging about gay bashing is a sick virus that runs through the genre. Superstar Lil Wayne raps,

> *You snakes, stop hidin in the grass,*
> *Sooner or later I'll cut it, knock the blades in yo ass,*
> *You homo niggas getting AIDS in the ass.*
> *("Go DJ")*

Allen Iverson makes clear his death wish for gay men in his hatemongering lyrics:

> *Come to me wit' faggot tendencies*
> *You'll be sleepin' where the maggots be.*
> *("40 Bars")*

And Eminem raps in "Criminal,"

My words are like a dagger with a jagged edge
That'll stab you in the head
Whether you're a fag or lez
Or the homosex, hermaph, or a trans-a-vest
Pants or dress—hate fags?
The answer's yes.

This music flows through our boys' earbuds at a time when violent hate crimes against lesbian, gay, bisexual, and transgender (LGBT) people occur at six times the rate of other hate crimes.[192] Although violent crime in general is down, LGBT violent hate crimes are up. For example, in Ventura, California, recently, gay fifteen-year-old Lawrence King was shot to death in front of a computer lab full of middle school students. The fourteen-year-old shooter asserted the "gay panic" defense, claiming that he flew into an uncontrollable rage when King allegedly said to him, "what's up, baby?" Nationwide, gays and lesbians of color are the most likely to be targeted for gay bashing.[193]

Early rap and hip-hop warned against the dangers of drug use. "If you get hooked, baby, it's nobody else's fault, so don't do it!" sang Grandmaster Melle Mel and the Furious Five in 1983. However, times have changed—dramatically. Celebrations of the joys of smoking, snorting, and shooting up litter the landscape of today's popular music. Between 1979, when the genre was in its infancy, and 1997, positive drug references rose sixfold. During that same time period songs with drug references were three times more likely to have themes related to glamour and wealth than were earlier titles, and they were seven times more likely to emphasize drug use as recreation or as an accompaniment to sex.[194]

Another 2012 top seller, "Young and Wild and Free," is a mild example, extolling the fun of cutting class and smoking marijuana. Its catchy, mesmerizingly harmonized refrain, known word for word by anyone who listened to a radio this year, is:

So what we get drunk
So what we smoke weed
We're just having fun
We don't care who sees
So what we go out
That's how it's supposed to be
Living young and wild and free.[195]

Drugs are commonly celebrated as symbols of the good life in popular music. In Rihanna's "We Found Love" video, not one but two drug montages feature gorgeous young lovers cavorting in bed after playing with handfuls of candy-colored prescription pills and blowing marijuana smoke in each other's mouths. This is typical of the industry's message about alcohol and drugs: *Good times! Fun! All the pretty, cool kids are doing it!*

Music's Powerful Impact on Children's Behavior

If you think the messages in popular music have no impact on kids, you probably also believe Coke commercials don't sell sodas—that Coca-Cola and other multibillion-dollar companies enjoy recklessly throwing money out the window for advertising, day after day. In fact, the entire advertising, public relations and marketing industries are based on the premise that media messages have a direct, profound impact on human behavior. Decades of research back this up. And many commercials employ popular music, knowing the emotional appeal it packs. The songs are carefully chosen to convey a mood, to fire us up, to get us to love a product and associate it with our favorite artist. (How quaint it now seems that musicians once considered licensing their music to commercials as "selling out.")

Taking it all a step further, many hip-hop artists embed product advertisements directly into their songs—for profit, of course. After Busta Rhymes's "Pass the Courvoisier" jacked up the liquor's sales into double-digit gains, others rushed to rhyme about Prada, Gucci, Burberry, Belvedere Vodka, Alizé Liqueur, Hennessy Cognac, Cristal Champagne, and then the rappers' own clothing and product lines, in what's become one dizzyingly long gravy train of advertising masquerading as music.[196] Why? *Because the audience, especially young people, model their words, their clothes, their personal style, and their behavior on rappers and other celebrities.* Not only does the music industry understand the power it holds to shape its listeners' values and preference, but this knowledge is also the very basis of hundreds of millions of dollars flowing through the business annually, as corporate deals are made with the artists and recording companies. Parents: ignore this truth at your peril.

I've focused primarily on rap and hip-hop not only because they are so popular with boys and young men but also because their emotional undercurrents make them somehow hypnotically compelling. (Personally, I enjoy the sound of much of these genres, though not the messages.) But other forms of music also compete to be the most violent, woman-hating, and jarring. Heavy metal, for example, spews out repulsive, savage images like "Sawing the neck, I am engulfed in fantasy / Chew the esophagus, cannibal delicacy" ("Hacksaw Decapitation," Cannibal Corpse), though it sells far fewer songs and has a much smaller audience. Television's top shows, like the top-rated C.S.I. series, depict gory acts of carnage. Many video games like *Carmageddon* or *Soldier of Fortune* are blood-and-gore fests. By the time the average US boy starts elementary school he will have seen eight thousand murders and one hundred thousand acts of violence on TV as well as countless representations of manhood as being swaggering, criminal, loveless, and cold.[197]

And the life glorified in thug culture spills out everywhere, well beyond the music industry. Once you see it, you see it everywhere. Certainly, basketball, football, and baseball stars have become less and less the role models little boys used to look up to and more and more just dumb thugs. NBA stars Gilbert Arenas and Javaris Crittenton allegedly pulled guns on each other during a 2009 locker room argument.[198] Escalating his criminal behavior, Crittenton was charged in 2011 with attempted murder after a fatal drive-by shooting of a mother of four.[199]

Boxer Mike Tyson, who has a second burgeoning career in film now with the popular *Hangover* movies—targeted at a young male demographic—is a convicted forcible rapist. Mike Tyson Halloween masks sold out on Halloween 2010. Actor Charlie Sheen, who some young men admire for his cocky, in-your-face attitude toward those he perceives to have wronged him, has pleaded guilty or no contest to two criminal incidents of domestic violence against a wife and a girlfriend. In four other incidents, women have accused him of assaulting them, and he even "accidentally" shot then-girlfriend Kelly Preston in the arm. Despite all this he remained on the CBS hit show *Two and Half Men* (who was the half man?) and was the highest-paid actor on television.[200] Though he was later fired for erratic behavior, he promptly launched a nation-wide tour that sold out in eighteen minutes—a Ticketmaster record.[201] *Winning!*

Celebrities model irresponsible parenting without any negative consequences to their lives. Left to their own devices, boys can model themselves on male celebrities who leave a stream of babies in their wake, progeny with whom they have little connection. Kevin Federline left a girlfriend very pregnant with their second child to take up with singer Britney Spears. After fathering two children with her and their subsequent divorce, at age twenty-eight he's now the father of his fifth child with a third woman. Not to worry! He's still landing modeling and reality show deals.[202] Boxer Evander Holyfield has fathered eleven children he can't support with an untold number of baby mamas.[203] Former governor and action film megastar

Arnold Schwarzenegger had sex with his family housekeeper, and then for over a decade hid the fact from his wife, family, constituents, and worst of all, from the child himself that he was the resulting baby's father.[204] (As if a boy is simply an inconvenient object, imprudently purchased on a whim, to be shoved in the back of a closet or discarded.)

The glamorization of gangs, homophobia, domestic violence, even murder as well as irresponsible baby making and disappearing dads—these are the waters in which our boys swim. Rappers and athletes often define manhood as thuggery, and the more sadistic and criminal, the more "gangsta," the better. In the real world crime leads to prison, as it has for many rappers, such as megastars 50 Cent or T.I. Of course, men in prison can't be there for their families, gain employment, participate in their communities, or support their children. Inmates' children are more likely to become criminals themselves.[205] And so the cycle continues.

Thug culture hits boys especially hard. Male adolescents—more so than girls—listen to music as a stimulant, as a way to "boost" their energy level, or to create a more positive image of themselves, according to the American Academy of Pediatrics (AAP).[206] But how can this music help boys create that positive image when rappers so often present themselves as women-hating, gay-bashing, violent assassins?

Children and teens who listen to rap, hip-hop, and heavy metal music are more likely to be aggressive, have behavioral problems, commit acts of violence, use alcohol and drugs, and become promiscuous.[207] Boys steeped in the genre are more likely to tolerate sexual aggression against women and have negative views of women. The problem is so acute that the AAP recommends that *pediatricians* routinely ask parents what music their kids listen to and what music videos their kids watch as well as become familiar with the literature about how dangerous these messages are to our kids—because thug culture twists and distorts our children's development.

There can be little doubt that when fame and fortune are

equated with hypermasculinized rich and famous rap and hip-hop stars who seem to have the world at their feet, boys will emulate them. And so, of course, young people will model their speech and behavior on music stars like 50 Cent or Kanye West. But beware to those who fail to understand the trap: *it's okay for them to talk the talk, but not for you!* Yuri Wright, the for-tieth-ranked high school football player in the nation, sought after by colleges in the Big Ten, Pac-12, ACC, SEC, and Big East, was expelled from high school for sexually graphic and racial Twitter posts in 2012.[208] Wright's tweets, calling people "niggas" and saying "I want some pussy," though offensive and inappropriate for a high school student online or anywhere, are tame by the rap and hip-hop standards we've just seen. Other than the vulgar language, the primary message Wright conveyed was his sexual interest in girls and their anatomy. Though he didn't advocate violence or rape or drug use, he spoke in the vernacular of the streets and thug culture, and for that, despite his athletic talents, he paid a heavy price. After his expulsion, his full-ride scholarship offer from the University of Michigan, Wright's first-choice school, was withdrawn. Jay-Z or Snoop Dog or the biggest record companies in the world can make millions from it, but a kid who merely mimics the language loses his future—a cautionary tale.

Thug culture creates a treacherous world for our kids, one in which emotional, compelling music set to insistent beats teaches values that will undercut them at every turn if they adopt them. So much of life in the digital world is antithetical to a healthy life in the physical world. In a music video a violent thug is revered; in the real world he's despised for the pain he causes. In some rap music rape makes a man admirable; in real life he'd be reviled and, one hopes, imprisoned. In some hip-hop music drugs and alcohol are the way to get happiness and girls; in real life underage drinking can get kids kicked out of school, and drug use often leads to addiction and harsh prison terms (as we shall see in a moment). In violent TV, movies, and video games, *bang bang! The bad guys are dead! Hooray!* In the real world gun violence is agonizing, excruciatingly painful, and leaves behind a trail of grief and misery.

Thug culture has snuck up on many parents. Insidiously, messages are being delivered to our children that directly undermine our values, our hopes and dreams for their future, and our kids' character. Though the music sometimes carries warnings, most kids download the music directly online, where no one checks ID. And a great deal of violence in film and television is not even considered inappropriate for kids, garnering only a PG-13 or TV-14 rating. The megacompanies that spew these messages don't even bother to pretend to care about the damage they are inflicting; there's so little outcry that they rarely have cause to defend their products. As long as they profit, thug culture will continue to grow like a parasite eating away at our culture, teaching all the wrong lessons to our boys.

CHAPTER FOUR

MASS INCARCERATION: YOUNG MEN LOCKED UP, LOCKED OUT

POORLY EDUCATED, trapped in a jobless economy, and bombarded by thug culture, many of our boys turn into rudderless young men—adrift and lost. No one has told them that the rules have changed and that the deck is increasingly stacked against them. And one mistake—one act of impulsive, youthful stupidity or one night of living like the millionaire thugs our culture reveres by getting high, robbing, or gangbanging—can radically alter the remainder of their lives because they happened to be born into the one developed country in the world most likely to incarcerate a young man and cut off his future for minor offenses.

Sympathy for criminals is as rare in America as a genteel rapper. *You do the crime, you do the time,* right? Our national ethic strongly emphasizes individual choice and personal responsibility: *If you want to stay out of prison, don't break the law.* Isn't it just that simple?

In some cases, yes. I've long been an advocate for long prison sentences for child molesters, for example, because their high rates of recidivism mean that the only way that we can truly be safe from their compulsive, destructive behavior is to lock them up for many years at a time. Murderers and violent felons also must be incarcerated for life or long terms because their crimes are heinous and we all deserve to live in safety.

But with little public discussion, a sweeping change has occurred in our criminal justice system in the last thirty years, one without precedent in our country's history or, indeed, in the history of any liberal democracy. Though this new order has radically changed families and communities as well as reshaped state budgets and spending, our mainstream media has been virtually silent on the issue. Sure, our news organizations cover crime stories, but almost entirely that coverage is of missing pretty white girls or sensationalized trials such as the Casey Anthony murder trial (not guilty of killing her daughter, the jury found) or Dr. Conrad Murray's involuntary manslaughter case (guilty of recklessness in administering a sleeping medication to singer Michael Jackson, negligently causing his death). These are highly unusual, outlier crime stories, either shocking in their facts or centering around a celebrity victim or defendant. Stranger abductions of American children are exceedingly rare. Female killers are not unheard of, but still, they are unusual, and as a result, they grab our interest and spike ratings. And a doctor to the stars, on call 24/7 to just one patient, administering a controlled substance in a private home? Something beyond the experience of nearly all of us mere mortals and entirely irrelevant to our lives. Yet entire networks and websites devoted wall-to-wall coverage to these sensationalized stories in 2011 while ignoring the biggest crime-and-justice story of them all: our mass incarceration of millions of our own people, overwhelmingly due to the War on Drugs.

America's War on Drug Users

IN THE 1970s and early 1980s drug use and sales were not considered evil but rather vices, low-level violations comparable to prostitution and gambling. At best, users were seen as experimenting kids; at worst, they were individual tragedies. Sellers were considered only minor threats to the public order. For example, in 1982 less than 2 percent of the American public viewed drugs as the most important issue facing the nation.[209] Nevertheless, our War on Drugs began under President Ronald Reagan in October 1982, in which we reclassified previously tolerated human behavior as criminal, imposing heavy sentences and a system of sometimes lifetime control on what had formerly been considered petty offenses.

So entrenched are we now in War-on-Drugs propaganda that it's hard to imagine that it didn't have to happen. We could have just as easily declared War on Prostitution, for example, and assembled SWAT teams to round up desperate impoverished women selling their bodies, locking them and their pimps up for decades or for life rather than the few days in jail now and then that most sex workers endure throughout their careers. Or we could have announced a War on Gambling and spent billions on police and prisons to send away compulsive bettors who were capable of bankrupting themselves and their families and who are sometimes connected to bigger fish, like organized crime. Or we could have chosen compassion over punishment, declaring a War on Drug Addiction and focusing on helping our citizens who struggle with substance abuse get clean and sober to lead productive lives.

But we didn't do any of that. Instead, we declared a War on Drugs, and the consequences for all of us, especially our young men of color, have been earth shattering.

Immediately under the new War on Drugs regime, law enforcement budgets soared and treatment programs were slashed, reflecting the new view that after-the-fact punishment was superior to before-the-fact treatment (there's that anti-prevention bias again). Between 1980 and 1984 FBI antidrug funding shot up from $8 million to $95 million. From 1981 to 1991 the Department of Defense's antidrug enforcement spending increased from $33 million to over $1 billion, the Drug Enforcement Administration (DEA)'s antidrug spending grew from $86 million to over $1 billion, and FBI's antidrug spending grew from $38 to $181 million. Meanwhile, as all these massive new law enforcement machines were ratcheting up to ensnare American drug users and sellers, the National Institute on Drug Abuse saw its budget slashed from $274 million in 1981 to $57 million in 1984, and antidrug funding at the Department of Education was slashed from $14 million to $3 million.[210] The message to addicts was clear: *we're not here to help you; we're here to arrest you.*

Hopped up on the national fervor of the new War on Drugs, in 1988 Congress got into the action with punitive legislation that allowed public housing authorities to evict anyone who allows any form of drug-related criminal activity to occur on or near public housing premises; eliminated many federal benefits for anyone convicted of a drug offense, including student loans; and imposed new mandatory minimums for narcotic offenders, including a five-year mandatory minimum for simple possession of cocaine, without intent to sell, even for first-time offenders. As Professor Michelle Alexander points out, until 1988, one year of imprisonment had been the maximum for possession of any amount of any drug in America.[211]

How radically things changed thereafter. An enormous surge in the American prison population followed, which continues today. As law enforcement budgets shot up, more of our citizens were rounded up, arrested, and incarcerated for longer terms than ever before. In 1991 activists warned that the number of people behind bars in the United States was unprecedented in world history. Yet it became career suicide for any politician, Democrat or Republican, to waver from a "tough on crime" position. No major political figure did. And our prison population continued to bloat.

In 1994 President Bill Clinton signed another multibillion-dollar crime bill, creating dozens of new federal crimes, mandating life terms for more offenders, and spending over $16 billion to build more state prisons and expand local police forces. The Justice Policy Institute says that Clinton oversaw "the largest increases in federal and state prison inmates of any president in American history." President Clinton also signed legislation to impose a permanent, lifetime ban on eligibility for welfare or food stamps for anyone convicted of a felony drug offense, including simple marijuana possession.[212]

Many otherwise law-abiding citizens have used illegal drugs, including President Barack Obama, who has admitted to smoking marijuana and using cocaine in his youth. Forty-two percent of Americans have tried marijuana, and 16 percent have tried cocaine. In one study of seventeen countries, including France, Spain, South Africa, Mexico, Colombia, and the notoriously drug-permissive Netherlands, the United States had the highest percentages of citizens who had tried marijuana and cocaine.[213] Nevertheless, we have become the most aggressive in arresting and incarcerating our own citizens who use or sell any kind of illegal drugs.

Where does all this leave us? In our new era of unprecedented punitiveness toward our own people, a half-million Americans are incarcerated for drug offenses today, compared to just forty-one thousand in 1980. A stunning thirty-one million people have been arrested for drug offenses since the War on Drugs began. And though many of us think that drug kingpins are the object of law enforcement's attention, four out of five drug arrests in 2005 were for *possession* and only one in five for selling narcotics. In fact, most people in state prison for drug offenses have no history of violence or significant selling activity;[214] they are there because they used. And although many believe we have become more tolerant of marijuana use since sixteen states and the District of Columbia have passed medical marijuana laws,[215] arrests for marijuana possession accounted for nearly 80 percent of the growth in drug arrests in the 1990s. A generation ago drug arrests commonly resulted in dismissal, community service, or probation; today, the number that result in imprisonment has quadrupled.[216]

In 1980 activists were concerned that an intolerably high number of Americans were behind bars—three hundred thousand. Today, the number of incarcerated adults is over two million. Another five million are under the direct control of the criminal justice system, either on probation or parole. And those numbers don't count the ninety thousand children under the age of eighteen incarcerated in juvenile detention facilities.[217]

Here's one stark way to understand our new normal of mass incarceration: if we wanted to return to 1970s level of incarceration, we'd have to release four out of five people behind bars today.[218] We now live in "the first genuine prison society of history."[219]

The typical mandatory minimum sentence for a first-time drug offense in US federal court is now five to ten years. In other first-world countries that offense warrants either no jail time or less than six months behind bars.[220] The War on Drugs is a prisoner-generating machine that has profoundly altered every aspect of our criminal justice system, with ripple effects on all of us. Annually we now spend $68 billion and growing on local, state, and federal law enforcement, while, as we've seen, in many towns we can't find the money for books for first graders, or street lights, or paved roads.[221]

And when we're talking about incarceration, overwhelmingly, we're talking about boys and young men. Our jail and prison population is 93 percent male; our juvenile detention population is 85 percent male. Put another way, a young male is more than ten times as likely to find himself incarcerated as a young female. Yes, males commit the majority of the crimes, but gender bias against men in sentencing is also firmly embedded in our system and compounds the problem.

University of Rhode Island sociology professor Jill K. Doerner reviewed the scholarly research of gender bias in federal and state courts and concluded that "a fairly persistent finding in the sentencing literature is that female defendants are treated more leniently than male defendants."[222] Some analysts have found that the odds of receiving a prison sentence are two and a half times greater for male offenders than for female offenders, after controlling for legally relevant factors. Reviews of Pennsylvania and Ohio state court sentencing has similarly found that male defendants get harsher sentences for the same crimes.[223] A Texas study found that female criminals are less likely to be sentenced to prison, and if they are, they get substantially shorter prison terms than do males sentenced for the same crimes.[224]

As a result, young males are in particular jeopardy any time they come into contact with the criminal justice system, and African American and Latino young males are most at risk. Though we hate to hear it, that drug laws are enforced in a racially biased manner is well documented and beyond dispute. Whereas whites and blacks buy, sell, and use drugs at roughly the same rates (and white youth are the most likely of any group to use and sell illegal drugs), Human Rights Watch reported in 2000 that in seven states African Americans were 80 to 90 percent of all incarcerated drug offenders. In at least fifteen states blacks are admitted to prison on drug charges twenty to fifty-seven times more than whites.[225]

How does this happen? Simple: drug roundups occur frequently in neighborhoods of color, especially inner cities, and rarely in the suburbs and rural areas, where whites predominate.[226] If you are white, you probably know people who smoke marijuana or regularly consume other illegal drugs who not only have never been arrested but are only faintly concerned about the possibility of being caught, if at all. If you are black or Latino, you are likely to know at least one family devastated by someone's incarceration on a drug offense. This is one of the single-biggest race markers in the United States today.

Nineteen-year-old pop superstar Miley Cyrus was caught on video in 2011 smoking what looked like marijuana, which she said was salvia, a legal herb. At her birthday party later that year, upon seeing the Bob Marley cake her friends had prepared for her, she said on camera, "You know you're a stoner when your friends make you a Bob Marley cake. You know you smoke way too much [expletive] weed."[227] As it is for most affluent white Americans, the threat of a drug arrest is so remote as to be laughable to her.

African Americans and Latinos, even celebrity musicians comparable to Miley Cyrus, inhabit a very different world. Singers arrested for drug use (mostly marijuana) in 2011 include Baby Bash (Latino), Big Boi (African American), Dice Raw (African American), Hynief (African American), Juelz Santana (African American), Juvenile (African American), Soulja Boy (African American), Wacka Flocka (three times, African American), and many others.

Probably the American celebrity most famous for seemingly never-ending trouble with the law is Lindsay Lohan, convicted of drunk driving, cocaine possession, and numerous probation violations, including theft and repeatedly failing to show up for court-ordered community service projects because, she said, they were not "fulfilling."[228] She's served only hours or days in jail now and then, none in prison.

Compare Lohan's minimal time in her local jail to that of Green Bay Packers Defensive Lineman Johnny Jolly, a young African American man who, like Lohan, violated his drug probation. Jolly had already been suspended for the entire 2010 NFL season for his offense, possession of codeine, a controlled substance that until recently was widely available in over-the-counter cough syrup. Both Jolly and his mother tearfully begged for rehab so that he could recover from his addiction. His judge was unmoved, sentencing him to six years behind bars.[229]

The noncelebrity world mirrors this same unequal treatment. Studies have shown that at every level of the criminal justice system, whites fare better than do people of color. Whites are less likely to be stopped and have their vehicles searched; if arrested, whites are more likely to be permitted to plead down to a lesser crime. And if convicted, whites are given lighter sentences.[230]

The impact of this uneven enforcement has been shattering in African American and Latino communities, as overall, African Americans are now incarcerated at more than twenty-six times the level they were in 1983, and Latinos are imprisoned twenty-two times more. Whites are incarcerated at "only" eight times the level they were thirty years ago.[231] Of particular concern to parents, the racial discrepancy is stark for juveniles. For first-time child offenders, African Americans are six times as likely as whites to be sentenced to prison for identical crimes. African American youth are significantly more likely to be arrested, more likely to be tried in adult court, and more likely to be sent to adult state prison.[232]

In Washington, DC, three out of every four black men can expect some time behind bars in their lifetimes. In Baltimore or Chicago the vast majority of young black men are currently under the control of the criminal justice system. Young black men in Chicago are more likely to go to prison than to college. In 2001 there were more black men in Illinois's penitentiaries *just on drug charges* than there were in state universities.

These are nauseating statistics in a country that prides itself on liberty, equality, and opportunity for all. So much squandered potential, so many families and communities devastated—there is no way to look at these facts without being appalled.

In sheer numbers more African Americans are under correctional control today than were enslaved at the time of the Civil War.[233] Because many states do not permit convicted felons to vote, more black men are disenfranchised today than in 1870, when the Fifteenth Amendment was passed, granting all men the right to vote regardless of race. Black men are "missing" fathers or "missing" from communities or "missing" as available partners for black women seeking them because they are locked up—a fact often excluded from public discussion. They're not really "missing"; we know where they are: behind bars. We just so rarely discuss our warehousing of our own people.

Because the War on Drugs is heavily concentrated in inner cities, residents there bear a grossly disproportionate burden. Even as crime rates drop, young men continue to be rounded up by police. In terms of the effect on these communities, the removal of these hundreds of thousands of young men has been compared to collective losses similar in scale to epidemics, wars, or terrorist attacks.[234] Incarcerating nonviolent first-time offenders removes fathers from families (the majority of state prison inmates have children under the age of age eighteen) and painfully strains families and social networks. When a young man is locked up, not only is a potential income earner removed from the family and community in his prime working years, but those left behind, especially women, also struggle with the shame, the increased burden of holding on to the connection, keeping the family together, paying burdensome expenses, and regularly traveling long distances with children in tow to visit the inmate.[235] Among African American children, 1.2 million, or about 11 percent, had a parent incarcerated in 2008.[236]

And some offenders say that prison isn't even the worst part; it's getting out and finding their options so limited, their civil rights so restricted. Most of us are entirely unaware of the sweeping limitations imposed on this huge class of Americans after they've "done their time." In ancient Rome the Plebeians had no legal status and few legal rights, though they walked among the general citizenry and their second-class status was invisible. Though we think of ourselves as a country without castes, today American ex-offenders are similarly legally barred from access to civic life and bear an invisible stigma of second-class citizenship.

A Civic Death

AFTER INCARCERATION, problems follow offenders for many years. Michelle Alexander calls this "parallel universe" of postin-carceration penalties "a form of punishment that is often more difficult to bear than prison time: a lifetime of shame, contempt, scorn, and exclusion...a civic death."[237] For example, thirty-one states and the federal government exclude felons from juries for life. (As a result, about 30 percent of black men are automatically banned from jury service for life, making it increasingly unlikely that an African American defendant will get a true jury of his peers.[238])

Let's say a young man pleads guilty to a first-time felony marijuana possession charge. He may get lucky and get his crime pleaded down to a lesser charge and avoid much jail time (especially if he's white). Or he may be unlucky and get hit with five or ten years in prison (especially if he's black). There will be court costs billed to him before, during, and after his incarceration. Upon release he'll become automatically ineligible for many federal health and welfare benefits. Where will he live? He's automatically banned from public housing for a minimum of five years.[239] Everything turns on housing: the ability to receive mail, a return address for a job application, a place to have custody or visitation with his kids, a roof, a bed, a sense of community and rootedness. Without access to public housing assistance, many ex-offenders quickly become homeless, according to Human Rights Watch, an international organization that normally brings to light human rights abuses abroad but also criticizes the United States for how difficult we make re-integration for our own citizens.[240]

Can he go back to school and try to improve himself? Unlikely. Ex-offenders are denied federal educational assistance—precisely the type of help that is sorely needed for an offender resolved to "go straight" and turn his life around. And how will he study while he's hungry? Drug conviction bars him from federally funded food stamps—the lifeline currently feeding forty-six million Americans—*for the rest of his life*, without any compassionate exceptions for say, the disabled, people with AIDS or cancer, parents of young children, those in drug treatment, or those who have been law-abiding citizens for decades after an early offense. His driver's license may be automatically suspended, making it difficult to go to work or job interviews. He will now be barred from certain jobs and forever denied some professional licenses. The military? Forget it. He cannot enlist, period. He is not permitted to possess a firearm, nor can he apply for a security clearance.

In an affront to democracy, the majority of states bar parolees from voting, and some deny voting rights for life. The United States stands alone in the world in so harshly disenfranchising so many of its own citizens, denying them the right to participate in their country's affairs. One in seven black men nationwide has lost his right to vote—one in four in some states. Many of those barred from voting are veterans or family members of military service members. No matter: one felony marijuana conviction is all that's necessary in many states to bar US citizens from taking part in our democracy.

Judges are not even required to advise defendants of this civic death that will tail them forever after they accept guilty pleas (which is how 95 percent of cases are resolved in our system). Indeed, even defense lawyers are often not aware of the full array of rights denied to offenders after they serve their time. Nearly every state, for example, permits employers to discriminate against those who "check the box" on job applications, admitting that they have been convicted of a crime, even if the offense is entirely unrelated to the job or it's thirty years in the past (and, of course, lying about a criminal conviction would always be legitimate grounds for termination). Without the ability to drive, get a job, find housing, or even qualify for food stamps, many ex-offenders lose their children. Though most offenders earn less than $12,000 annually at the time of arrest, they are required to pay a panoply of new fines, such as jail booking fees, jail per diems, public offender application fees, presentence report fees, and parole and probation service fees. When, as is usually the case, they can't afford to pay these fees, offenders find their paychecks, if they have them, garnished—up to 100 percent of their earnings. When no more blood can be extracted from the stone and moneys are still due and owing, ex-offenders are often sent back to prison, more fees are imposed, and the cycle continues.[241]

Clearly, we don't care what happens to offenders upon their release. Treating criminals fairly is nonexistent on policy makers' to-do lists. We load ex-cons up with challenges and create a disincentive for them to work and reintegrate into society. We can hardly be surprised that given all these hurdles, 44 percent relapse within a year of release.[242] Many ex-offenders are re-incarcerated simply because they could not pay back thousands of dollars in court fines, fees, and child support.[243]

The argument for imprisoning vast swaths of our population is a no-lose position: if crime rates are down (as they have been since the 1990s), mass incarceration is working; if crime rates are up, we need to "get tough" and lock up more people! In fact, there is substantial evidence that mass incarceration is crimogenic; that is, it *increases* crime, because minor offenders become hardened criminals during their incarceration, the barriers to re-entry into society after release are so high, and mass incarceration decimates the communities left behind. Children of inmates are more likely to grow up and become offenders themselves.[244] And these are only the direct reasons why mass incarceration can be crimogenic. Siphoning money from schools to pay for prisons, as we have seen, leaves our schools underfunded, producing a generation of often illiterate, unemployable young people into jobless inner cities, a generation for whom drug sales, prostitution, and petty crime becomes the most viable income-producing option. And thus the prison population swells further.

We've become a nation that's turned our backs on millions of our own people, even young nonviolent offenders. Our national mood has soured toward all arrestees, as we lump together drug users with violent thugs, as if there were no difference between them—locking them all up, throwing away the key, and leaving them on their own once released, as we throw obstacles in their path. Human Rights Watch's sober assessment is that there is "a widespread belief in the United States that people who have broken the law do not deserve a second chance and are the legitimate target of policies that are little more than expressions of disdain and hostility." And thus these policies continue unabated, with no political will to change them, even as the costs are destroying other worthy programs like education. We once believed that after an inmate served his time, his debt to society was repaid and he deserved a new opportunity to begin again. Human Rights Watch's report title encapsulates the new American view toward even petty offenders: "No Second Chance."[245]

What's remarkable is that millions of us—mostly young men—have disappeared from American life in just one generation, with so little public discussion. The United States currently has more prison inmates than the leading thirty-five European countries combined.[246] With just over 4 percent of the world's population, the United States accounts for a quarter of the planet's prisoners. A generation of young men have been lifted whole from our communities, locked into cages, and there's no outcry, barely even a mention of their absence. Few parents understand the harshness of the system that awaits a boy who breaks the rules, even once, even as a minor.

New prisons are being built every year. State legislators eager to appear "tough on crime" are constantly dreaming up new restrictions on ex-offenders' rights. Boys and young men and others are being plucked from their communities every day, in every town, sentenced to long prison terms disproportionate to their crimes.

As this book went to press, amidst the 2012 presidential election debates, the issue of the mass incarceration of US citizens was not even a blip on the candidates' radar.

PART TWO

TEN RULES FOR RAISING BOYS RIGHT NOW

"It is easier to build strong children than to repair broken men."

—FREDERICK DOUGLASS

IN AN airport in Manchester, England, I saw him: a wild-haired, noisy, chubby boy of about eight, sporting a T-shirt that said it all:

I BLAME THE PARENTS

After laughing out loud in a waiting area full of strangers, I surreptitiously attempted to get a photo of him. *You* try snapping a photo of a boy wriggling up, over, and under bolted-down seats, hollering nonstop.

Oh well. I got a mental snapshot, and I've never forgotten little Piers or Giles or Geoffrey, nor his mum's admirable self-mocking sense of humor.

Parent blaming is all the rage on this side of the pond. *How could she bring a crying baby on a bus? Can't they see he's outgrown those trousers? He's overweight/underweight: the parents' fault! Can't they make that kid sit still?*

Most of this comes from people who aren't parents themselves or who may have forgotten that children are independent human beings who can never be 100 percent controlled. When I hear a screaming child on a plane, I close my eyes and remember my daughter, at age two, who once spent an entire transcontinental flight kick-kick-kicking the woman next to her, interrupted by mad bursts of running up and down the aisle, pointing out loudly who was "fat!" and who was "not fat!" (*Why, oh why, had I just taught her that word?*)

Parenting is humbling. When I was pregnant, I decided my children would never eat in the car. I would not be one of "those" mothers. Cut to our crumb-filled, leaky-sippy-cup-filled station wagon a few years later. I also vowed not to give them candy, or to succumb to tantrums, or to resort to bribery.

Oh, sure.

After a bit of experience, most of us upgrade to Parenting 2.0, a new, revised program that takes into account the limitations of actual human beings (and the fact that bribing them with sugar is so darned *effective*). After a few years, my parenting philosophy evolved, and I decided not to sweat the small stuff and, in fact, to revel in the antics of childhood. They're not going to be crawling under the furniture or wearing those ridiculous pants or making inappropriate remarks about strangers forever (hopefully not, anyway, unless they grow up to be Perez Hilton). They'll outgrow all that in due time, with little effort on your part. In the meantime try to teach them some manners, take them out of the public space if they are frothing at the mouth, and otherwise make a lot of videos that you'll all laugh at later (or, failing that, that you can use to blackmail them when they are choosing your nursing home).

Focus on the big picture: preparing your son now for a bright future, giving him a clear-eyed view of the world he's living in. As we've seen, our boys find themselves in the quagmire of failing schools, a country that no longer prioritizes education, a hostile economy, a culture that defines literacy as "girly," and a justice system that harshly penalizes their every misstep. As a result, they are flunking out, dropping out, and checking out. These are major issues that cannot be ignored.

Although small matters should essentially be overlooked, please don't pull away from the big ones in despair. Yes, the forces we've seen aligned against your boy are mammoth. The problems can seem huge—insurmountable—and we are tempted to turn away, defeated. But don't. The only question for parents is: now that we are aware of the forces battering our boys, how can we protect them?

Because that's our real job, and because we can. Protecting them, raising them right, shoring up a healthy future for them is possible. It is eminently doable. We may not be able to turn around our thug culture, our schools, or our unemployment rates single-handedly, but we can create profound, life-changing solutions in our children's lives once we decide that this will be our focus.

While powerful forces have been blasting away at our sons, a strong body of knowledge has also emerged, offering a way out. Researchers and educators and parents know what works and what fails. On an individual level, practical solutions exist. Regardless of our circumstances, we can create strong families, homes that reflect our values, and instill in our boys both intellectual curiosity and a healthy dose of cynicism for the parts of our culture that have veered off in the wrong direction.

To answer the question of how we can best protect our sons, I not only waded through all the latest scientific and social science research; I also interviewed teachers, administrators, parents, and a diverse group of boys, and of course, I drew from my own experiences. There is always more work to be done, more research to be conducted, more boys to study, but clear patterns emerge, and there are many things we now know for sure. Blessedly, not only are most of the answers relatively simple, inexpensive, and readily available, but you are also going to enjoy your new and improved family life immediately.

Fellow parents, I'm not interested in blaming you. I want to empower you.

Here's what I found.

RULE 1:

LOSE THE SWAGGER, KID

"Even if you be otherwise perfect, you fail without humility."

—THE TALMUD

"If I only had a little humility, I'd be perfect."

—TED TURNER

BEFORE WE get to the more nitty-gritty practical advice, let's start with a major *attitude* adjustment that's a necessary precursor for all the steps that follow.

To begin, ask your boy this question: would you say you're a "very important person"? Yes or no? Then, hold that answer for just a moment.

The Lost Virtue of Humility

OUT OF the blue, it seems, we Americans have become quite full of ourselves. In the 1950s only 12 percent of high school

seniors said they were a "very important person."[249] Back then
self-effacement and modesty were virtues of the highest order,
taught by clergy and parents alike, passed down to the kids as
characteristics that were expected in every decent person, like
neatness or good grooming. One didn't brag or show off. That
was *not done.* One projected an air of humility.

The Bible, in particular, is filled with exhortations for us all
to take it down a notch. Commonly referred to as "pride goes
before a fall," the actual quote is "Pride goes before destruction, and a haughty spirit before a fall" (Proverbs 16:18). But
also: "God opposes the proud but gives grace to the humble"
(Proverbs 3:34). And: "When pride comes, then comes dis-
grace, but with humility comes wisdom" (Proverbs 11:2), as
well as "Blessed are the meek, for they shall inherit the earth"
(Matthew 5:5). The entire Book of Job is commonly understood as a morality tale about the sin of pride. And so on.

The Judeo-Christian God does not brook arrogance.

The word "humility," some etymologists believe, comes from
the Latin root "humus," meaning soil, dirt. To be humble is
to be grounded, feet firmly rooted on earth. Humility is a recognition that one is not the center of the universe and that
the needs of others must always be considered. "Humility is
not thinking less of yourself, it's thinking of yourself less," says
Pastor Rick Warren.[250]

Such sensible advice, right? Yet we're teaching our boys just
the opposite.

Just as popular books and magazines once admonished
girls to avoid vanity, boys were taught to eschew pride. Now
the multibillion-dollar beauty industry that funds magazines,
television shows, and websites exhorts girls (and, to a lesser
extent, boys) to stare endlessly in the mirror at our hair, eyes,
skin, and bodies, zeroing in on every imperfection so that we will
buy, buy, buy products to reduce, enlarge, darken, lighten, or
obscure. Not vanity but rather "letting herself go"—insufficient
attention to cosmetics, fashion, and plastic surgery—is the new
sin for females.

Similarly, we now teach our boys (and, to a lesser extent, girls) that they rock, they rule, they are the best! Simply for breathing. We tell them to stand tall, shoulders back, and stride proudly. Self-doubt is the new sin for males. For them, humility has gone the way of dial phones and turntables—so old school. There's something wussy about a modest boy who isn't constantly crowing about his awesomeness, now, isn't there?

Pop Culture: Bursting with Braggarts

POPULAR CULTURE is now teeming with boasters, a category that includes all of thug culture and many other athletes and celebrities as well.[251] As *New York Times* columnist David Brooks points out, a generation ago "it would have been unthinkable for a baseball player to celebrate himself in the batter's box after a home-run swing. Now it's not unusual. A few decades ago, pop singers didn't compose anthems to their own prowess; now those songs dominate the charts."[252] The explosion of social media has fed the craze: there we are, each of us, especially teens and young adults, tooting our own horns on Facebook or Twitter, hour by hour, minute by minute.[253]

Celebrities model breathtaking braggadocio. Boys look up to athletes and musicians whose heads are so swollen that one wonders how they make it out the door in the morning. Dallas Cowboys Wide Receiver Terrell Owens, who enjoys calling the press to his driveway while he does sit-ups, shirtless, not only proclaimed joyously, "I love me some me"; *he filed for trademark protection for the phrase.* "I love me some me" or the simplified "I love me" or "I heart me" T-shirts, mugs, and stickers sell on myriad websites. The perfect gift for Valentine's Day to your beloved...you!

Megastar rappers set the tone, with three of the top-selling artists today, T.I., Jay Z, and Kanye West, boasting lyrics like,

"Ain't nobody hot as me even if they rap they ass off," bragging with all they've got in "Swagga Like Us":

> *No one on the corner have swagga like us*
> *Swagga like us, swagga swagga like us*
> *No one on the corner have swagga like us*
> *Swagga like us, swagga swagga like us*

This is a refrain repeated fourteen times in the song. *Yeah! Even our swagger is better than yours! We're the biggest braggarts of all!*

This is something to be proud of?

Performers make preposterous boasts, and no one blinks. Trey Songz boasts, "I invented sex," which has to take the cake for out-and-out chutzpah. Kid Rock's song "Cocky" puts it right out there:

> *Now who the f* are you?*
> *I'm Kid motherf*' Rock from the old school*
> *Got more money / than Matchbox 20*
> *Get more ass than Mark McGrath*
> *They say I'm cocky, and I say What?*
> *It ain't braggin' motherf* if ya back it up.*

Ah. Thanks for that nuanced distinction.

Best-selling rapper Lil Wayne insists in "Best Rapper Alive" that he *is* the best rapper alive—twenty-four times.

"Swagger," especially rhymed with "like Mick Jagger," has been called *the* most used song lyric of the last decade. Every major act, across several genres, has proclaimed allegiance to swagger, from Ke$ha to T.I. to Kanye to the Black Eyed Peas and even the Jonas Brothers.[254] One might argue that an artist who merely copied the exact rhyme everyone else is singing should have less reason to swagger than one who came up with an original verse. But none of that matters. Swagger doesn't have to be earned or even original; the important thing is to do it, because everyone else is..

Psychologists and Parents: Well Intentioned but Not Helping

ATHLETES AND artists aren't alone in telling our boys to puff and strut. Since the 1969 publication of Nathaniel Branden's *The Psychology of Self-Esteem*, which argued that self-esteem was our most important characteristic and thereby launched a pop psychology movement, well-intentioned therapists, counselors, teachers, and just about anyone who works with children has fed, stoked, and stroked kids' egos, constantly telling them how brilliant, attractive, and all-around terrific they are, honoring them just for *existing*. Recall the scene in the film *Meet the Fockers* when Ben Stiller's character is humiliated by his parents' display of his childhood "achievements":

> JACK BYRNES: I didn't know they
>   made ninth-place ribbons.
> BERNIE FOCKER: (missing the mockery) Oh Jack,
>   they make them all the way up to tenth place.

Audience cringes.

The result of all these atta-boys we give our kids just for showing up: an astonishing cultural shift. If your boy agrees that he's a "very important person," he's in good company: 80 percent of high school seniors now believe that too.[255]

Parents have stoked these swollen egos. From birth we pump our kids full of the idea that they are amazing, superlative creatures, even if all they did that morning was tie their shoes after being begged, bribed, and threatened. Following along with the program we thought was expert advised, we're well meaning, for sure: build up your kids' self-esteem! Love means lots of praise! It's good for them, right? Most of us think so. A

Columbia University study found that 85 percent of American parents think that telling their kids they're smart is important.[256] And so we do, day in and day out, thinking we're doing the right thing. (I did it too when my kids were little. Mea culpa. I didn't know then what I know now.)

How Swagger Harms Our Boys

SO HOW does this affect our kids? The impact has been seismic. Having been told since birth that they are not only as handsome and talented as Jamie Foxx but also naturally smarter than Einstein, 85 percent of American teens are confident of their math and science abilities (43 percent "very confident" and 42 percent "somewhat confident"). Gosh, that must feel good! Except for the uncomfortable truth that this attitude is completely unmoored to reality. American kids, in fact, embarrassingly rank twenty-first in science and twenty-fifth in math out of thirty developed countries, with a proficiency rate of 20 to 30 percent, as we've seen.[257] As the disturbing documentary film *Waiting for Superman* pointed out, our kids can't hold a candle to kids in other first-world countries in math, but in just this one area we score the highest: math confidence.

We are raising our kids to be delusional, boasting about nonexistent skills. On some level we have to know this isn't healthy.

Citizens of the United States are at the top of world indexes for swagger. In the manner of the fictional families of Garrison Keillor's Lake Wobegon, we insist that all of our children are above average. The humblest? Folks from South Korea, Switzerland, Japan, Taiwan—nonswagger nations that routinely trounce us in international academic competitions.[258] (It turns out that that's not a coincidence. More on that in a moment.)

When we break down swagger by gender, it's overwhelmingly a male trait. So often it's our guys who wrongheadedly believe they are the best when, measurably, they are not. Boys have far more confidence in their math skills than girls, for example, though girls perform at the same level as boys in math and science today.[259]

Males overrate their math abilities, but it doesn't end there. In one study of men and women across twelve countries—Australia, Austria, Brazil, France, Iran, Israel, Malaysia, South Africa, Spain, Turkey, the UK, and the United States—participants were asked to rate themselves on seven specific types of intelligence, including verbal, logical, interpersonal, musical and spatial, and emotional intelligence.

Guess which gender swaggered and which was more modest?

Yeah. "We found a consistent difference in how intelligent men and women believe themselves to be; with men giving themselves significantly higher levels of intelligence in all twelve countries. Not only did men award themselves high scores in traditional male abilities like spatial and logical reasoning, they also gave themselves higher ratings in verbal ability," said the authors of the study, published in the *British Journal of Psychology*.

"These results do not reflect any actual differences between men and women's levels of intelligence," said researcher Tomas Chamorro-Premuzic. "Rather, our study shows that men like to have a high opinion of themselves and are prone to over-estimate their level of intelligence while women are more modest, and even under-estimate their own intelligence."[260]

Where does all this male arrogance come from? I can't say whether it's hardwired with the XY chromosomes, but once the baby is wrapped in a blue blankct, we all seem to reinforce it. A toddler drags a heavy toy into a room. If told the kid's a boy, adults say, "what a strong boy you are!" If told it's a girl, "be careful of your party dress!" Researchers at Penn State in 2010 found that moms and dads interact differently with their children, setting up different gender expectations. Usually unwittingly, parents teach children about gender roles and reinforce stereotypical patterns.261 A Toronto couple who named their newborn "Storm," refusing to reveal the baby's gender for the first few months of his/her life, set off a storm of controversy, with talk show hosts and bloggers bloviating angrily about how the child would be scarred for life, how the parents were selfish narcissists...for asking strangers simply to treat Storm as a baby human.[262] Our approach to kids is so rooted in gender expectations that even an infant whose gender is not instantly apparent completely unnerves us.

We don't just encourage swagger in boys: most of us—both men and women—prefer confident men. In one study both male and female interviewers liked modest guys less.[263] And, yes, we females surely reinforce swagger with our attention, even lust. In popular magazine surveys "confidence" rates high on single women's lists of desirable personality traits. Entire books have been written on to how to have that self-assurance that drives women wild with desire.

No one understands the lure and destructive power of swagger better than Joe Loya. A once-cocky bank robber who served nine years as a young man in California penitentiaries for multiple felony convictions, he turned his life around upon release and became an author, playwright, and columnist whose work has been praised by literary greats like Frank McCourt and Abraham Verghese.[264] He lectures to juvenile offenders as one who's been there himself, exhorting them to give up a life of crime before it's too late, teaching them nonviolent ways to confront their anger and pain.

The hardest part of his transformation? "Women," he says, without hesitation. "They flocked to me when I was an arrogant bank robber. When I got out of prison and told them I was done with that life, for real, they lost interest," he said.

We're all implicated. Unless we're careful, we're all underwriters of our boys' swagger. But as with Joe the bank robber, arrogance is leading our boys down the wrong path.

A few voices in the wilderness have been clamoring for our attention to tell us that no, contrary to popular thinking, all this empty praise isn't building our boys up. Surprisingly, actually, it's slowing them down. Boosting kids' self-esteem when they haven't earned it can be harmful, according to a University at Buffalo researcher who found an inverse correlation between confidence and mathematics achievement in a large-scale international study spanning the globe. "In all thirty-four countries studied, overconfident students were less likely to have above average math scores, and under-confident students were more likely to have above average math scores," says University at Buffalo Professor of learning and instruction Ming Ming Chiu, the lead author.[265]

Your kid? "Sure, he's special," say Po Bronson and Ashley Merryman, reviewing the scientific research in *NurtureShock: New Thinking about Children*, "But new research suggests if you tell him that, you'll ruin him. It's a neurobiological fact."[266] Kids praised for being smart give up easily, suffer defeat harder, and are more likely to do poorly in school overall. Beset by a false sense of their superior skills and brainpower, they slack off. If he's already the best, why should he apply himself? If he's so smart, why does he need to study? If he's already perfect, there's no room for improvement.

WHEN SWAGGER meets another male tendency, risk taking, trouble often results. Testosterone already correlates with thrill-seeking behavior. Women have on average more long-range neural connections than most men, enabling them to more readily grasp the long-term consequences of their actions. As a result, boys and men tend to focus narrowly on the short term or the present.[267] Add an unhealthy dose of bravado to the mix, and disaster can follow.

High-flying politicians who went down in flames for sexual risk taking immediately spring to mind: former Congressman Anthony Weiner sending racy photos of himself to strangers on Twitter, former Governor Elliott Spitzer sleeping with hookers after making a name for himself prosecuting prostitution rings, former Governor Arnold Schwarzenegger philandering with his family housekeeper, former Senator John Edwards hooking up with a campaign videographer, former President Bill Clinton's trysts with an intern. The lies, denials, blaming of others, ultimate teary confessions and apologies, often with the wife standing mutely by him—this crowd has so much swagger that they make the fellows on *Jackass* look like trembling milquetoasts.

Hey, at least the *Jackass* guys call themselves what they are. What else can you call young men who really need to know, say, what happens if they staple their scrotum to their legs? Surely you know *Jackass*, the phenomenally successful MTV television show that's spawned five television spinoffs, three feature films, popular DVD boxed sets, websites, and a video game, featuring antics like a young guy diving into a vat of excrement in nothing but duct-taped tighty-whities and a snorkel, or a guy being pulled over a hill on a plastic sled by a four-wheeler, and—surprise!—smashing his tailbone. On one episode a cast member was moved to don a hot-dog suit and ride a BMX bike down a skate ramp to a spectacular crash. As he lay on the ground, a crew member ran up and squirted mustard in his mouth and all over his face. That's how they roll on *Jackass*.

The show captured boys' creative zeal to rig up odd machines—especially with wheels and engines—along with their enthusiasm for crude humor and a "what if we…" *joie de vivre*, all with comic-book effects. How about if I pack my parents' indoor staircase with snow and ski down it? *Crash!* Will an alligator bite directly to the nipple leave a mark? *Ow!* What happens if we fill a car full of bees and then throw marbles on the ground as our buddy tries to escape? *Bam!* Or if we put a lit firecracker between our butt cheeks? *Ka-boom!*

What happens is injuries, naturally, coming fast and furious to the cast members over the years: a torn urethra (that's in the penis, folks), concussions, permanent nipple damage, a broken clavicle, shattered hand, broken ribs, a broken foot, broken bones of every kind imaginable, giant chunks of scraped-off

flesh, a torn liver (*a torn liver?*)—and these are just so ⌐
the "top" injuries to the cast members reported on MTV': ₍₁
website.[268]

I don't often feel sorry for my fellow lawyers, but I can only imagine the show's legal department begging, pleading to tone this stuff down, then having to limp off, tails between their legs, having no choice but to accept the network's decision to air the show anyway, albeit with frequent warnings sprinkled throughout. Despite those aggressive disclaimers, *Jackass* devotees could not resist trying these stunts at home, causing young people's predictable pain, destruction, and, sadly, deaths. Thirteen-year-old Wisconsin boy Aaron Brown, for example, died when a van driven by his teenage friends sped over railroad tracks, tapes of the show in the vehicle alongside homemade videos of the copycat stunts that the boys were attempting.[269]

One of the *Jackass* stars, Ryan Dunn, himself died in 2011 in a fiery car crash just outside of Philadelphia, hours after tweeting a picture of himself drinking. Police say that his blood alcohol level was twice the legal limit and that he was driving over 132 miles per hour. He was thirty-four years old.[270] Cast members and fans ripped film critic Roger Ebert for tweeting after the crash: "Friends don't let jackasses drink and drive."[271]

Jackass is one of the most colorful and tragic pop culture examples of male swagger mixed with thrill seeking. But once you're aware of this toxic cocktail, you'll notice it everywhere. Forget the stereotypes about female drivers, for example. Behind the wheel, mile for mile, male drivers are 77 percent more likely to get in a fatal accident, according to a major traffic analysis done at Carnegie Mellon University. Why are males so accident prone? Overconfidence in their driving ability and foolhardy risk taking. (Insurance companies have known this for years. Males under twenty-four drive so recklessly and aggressively that, of any group, they are the most likely to die in highway accidents.[272] The author of the study was so moved by his findings that he now has his wife drive. "I put a mitt in my mouth and ride shotgun," he said.[273])

Swaggering boys grow into overconfident men ill served by their superiority complex. Men are overrepresented in high-risk professions, such as stock trading, for example, but that doesn't mean they're better performers in those industries. I was fascinated at the underreported news that female fund managers outperform their male counterparts. Male investors, for example, execute more trades—apparently wanting more *action*, more *zazz*, even if trading is ill advised at that time. Holding firm in tough times, minimizing costs, buying low and selling high are the common-sense hallmarks of profitable portfolio management, but during a financial crisis men are more likely to sell low, and conversely, they are more likely to buy high.[274] Male investors are just so darned *overconfident*, according to the study, by mutual fund company Vanguard, they think they know what they're doing, but they don't. Women more readily acknowledge what they don't know and ask for help.

Ah, the proverbial woman, who's not afraid to stop and ask for directions. And the image of a cocky Wall Street trader, brought low by a patient, nerves-of-steel female fund manager: in a nutshell, that's the consequences of swagger.

In another study of thirty-five thousand households of people who bought and sold stock, men traded 50 percent more than women—driving up fees and lowering their returns.[275] Men may brag about their prowess, but their female counterparts quietly outperformed them.

The rooster crows, but the hen delivers.

Remember that girls have less math and science confidence than boys, even when they perform at the same skill level? That swagger differential may explain why girls now have closed the gap with boys on math and science proficiency.[276] The 2011 Google science fair winners? Shree Bose, Naomi Shaw, and Lauren Hodge—all girls. Those girls are living the philosophy behind the old Avis Rent-a-Car commercials: *We're #2. We try harder.* While boys are resting on their imagined laurels, the girls are putting in more effort—effort that leads to results. As we've seen, girls, who have more humility, are destroying boys, who have more swagger, at every level of school, outperforming them in every grade, filling AP classes, and graduating in greater numbers.

The bottom line? Swagger is holding our boys and men back, giving a false sense of security that they are *all that* when, demonstrably, often they are not. The first step toward protecting your boy: instilling in him recognition that there is work to be done. Tell him to lose the swagger. Point it out when you observe it in his attitude, words, or behavior. Teach him that effort precedes rewards, that self-esteem must be earned, not bestowed. Prize humility—a return to what the human race has known since the days of the ancient Greeks: that hubris is folly and has brought down arrogant mortals for centuries. Sure, you can still praise him. Every kid needs kind words of recognition. But *praise wisely.* Kids given empty compliments, say, for being "smart," are actually hindered in their school performance and take more foolhardy risks, as we've seen. Those praised for honest effort, however, stay on task more doggedly, choose harder assignments, and are able to overcome academic setbacks with more persistence.[277] And that diligence, that resilience when faced with obstacles or failures, is the key to success not only in school but also in life.

As a kid, I bristled at phony adult compliments. I knew I couldn't sing or draw, for instance, and when grownups looked in my eyes and told me I was a wonderful musician or artist, I knew they were full of it and doubted their credibility on every other subject. My own children always despised the "everyone's a winner!" mentality, attempting to boost their self-esteem by, say, pretending that all the kids won the race. No, the one who crossed the finish line first won, my son and daughter always insisted, miffed by the insult to their intelligence. Were they not to believe their own eyes? *What are we, morons?* was the undertone. *We see what you're up to. And it's not helping us. Knock it off.*

Children don't need the ninth-place ribbons. They know they're not super-fantastic just because they rolled out of bed.

Innately, they want what's best for them: recognition that when they really did sweat out a hard math test, when they did the dishes without being asked, when they stayed on task in history though their friends tried to distract them, when they accepted a tough reading challenge, when they stuck out the hockey team all the way through the semester...*then* they deserve our praise.

As a mother, I get that every tiny thing our angels do is amazing to us. They started out drooling, babbling, and incontinent, and each step forward is a miracle of developing life. But part of our job as parents is to squelch our natural desire to fawn all over them, spoil them, and overdo the praise. Instead, let's go back to basics and teach the core value of humility. Your son *is* an important person, a child of God, with the spark of the divine animating him. But so is every other person on the planet—no more, no less.

"With humility comes wisdom" (Proverbs 11:2). And with humility comes better grades, higher graduation rates, a more stable career, safer driving, fewer injuries, and better money management in adulthood. That's a fat payoff for one little attitude adjustment.

And let's face it: your boy will be a lot less of a jackass.

RULE 2:

SET COLLEGE EXPECTATIONS EARLY AND OFTEN

"A human being is not attaining his full heights until he is educated."

—HORACE MANN

DIDN'T YOU love board games as a kid? I did. My Dad, my brother, and I played endless cutthroat games of Scrabble, Monopoly, and poker. At home with my girlfriends, we played the Milton Bradley game Life. Slower paced and less exciting than the others, it nevertheless managed to teach us an indelible lesson. If you've ever played it, you know that early on in the game you make a choice (or it's made for you) about how far you'll go in school. High school graduate? College graduate? For the rest of the game you regularly hit a square marked "payday," and the amount of colorful paper money you receive depends on whether you attained a high school degree or, better, a college diploma. College graduates get marginally more money each "payday," and after a few rounds, that difference starts to add up. With more money comes more options. As you continue along the circuitous, windy path on the playing board, your tiny plastic car moving over bridges and hills, with pink and blue pegs in your car representing your family, one thing is clear: it's almost impossible to win at Life without a college degree.

A College Diploma: The Golden Ticket to a Middle-Class Life

MILTON BRADLEY was apparently ahead of his time. Because in life, as in Life, payday after payday, year after year, the income differential between college graduates and those with less schooling mounts. In fact, it's snowballing much faster now than it did back in the seventies when I was sitting on my burnt orange shag rug, spinning the plastic wheel. In 1979 college grads earned about 38 percent more than those with a high school diploma. Today, they earn a whopping 75 percent more.[278] Milton Bradley may need to print more pastel paper money.

Here's recent US Census data for the average earnings of workers eighteen and older:

> $83,144 workers with an advanced degree
> $58,613 workers with a bachelor's degree
> $31,283 workers with a high school degree
> $21,023 high school dropouts.[279]

Paycheck after paycheck, year after year, the difference is enormous. In a dozen years those advanced degree holders have earned a million dollars, on average, while high school graduates, also working full time at their jobs, have grossed less than $400,000. That's the difference between being able to buy a home, provide for one's children, and save for the future versus living paycheck to paycheck or going deeper into debt. And that's assuming no promotions, which are far more likely to come to degree holders than they are to high school grads or high school dropouts, who often labor in dead-end jobs.

As a middle-class income becomes more elusive and the gap between rich and poor widens in America, a college degree is essential for our boys (and girls) if they hope to support a family, own a home, or simply attain a modest level of economic security. We hear a lot about income inequality between the 1 Percent and the 99 Percent, and we should. But there's another, equally glaring inequality in America today—between those with four-year college diplomas and those without.

That college grads earn a whole lot more than high school grads is only part of the story. Job security is much higher for those with college degrees. If your son has a college diploma, he's far more likely to land a job and *stay employed*. As this book went to press, unemployment in the United States was at 15 percent for high school dropouts, 10 percent for high school grads, but only 4 percent for college grads. Those numbers may fluctuate a bit, but the gaps appear to be entrenched. Historically, college grads have consistently had a far easier time landing a job during tough times, and they rise to the top in a strong economy. A college degree is a clear economic win for your child, no matter what.[280] As Martin Luther King, Jr. said to protesters years ago: "You say burn, baby, burn. But I say learn, baby, learn, so you can earn, baby, earn!"

But it's not only about money and job security. Most important but least measurable are the knowledge and critical thinking skills that will last your son a lifetime. He'll be more likely to be able to solve the problems that come his way, he'll know how to research issues, he'll be a better communicator—all skills that will serve him no matter what path he chooses for his life.

And there are myriad other perks, loosely grouped under the category of "social benefits." In fact, the social divide may be even starker than the income divide. In the 1970s high school and college grads had very similar family structures. Today, college grads are much more likely to get married, much less likely to get divorced, and significantly less likely to have a child out of wedlock. Compared to high school grads, they are far less likely to smoke, are less likely to be obese, are healthier overall, are more likely to be active in their communities, have much more social trust, and speak many more words to their babies and children at home, thus ensuring an early start and a better future for the next generation. Some research suggests that college grads have much bigger friendship networks than do high school grads. And on and on it goes.[281]

Have you ever heard someone say, "I wish I hadn't gotten that college education"? No, and you never will.

As we've seen, as our nation has de-industrialized, most unskilled jobs that can be replaced by a machine or a computer or sent oversees have been. The jobs that remain require the higher learning and analytical skills that come with a four-year college degree. And the trend—just as more of our young people are dropping out—is toward a need for even *more* college-educated workers than ever before. In just ten years, more than 60 percent of all new jobs will require a college degree, according to Complete College America, a nonprofit committed to raising awareness about college dropout rates.[282]

Apple, the most valuable company in the world as this book went to press,[283] is a perfect example. An American company that once employed Americans to assemble its computers, it has now almost entirely outsourced the manufacturing of its phenomenally successful products to Asia. "Those jobs aren't coming back," Apple founder, the late Steve Jobs, once told President Obama.[284] Almost all of the seventy million iPhones, thirty million iPads, and fifty-nine million other products Apple sold in 2011 were manufactured overseas, primarily in China, where seven hundred thousand workers toiled away in sometimes substandard conditions as they assembled these devices.[285] Its remaining US jobs are in design, engineering, and executive positions that require higher education.[286] It's the Information Age now, or as the Organisation for Economic Cooperation and Development calls it, the "knowledge-based economy."[287] Where does your son gain that knowledge? College.

A college degree is now the required golden ticket to the middle class. It is critically important to your boy's future. And by "a college degree," I do mean that he needs that diploma in hand. Beware of news stories or statistics about large numbers of young people *enrolling* in universities. Many do, but, sadly, most don't graduate, as we've seen. It's not about signing up; it's about *finishing* and getting that degree that will get him past the velvet rope and onto the higher paying, more satisfying, more stable and lasting jobs.

But it's expensive! You say. You don't have to tell me. I just put two kids through private colleges as a single mother, and I'm scarred for life from the financial bleed-out of that experience. Yes, college costs are insane, offensive, a slap in the face to working families, as we've seen. Congress should require, as a condition for tax exemptions, that schools with bloated endowments charge more reasonable tuitions. State governments should reprioritize and fund education over prisons. We should all be occupying state houses and the capitol building until this happens. (*Who's with me?!*)

But in the meantime your kid is growing up, and he still has to go to college. Tick tock. So how do you make that happen in this hostile environment?

If money is tight, he should go to a public university in your state. Although their fees have risen steeply, your local State U is still a fraction of the price of private schools and the best bang for your buck. For the 2011–12 school year, public four-year colleges charged, on average, $8,244 in tuition and fees for in-state students, according to the College Board, which tracks these numbers.[288] (Compare that to $28,500 per year in tuition and fees at private colleges.)

He can live at home in order to save on housing and food costs.

Will he be missing out on dorm life? Yes, he'll be foregoing the drunken sexual revelry of twenty-first-century college residence halls, just like the three-quarters of other college kids who don't live on campus. That's okay. He's there for the education.

Still, even $8,244 a year (not counting those pricey text-books!) is an enormous amount of money. Here's more good news: *most* students receive financial aid. In 2010–11 about $178 billion in financial aid was awarded to undergraduate students. The average amount of aid for a full-time undergraduate student was about $12,455, including more than $6,500 in grants that don't have to be repaid.[289] If you are struggling financially, a great deal of financial aid will be available to your son.

Often left unsaid in college discussions is the fact that the *majority* of students get grants, tuition breaks, and, yes, those dreaded student loans.[290] Yes, some students graduate with six-figure debt, which should be appalling to all of us. No young person should begin life that deeply in the hole, punished simply for wanting an education. But those stories are, thankfully, still outliers. Although college loan debt is up, it now averages $25,250 per graduate—a large amount of money, especially for a young person, to be sure. But that amount is still less than the $27,330 difference between what the average college grad and the average high school grad earns in *one year.*[291]

So pay no attention to all those earnest "Is a College Degree Worth It?" fear-mongering stories. Purely as a matter of dollars and sense, there is no question about it: a college degree is *well worth it.* It is by far the best investment you can make in your child. Along with vaccinations, seat belts, and bicycle helmets, college should be seen as a necessary protection for your son's future. Do not let him leave home without it.

And Mom, Dad, Concerned Adult: he needs to go full time. Why? Because here's a fact almost no one tells you: there's a name for part-time college students—dropouts. In a comprehensive study of ten million college students, less than 8 percent of part-timers trying to get a two-year degree in four years actually got that diploma. For part-timers working toward a four-year degree in eight years, only 24 percent were successful. It's just too damn difficult to work and go to school, and so part-timers, even when they're given double the normal time to finish, hardly ever do. More years to finish school actually decrease your son's chance of getting his degree, though that may seem counterintuitive. But here's what happens: life gets in the way. Job hours are difficult or impossible to schedule around class time. (Try telling *your* boss, "Hi, I can only work Tuesdays and Thursdays from 4 to 9 p.m. for the next four months. Then after that I'll get back to you with an entirely different schedule.") Young people form relationships, get married, have babies, and take on mortgages and additional work responsibilities. Money becomes increasingly important, and college feels more and more like a luxury and a diversion. And we've seen that the number-one reason most of our college students drop out—and remember, *most* drop out—is that the stresses of working and going to school at the same time are too overwhelming.

If your son attends a four-year college full time, he *triples* his chances of graduating over part-time attendance. You want to give him those odds.[292] You also want him to be able to focus on his classes and studying. Every single part-timer I have spoken to has bemoaned being pulled in multiple directions when all they wanted was a block of time and some peace and quiet so that they could study. They envied their peers who didn't work through school and who could complete reading and class assignments without distraction and with a good night's sleep. Give your son that benefit.

How do you get your boy there? You need to deliver two messages to him frequently:

> College is expected.
> College will be doable.

First, expectations. The expectations you set for your son have a tremendous impact on his mindset. Most college graduates tell me that, from their earliest memories, their parents always made it clear that they would be going to college. There was no discussion about whether it was going to happen or not. It was going to happen, period. However, there was a lot of talk about *which* college, *which* major, *which* college teams the family rooted for, and so forth. College grads often tell me that they had no choice in the matter (though, of course, they did, as legal adults): they were going to graduate from the best four-year school they could get into and that was that. Their families would never have accepted anything less.

The two ethnic groups with stratospherically high college graduation rates relative to their small numbers in the population are Jews and Asian Americans. Both groups come from cultural traditions that strongly emphasize the importance of education. From the beginning, many Jewish and Asian American children get a clear message that not only is their number-one job to do well in school each and every day, but also that college graduation is firmly expected of them, a given.[293] This expectation is constantly reinforced throughout their childhood, with casual conversation about "when you go to college…"[294] No other options are discussed or considered.

In many Asian or Jewish homes, choice of university begins to be discussed when a child is in middle school or even younger. "You're interested in journalism? Syracuse has the Newhouse School." "Business? You'd love Wharton. Let's go check it out!" The family attends every college prep seminar offered at the child's school or in the community. The family visits dozens of potential colleges. There's no question of whether or not the child will go to college. The only question is, *which* college. (And, often, law, business, medical, or other graduate or professional school. As the joke goes—Jewish birth announcement: Mr. and Mrs. Weinberg are pleased to announce the birth of their son, Dr. David Weinberg.)

The payoff? Asian Americans make up 15 to 20 percent of Ivy League classes, though this group is only about 5 percent of the population overall.[295] Jews, less than 2 percent of the US population, make up an astounding 31 percent of the students at George Washington University and 30 percent of the kids at the University of Pennsylvania.[296] Why did I pick those two schools? Because they are academically strong universities and because my children recently attended them. And the many times I visited them at these colleges it really did seem as if everyone was Jewish, Asian, or, like my kids, both.

An eleven-year-old recently graduated from a California community college. Moshe Kai Cavalin is half-Jewish, half-Asian. His idols are Albert Einstein and Bruce Lee.[297] Sure, it's an extreme example. But cultural norms and family expectations really do go a long way.

Anyone can decide to inculcate these values, regardless of ethnic background, of course. I visited the East Harlem Tutorial Program (EHTP), an inspiring, well-run after-school project and charter school that's been working for forty years with some of the poorest kids in New York City, most of whom are Hispanic and African American. Fifteen thousand kids have gone through the program, in a neighborhood known for poverty, junkies, and boarded-up, abandoned buildings some call "haunted houses."[298] By instilling high academic standards and college expectations from kindergarten through senior year— classrooms are decorated with Harvard's fight song or SUNY Buffalo's school colors, and children are always addressed as "scholars" — an amazing 98 percent of kids in the program go to college, and they complete college at double the national rate. Over three hundred volunteers work relentlessly with the students to prepare them for higher education, providing frequent one-on-one college mentoring and even following up with them once they leave the program and go to universities. EHTP is a testament to the success that comes from setting high standards early and being clear with children about college expectations.

On the other side of the country a low-performing, predominately Hispanic public elementary school in San Diego, California, decided to get on this bandwagon of setting college expectations early. To drive home their point, they changed the name of the school from Los Peñasquitos Elementary School to No Excuses University at Los Pen. Instead of numbers, classrooms are now identified by college names like Ohio State or the University of Michigan. School colors and flags are displayed to get kids in the college spirit. Youngsters learn all about their assigned school, make up a cheer for it, and enjoy visits from "their" school's alumni.

"From the minute students walk in the door, we want them to feel like they are on a college campus. It's all about the spirit," Damen Lopez, a former principal at the school and the founder of the No Excuses University Network of Schools. "We want to expose them to the possibility of a four-year university. That it's not something far, far away."[299] Parents come to meetings to learn to set college expectations for their kids.

How's it working out? Five–hundred–student Los Pen has gone from being the lowest-performing school in the thirty-three thousand–student Poway Unified School District to one of the top schools in California and a recipient of the National Blue Ribbon School Award. Eighty-eight other schools have joined the No Excuses University model.[300]

You don't have to wait for your kids' school to follow suit; you can start your own No Excuses University at home, today. Explain to your boy that regardless of the choices you may have made, a four-year college degree is essential to his future. You expect him to go. He *will* go. Any other alternative is a nonstarter. You will give him the support he needs to apply, register, attend full time, and graduate. Not only will you make whatever sacrifice is necessary for him to complete college, but you also expect him to do the same. Any shortfall that the family cannot meet will be taken out in loans, and he can live at home upon graduation until the loans are paid.

Those of us who have looked at the data are motivated to take bold moves to get kids to college. Frustrated by the fact that only 6 percent of foster children earn a bachelor's degree, philanthropist Peter Samuelson realized that familiarizing foster children with a college environment at an early age was key to getting them to see themselves as future collegians. So he created First Star, Inc., a nonprofit that set up a boarding school for middle school and high school foster kids—located smack in the middle of a local university campus. At first, he says, the kids are bewildered by their new environment, the University of California at Los Angeles. But as the weeks go by they become comfortable there and begin to see a college future for themselves. *But I could never afford college!* many say. Samuelson breaks down the scholarships, grants, and loans that are available, explaining that in fact the UC college system will not charge most of them anything due to their low economic bracket. A light switches on in their minds, he says: *Whoa. Maybe I could do this.* As the program just began for ninth graders in 2011, it's too soon to tell what First Star's end results will be, but having higher education surround them will surely change their hearts and minds, making them literally see themselves in college every day they go to school.

Hey, if you wanted to take up residence inside the parameters of your local university, I'd be impressed. Short of that, make your home college-friendly and college-positive. His first stuffed animal? A college mascot. Buy your boy State U hoodies and T-shirts. Decorate his room with college pennants, posters, and flags. Take him to free lectures and book events at your local university, and then stick around afterward to chat with students who attend. Take him to readings and just to browse at the college bookstore. Root for one college team against another. If he's a sports fan, take him to games— they're filled with college students. When adult friends come over, have them recount their college experiences—the fun, the challenges, the favorite classes, the silly antics. The mystery of how an intact, hollowed-out pumpkin appeared atop a 173-foot-high spire at Cornell University in 1997 has never been solved, for instance.[301] And how did those Massachusetts Institute of Technology students manage to get a police squad car, complete with Dunkin Donuts and flashing lights, atop the engineering library's dome?[302]

Your message: college is fun. It's a time of your life you'll always remember. You're going to have a blast. You're going to expand your brain and make lifelong friends. Sure, there will be challenges as well as late nights of studying and difficult exams. You may end up loving it or hating it.

But no matter what, kid, you're going, and you're graduating.

RULE 3:

MAKE YOUR HOME A READING MECCA

"It is what you read when you don't have to that determines what you will be when you can't help it."

—OSCAR WILDE

OF COURSE, once you've reset your son's expectations to include college graduation, he'll need to be *prepared* for college. He'll need to excel in high school well enough to be accepted to college, and he'll need skills that will get him through the more rigorous demands of higher education once he's there. Thanks to our culture's deprioritization of education and our failing schools, *half* of all students entering community colleges and 20 percent of incoming four-year college freshmen now require remediation—catch up classes to get them up to the reading and writing level they should have had before entering college. (Recall that one-fifth of our high school graduates are functionally illiterate.) A city college president told me that, after budget cuts, the biggest problem facing her school, year after year, is trying to bring incoming students who can't read or write up to speed. This large group of people starts out far behind the starting line, often becoming stuck in remediation classes, unable to move forward. The vast majority of remediation students nationwide never graduate from college.[303] As we've seen, boys fill these classes.

Don't let that be your boy.

Let's work backward. To be sure that he enters college ready, willing and able to succeed, he'll need to excel in high school. Of course, to lay the foundation for high school success, he'll need to master his subjects in middle school. To do that he'll need to develop strong reading, writing, math, and communication skills in elementary school. (And even when he's a preschooler, you'll want to get him away from video screens, talk and read to him, and prepare his brain, as we'll see.)

We know that our schools undereducate our boys, so it's imperative that parents ramp up at-home learning by creating an environment that stimulates intellectual curiosity and, most of all, supports reading. Turning your boy into a strong reader, an articulate writer, and an eloquent communicator isn't just a matter of boosting his school performance; solid reading, writing, and communication skills are so critical for your boys' future that they can hardly be overestimated.

His Future Turns on Literacy

LET ME be very clear: *without strong reading, writing, and communication skills, your boys' future is bleak. His future flows from developing these skills early.* We've seen how dismal the job market is for blue-collar trade jobs, how many young men are competing for the few that remain. Nonreaders cluster at the bottom of all those sad statistics, dominating the unemployment rolls and filling our jails. Recall all those young men locked up in our prisons: 70 percent of them are illiterate.[304] For our incarcerated boys it's even worse: 85 percent of all American juvenile offenders are functionally or marginally illiterate—truly, an astounding number. And the stakes could not be higher for our nonreading kids because the American criminal justice system is harshly punitive toward juvenile offenders, compared to other first-world countries, often trying them as adults, trusting them to sign waivers of their constitutional rights, and meting out long sentences to minors. We are one of the last countries in the world, for example, to sentence juveniles to life in prison without the possibility of parole, a cruel and unusual punishment that I am confident will one day be found unconstitutional.[305] Mistakes that juvenile offenders make when navigating through the judicial system can literally cost them a lifetime of freedom.

After just one brush with the law, nonreading boys have few options—burdened by their illiteracy, shut out from opportunities to connect with their communities, being forced to "check the box" that they have a criminal conviction, thereby rendering them unemployable. Illiteracy sharply increases the chances of recidivism and re-incarceration. The ability to get a job upon release from prison is the single-biggest determinant of whether an ex-con lands back in prison.[306] Thus, most ex-cons who can't read are back in prison within two years of their release, largely because they are unemployable.

The Department of Justice says plainly, "The link between academic failure and delinquency, violence, and crime is welded to reading failure." Two-thirds of students who cannot read proficiently by the end of the fourth grade will end up in jail or on welfare. The fourth grade is the watershed year.[307]

Some in the literacy and education community say that Texas and Arizona use fourth-grade reading scores to project how many prisons they'll need to build in ten years.[308] Though many well-meaning sites tout this story, I hunted it down to the source and it's not accurate. Prison construction planners are not reviewing elementary school test results in assessing their future needs. It's one of those gripping statements that gets copied and pasted, but there is no solid evidence to back it up.

But it may as well be true. There is a straight-line correlation between boys who don't read who then do poorly in virtually

all subjects, hate school, drop out, and become juvenile delin-
quents, unemployed, and even incarcerated. If I were in the
business of projecting future prison construction needs, I
would take a hard look at fourth-grade reading scores because
they are highly predictive of children's futures.

Reading is that critical.

And it doesn't end there. Even if our nonreading boys somehow manage to grow into men who find a decent job and stay
out of prison, they lose out on the myriad lifetime benefits of
literacy. Readers have healthier habits and lifestyles, happier
personal lives, and live longer. Readers are more connected
with their communities, vote more, and even exercise more
and play more sports. The National Endowment of the Arts's
comprehensive report on the subject concludes, "Reading
correlates with almost every measure of positive personal and
social behavior surveyed."[309]

Is literacy a cure-all for what ails our boys and men? In a
world without panaceas: just about.

How to Make Your Home a Reading Mecca

SO YOU'RE in. Perhaps you didn't need much convincing anyway. Eighty-two percent of parents say they'd like their kids to
read more for pleasure.[310] But how do you get him there? The
first step should come as a lovely bit of good news for parents
and caregivers, because the solution should be a joy to you too.

Mom, Dad, Caring Adult: *you* must read more. Not when
he's in school. Not when he's asleep. Not when you're waiting
alone in the carpool line. Here's one of the most important
pieces of advice I can give you: *read when your child is awake and
around.* Don't sneak off into your bedroom as though you're
doing something faintly shameful. Bring your book out into
the light of day, into the family room or living room, and plop

down in your favorite chair, relax, and enjoy your book "openly and notoriously," as we say in the law. The key is for your boy to observe you, on a regular basis, reading avidly. If he does this, he will be *six times* more likely to read on his own for pleasure.[311] How about that? Be a show-offy reader.

Children of parents who openly read for pleasure learn that reading *is* a pleasure. Most of us know that reading to young children is important—and it is. But reading *with* older children is equally important. Pat the sofa cushion and invite him to join you with his book. Or lean up against a tree in your backyard or park and pull a bunch of books out of your picnic basket, some for him and some for you. Read the good parts aloud to each other. Laugh at the funny bits; brood over the sad chapters. When you're called to dinner, beg permission to finish your chapter. Look at the clock and say, "Wow, does time fly when I'm reading a good book!"

Sell reading as though your boy's life depends on it, because it does. Read fiction, nonfiction, history, biographies, romance novels...your choice! Sure, intelligent books are better, and dipping across to unfamiliar genres is better for you.[312] But mainly you need to convey through your behavior that books are a treat, that reading is your default pleasure activity, that you pick up books eagerly and put them down reluctantly.

"Where do I find the time for not reading so many books?" the Austrian writer and journalist Karl Kraus said a hundred years ago.[313] Adopt this philosophy of life and mention it to your boy. "Why am I wasting my time vacuuming when I could be finishing my amazing book?" "Hey," you say to him, "While we're waiting in line here at the supermarket, let's take out our books!" Listen to audiobooks together in the car, and when you arrive home, sit in the driveway to savor the end of the chapter. Everything else can wait. Literacy is more important.

Put up bookshelves in every room in your house and fill them with new or used or borrowed library books. Yes, you should even have a few volumes in your bathroom, a beloved male reading locale. If, like me, you need reading glasses, buy ten cheap pairs and put one in every location where you might want to read something. Eliminate every excuse for not reading. Make books a constant presence in your home and in your life. Make sure there are one or more comfortable child-sized places in your home for your boy to read for good, long chunks of time. A bean bag chair, a kid-sized recliner, a futon on the floor—if it keeps him reading longer, it's the perfect accompaniment for any décor.

Acquaint yourself with your local library, the last public institution in America where you need no special credentials, license, or sticker for admittance. Just walk right in, sit down, and revel in the books—with your son in tow, of course. Bring home armloads of them.

Invite over reader-friends and *talk* about your love of books in front of your kids. "Oh! I just finished the greatest book! Have you read this?" Tell your friends in advance you'd love it if they'd get with your new program. Everyone is to enthuse about books in the presence of your son.

Men, especially, must model reading for pleasure in the presence of your boy. As we've seen, Mom on average reads for pleasure almost twice as much as Dad. Your son is used to book people, such as teachers and librarians, being primarily female. If there's a book club member in your house, dollars to donuts it's Mom. When asked who is most likely to recommend books to them, children ranked their fathers dead last on a list of five possibilities, after mothers, friends, teachers, and librarians.[314] So you must create a world in which men and books go together like rice and beans. *Dads: read to your boys.* Read in the presence of your boy. Take him to the library, the bookstore, author readings, and book festivals. Be a male reading role model for him daily.

As always, he will do as you do, not as you say. Don't tell but *show* him how to incorporate regular reading into his life.[315] You may think that sports figures are his idols, but when one thousand boys were recently asked who their number-one role model was, Dad beat out all those athletes by a landslide.[316]

This is consistent with many surveys. In kids' minds, parents always come in first on the role model contest, followed by teachers. Sports stars, celebrities, and even the president lag far behind, getting only single-digit responses.[317] Absorb this. Even a brooding teen is watching you beneath that long hair and hoodie. He's listening to you from behind those earbuds. He won't admit it, but he wants to be just like you. Boys imitate their dads—or other male role models in their lives.

Recognizing the urgent need for male reading role models, some schools are bringing in "manly" role models like firefighters—in full uniform and regalia—to hunker down on the rug and read with the kindergartners.[318] Brilliant. Yes. Whatever works.

Ask your boy what he's reading, and listen, rapt, to every word he has to say about it. Nudge him with open-ended questions: "Why didn't you like it?" "What was the best part?" "What did you relate to in the lead character?" "What was different about the setting of that book?" "Did any of that book hit you on an emotional level? Why or why not?" You don't want to sound like you're pushing him to give you a book report, but you do want to create a conversation about stories and ideas, to reinforce the fabulousness of reading. Ask him to read you his favorite parts aloud. And make sure he understands it and isn't just sounding out the words.

Despite all your positive role modeling, he may say he doesn't like to read or that he doesn't know of any good books. Boys of all ages say they have trouble finding books they'd like to read more often than girls do, which is one of the key reasons why they read less and perform less proficiently in school.[319] With boys generally it's about finding the right book to spark some curiosity. Knowing your boy's interests and zeroing in on books that will excite him, reading the book with him, or, especially, suggesting that the book "may be inappropriate for him" are surefire ways to get him to crack it open. Check out the Books Boys Love Appendix at the end of this book for a list of tried and true appealing books for boys of all ages. Of course he

doesn't know of many good books—that's your job: to help
him find them.

Spurring your son to read begins in his infancy, when he
teethes on plastic chew-up books and then continues for life.
When he's little, of course, you need to read to him. Many parents do this at bedtime, and huzzah for that. But the newest
recommendations call for reading to him not just once but
three times a day.[320] And don't stop reading with him after he can
read on his own! Parents sharply drop off reading together with
their children after age eight.[321] At that age they are only beginning readers. Your job is far from done. Yes, we all thank the
Lord when we can stop reading *Goodnight Moon* after the twelve-
thousandth time. But move on to more sophisticated chapter
books that you can enjoy together. Be relentless in stoking the
reading flames, week in and week out, throughout the elementary, middle, and high school years and beyond. (My children
are young adults, one a recent college grad and the other a
junior in college, and we talk about books constantly, sharing
an e-book account so that we can read the same books on our
different devices, though we may live thousands of miles apart.
They know that I consider it a lifelong job to keep them reading—and that I eagerly await their book recommendations.)

Your boy's brain is blossoming while he's hanging upside
down off the arm of the sofa, turning pages of a book he's
chosen. If he's doing that, you've largely succeeded as a parent,
so give yourself a big smug pat on the back. His brain matters
more than the upholstery. Bring him a snack so he has no reason to stop. Resist the temptation to interrupt him, to ask him
to take out the trash, to tell him what your mother just said. His
future is based on literacy and is more important. Unless the
house is on fire, let the boy read—his books, his way. And if the
house does catch fire, I hope the first thing you grab after your
family and pets are the books.

RULE 4:

ELIMINATE THE COMPETITION

"I must say that I find television very educational. The minute somebody turns it on, I go to the library and read a book."

—GROUCHO MARX

RANGY THIRTEEN-YEAR-OLD Cosmo Cothran-Bray reads two years above grade level, as does his ten-year-old brother, Tennessee. Just for fun, Cosmo recently challenged himself to reread the entire *Harry Potter* series—all 4,182 pages—in one week. He didn't quite make it. It took him ten days.

The Cothran-Bray home is littered with books, spilling out of a large, comfortably messy bookshelf front and center in the living room, stacked on tables, dog-eared in the boys' beds. If you ask Cosmo or Tenny to recommend a book they've read recently, be prepared to sit down for an excited, lengthy, detailed explanation with constant self-interruptions to describe other books that wait—now that they think about it—are even better.

When I told Cosmo that I was writing about boys uninterested in reading, he was mystified. "I can't believe there are people who don't like to read," he said, looking askance at me as if I'd proposed that some people have gills. My credibility was now in question. "*Come on*, Auntie Lisa!"

Yes, Cosmo and Tennessee are my brother's sons.[322] As you may have guessed from their children's unusual names, Peyton and his wife, Ellen, have the courage to forge their own path in the world.

That includes chucking the "electronic hearth" that flickers an average of five hours per day in other American households.[323] They didn't just rule out TV sets in their sons' bedrooms; they rejected the medium entirely. "I'd done my homework before Cosmo was born and learned that no matter how good the programming, at the core *Sesame Street* teaches children how to watch TV," Ellen says. It took some convincing to get Peyton to agree to this. The thought of *actually not having a TV from then on—forever!?*—was unnerving to him, and the couple had many conversations on the topic over a period of several months during her pregnancy with Cosmo. Ellen kept the focus on their future children's health. Ultimately, she prevailed.

"We got rid of the TV the day after Cosmo was born," Peyton says, now clearly pleased with their decision. "It's not like when we were kids, when there was a good show on maybe once a week," he reasons. "Remember? We'd sit down and watch *Taxi* or *M.A.S.H*, and when it was done, we'd turn it off and go out and play. Now there are hundreds of channels. Several round-the-clock, kid-only channels. And the shows are *better*. They are funny and thrilling, with dazzling graphics and chase scenes and compelling plots and characters. We didn't get rid of the TV because it was all bad. We dumped it because some of it was *too good*, too alluring. We knew that books would be less appealing if the TV was always available."

Ellen learned early what many parents learn only after tense TV wars in their own homes. To make books more appealing you must ruthlessly eliminate the competition. That flat-screen on the wall of your child's room or that box in your living room, with all furniture facing it expectantly, is a relentlessly seductive temptress, and your son cannot be expected to resist her siren call. *American Idol* is just too addictive. *Sponge Bob* is too much fun to watch.

You cannot match the resources of, say, Disney, when it decides to roll out a new show designed to grab your boy's attention and get his eyeballs in front of their advertisers. When the network launched *Phineas & Ferb*, for example, targeted at six- to eleven-year-old boys, Disney put the new cartoon characters on Kraft Macaroni & Cheese, Johnson & Johnson's Band-Aid bandages, and Kellogg's Fruit Snacks. *Phineas & Ferb* showed up on skateboards, guitars, and raincoats sold at stores like Walmart, Kohl's, and Target. Two million *Phineas & Ferb* T-shirts have been sold since 2008, according to the *Wall Street Journal.*[324] Unless you're a billionaire who intends to roll out a multilevel marketing campaign for the next book you'd like your son to read, you cannot compete with this. But you can pull the plug on your son's TV, removing this option entirely from his equation.

Because my brother and sister-in-law's instincts were right: the research is crystal clear that the more TV time kids enjoy, the worse they'll do in school and later in life.

TV: Can You Handle the Truth?

LET'S START with little kids. American infants and toddlers today spend twice as much time watching TVs and DVDs than with they do with books.[325] Show me a tiny tot, and I'm looking at a kid who's mentally plugged into a screen.

But isn't a lot of that stuff harmless and even educational? We all want that answer to be yes. I raised two kids mostly as a single mom, and I was not above sitting them in front of the *Little Mermaid* or *Barney* so that I could get dinner simmering.

More challenging—more advanced parenting, if we're honest with ourselves—is Peyton and Ellen's style because parents don't get the benefit of the kids sitting blessedly quiet and still and being entertained for an hour or two at a time. Without the TV and videos, they're crawling up the walls, and we start sounding like our own parents: "I can't hear myself think!"

But after looking carefully at all the science, the answer is that Peyton and Ellen's way is clearly superior from the standpoint of producing kids who are smart, literate, intellectually curious, and alive—and college-bound. It pains me to say this because our childhood rivalry has never died, and now he gets this admission from me in print. But although some television shows and videos may be okay for older kids—in limited amounts—that's about the best one can say about them. Overall, the less TV the better. Zero is best of all.

For babies under age two there is no doubt left that screens are just glowing, noisy, brain-dulling machines. After reviewing fifty studies on the subject, the American Academy of Pediatrics says babies should not have any screens before them. None. None at all.[326] During this important period of brain development they need as much interaction and talking with real, live, flesh-and-blood humans—adults and kids—as possible. It would be nice if plopping them in front of an iPad with a Baby Einstein or educational app teaching them colors or letters or lessons in sharing benefited them. But wishing doesn't make it so.

Researchers can tell pretty quickly what television does to kids. University of Virginia psychologists had a group of four-year-olds watch nine minutes of *Sponge Bob*, an enormously popular, fast-paced kids' show—and one that, even to me, can be charming and funny. (How can you not love a theme song with the line, "absorbent and yellow and porous is he!"?)

The children in the study were tested immediately afterward for how well they solved problems and followed rules, remembered what they had been told, and were able to delay gratification. The big finding was that the *Sponge Bob* watchers suffered "severely compromised" executive functioning: the ability to pay attention, solve problems, and moderate behavior.

Translation: popular kids' TV messes with kids' minds, first, because they come to emulate the characters frenetically racing around in fantastical, nonsensical worlds, and second, because children's developing brains are just not able to process all the noise, lights, graphics, flashbang-kazaam split-second lightning-fast speed of it all. Their brains slow down like hard drives with too many applications open.[327]

That's the short-term harm. But how long does it last? A few hours or a few days? The surprising answer: early television watching has *long-term* damage for kids. Years later they are struggling in school as a result of zoning out in front of the flickering box during their toddler days. The Social Science and Humanities Research Council of Canada followed two-year-olds through their tenth year, assessing their psychosocial, academic, and health status as they developed. It turns out that even a little TV in the early years harms, says the study's lead author, Dr. Linda S. Pagani: "Between the ages of two and four, even incremental exposure to television delayed development." As your boy gets older, it gets worse: "We found every additional hour of TV exposure among toddlers corresponded to a future decrease in classroom engagement and success at math, increased victimization by classmates, a more sedentary lifestyle, higher consumption of junk food and, ultimately, higher body mass index."[328] Wow. When trying to figure out why a nine-year-old struggles with multiplication or bullying, how many of us link it to television watching when he was a toddler?

And that doesn't even touch the important issue of values. Few parents are aware of the profound shift in the core principles children's television now promotes. Think it's all friendship and sharing time and "Kumbaya"? University of California at Los Angeles researchers assessed the values espoused by leading characters in the most popular television

shows for preteens in each decade from 1967 to 2007, two per
decade, including *Andy Griffith* and the *Lucy Show* in 1967,
Laverne & Shirley and *Happy Days* in 1977, and *American Idol*
and *Hannah Montana* in 2007.[329] The researchers were stunned
with what they discovered.

"Community feeling" (being part of a group) and benevolence (being kind and helping others) were ranked first and
second as the most desirable values portrayed by the lead
characters in the top preteen shows for the first four decades
surveyed. That's nice, isn't it? We adults grew up with shows
that may have been goofy, but doing the right thing usually
won out in the end, getting along with friends mattered, and
the good guy or girl was reliably, predictably rewarded. It was
an aw-shucks kind of era. "Achieving fame" ranked near the
bottom, fifteenth out of sixteen possible in the 1987 and 1997
television surveys. It wasn't really on the radar. The actors were
stars, sure, but they were playing roles of everyday working
people, like Laverne and Shirley. We admired the *characters*,
the waitresses, for their helpfulness and honesty and working-
girl pluck.

Then, in the decade between 1997 and 2007, something
dramatic happened. Fame became the number-one value
emphasized on the most popular adolescent shows. Shows like
Hannah Montana or *American Idol* (and now *iCarly* and many
others in the regular-kid-becomes-a-star genre) are about *everyday people becoming celebrities*, a completely inverted model in
just one decade. When they are just ordinary folks, we don't
care much about, say, *Idol* contestants. Viewers root for them
to become famous because that's when they'll be someone—
that's when they'll *matter*. And because characters like Hannah
Montana or Carly (or, say, the Kardashians or the cast of *Jersey
Shore*) don't achieve fame through working hard or developing skills, fame becomes an end in and of itself—a superficial,
empty end.

"I was shocked," researcher and lead author Yalda T. Uhls
said. "I thought fame would be important but did not expect

this drastic an increase or such a dramatic decrease in other values, such as community feeling." How did this happen—and so quickly? "If you believe that television reflects the culture, as I do, then American culture has changed drastically. The biggest change occurred from 1997 to 2007, when YouTube, Facebook, and Twitter exploded in popularity," she says. "Their growth parallels the rise in narcissism and the drop in empathy among college students in the United States, as other research has shown. We don't think this is a coincidence. Changes we have seen in narcissism and empathy are being reflected on television."[330]

The top five values promoted on the most popular shows preteens watched in 2007 were fame, achievement, popularity, image, and financial success. (In 1997 the top five were community feeling, benevolence, image, tradition, and self-acceptance.) Positive values we cherish are almost entirely absent from kids' shows now. In 2007 benevolence dropped to the twelfth spot and community feeling fell to eleventh.[331] Being kind to others is just so passé, so twentieth century.

For teens and older, reality shows are the most popular genre. There, more negative values are celebrated, mirroring the thug culture we've seen in rap and hip-hop music. Meanness reigns supreme in the reality genre. In fact, averaging in at fifty-two acts of aggression per hour, shows like *The Apprentice* have more hostility between the actors—oops, "reality show stars"—than do popular dramas, soap operas, or comedies, according to a study from Brigham Young University. Researchers found that at least half the meanness is obviously baited by producers, who, for example, put the contestants in a box and prod them to make cruel comments about other contestants, from whom they then provoke angry retorts, and so on, back and forth.[332] (In my experience representing a number of reality show performers, I'd say that more like 90 percent of the reality shows are loosely scripted by producers, who constantly push the performers to the ugly extremes of negative human behavior.) And, thus, shows popular with young people, like

Teen Mom and *Kourtney & Kim Take New York*, featured "caught on camera" incidents of domestic violence in 2011, in which performers angrily punched each other, with no moral or legal consequences following. Expect to see more overt acts of physical aggression as reality programming competes to become more and more outrageous.

Show me a study about children and television watching and I'll show you research that points to only one conclusion: turn it off. Even having the TV on in the background, tuned to adult shows, while young kids play on their own, impedes children's development. Kids played with their toys for shorter periods of time and were significantly less focused when a show as seemingly benign as *Jeopardy* played in the background, even when the children ignored the show. The "ever-changing audiovisual distractor" posed "a chronic environmental risk," according to a National Science Foundation study.[333]

How about inoffensive shows that purport to be educational? *Teletubbies* or *Sesame Street*, for example, teach children new letters and words. Doesn't that build their vocabularies? Nope. Kids under two don't learn words from even well-intentioned shows, despite what parents may hope; they pick up vocabulary from the adults in their homes. "The idea that television can help teach young children their first words is a parent's dream, but one not supported by this research," a Wake Forest University researcher concluded.[334] Many parents park their kids in front of educational videos, but unless you're sitting next to them, teaching alongside the video, they're not getting much out of it.[335]

Kids' minds aren't the only part of them that television viewing harms. Child TV watchers have increased preference for fatty and sugary foods.[336] Of course they do. Fast food companies are major contributors to the $121 million spent on television commercials aimed squarely at our children annually, and they carefully track their ad dollars to be sure they're producing results: kids clamoring for more junk food.[337] Obese kids *double* their food intake after watching boob-tube food commercials.[338] High school kids who watched a lot of TV in their younger days have significantly less healthy eating habits *five years later*.[339] They're not watching commercials for broccoli, folks. (Can you think of a single jingle for a healthy food?) Habits formed during teenage years tend to stick with us throughout young adulthood, and all those McDonald's and Coke commercials leave lasting habits: *Must...buy...French fries.* That Big Mac attack you're experiencing? That's not a naturally occurring phenomenon; it was programmed in during your early years, and for many, deprogramming now requires Herculean will power.

In short, if we were child haters and wanted to come up with one magic device that would make them stupid, mean, narcissistic, fat, and sick, we would have invented the television and twenty-first-century programming and put them in every home, even in kids' bedrooms (and given them lots of time off from school to sit in front of the box). We'd persuade parents that because everyone else does it, it must be okay. And we'd spread around a myth that it doesn't harm children—in fact, it could be educational!—and make parents feel like pariahs or freaks for seeking to cut down or eliminate the magic box.

But now you know the truth.

We've seen how rarely boys read for pleasure or even for school. (Seven minutes a day, and usually with a TV or computer on at the same time.) That's not the only worthy activity that's been cut out of their lives to make way for TV. The hours boys spend attending a concert, dance, or theater performance or going to a museum have plummeted. So has the amount of time they spend outdoors. Those mentally stimulating activities have almost entirely been replaced by TV and, to a lesser extent, playing video games, which I'll examine in a moment.[340]

Watching TV Sports with Your Boy

WATCHING TELEVISION sports deserves a separate mention because so many fathers and sons do this together, considering it bonding time. What about kicking back and taking in the football game with your boy on a Sunday afternoon, nachos on the coffee table, cheering for the home team? Watching sports on television is a beloved American, mostly male pastime. Chicago's Jeff Miller won a recent title for longest nonstop sports watching in one sitting, clocking in at seventy-two hours. He was permitted only five minutes' stretch time hourly, thrice daily bathroom breaks, and no sleeping. Brandishing his "couch potato" trophy awarded to him by ESPN, Jeff gloated, "It's all about determination." "He's driven in everything he does," his girlfriend gushed.[341] (*He has a girlfriend?*)

American men watch an average of three hours a week of televised sports—but many, like Jeff Miller, proudly watch much, much more. Many dads watch sports with their sons, of course, and it's a moment—or many hours—of father-son bonding time, rooting for the local team. The problem isn't sports per se—shows of athletic prowess, combined with strategies, sideshows, and backstories aren't inherently mind rotting in the way, say, phony reality shows or *Jackass* are. One could argue that cheering wildly for some steroidal millionaire who doesn't give a whit about you as he runs around the bases is mildly deranged, but I'm not going there. From the standpoint of your son's brain, NBA playoffs are definitely a better choice than *Flavor of Love*. The issue is *time*. Mainly it's just more TV watching—something men spend more time on to begin with (nearly three hours a day for American men versus two and a half hours a day for American women[342]).

Parents deserve a break, and father-son bonding time is a wonderful thing. If you truly love watching sports together with your son and it's done in moderation, I'm not going to talk you out of it entirely (especially if you're rooting for *college* teams!). There's some math involved in scoring and, say, working out baseball statistics. But consider what you are modeling: that relaxation equals television watching. My brother, Peyton, once a great TV sports watcher, says the main reason they gave up TV entirely is "we wanted to avoid training them to *watch* the world. It's too easy to default into being spectators." All those days of your life spent *observing* are days you're not getting back. You're losing more time, in fact, than the actual hours you're losing sitting on the sofa staring at Sports Center. One new Australian study says that for every hour we spend watching television, we lose an additional twenty-two minutes of our lifespan.[343] Those who watch six or more hours a day (a larger group than you may think) lose *five years* of their lives, largely because all that sitting leads to obesity along with all the gloomy, dire health consequences that flow from obesity: diabetes, heart disease, hypertension, cancer.

We've come to define almost every spare minute of free time as TV time. Americans spend nine times as much time sitting and watching TV and movies than on all physical leisure time activities combined. In 60 percent of our homes, the television set is always or sometimes on during dinner; in 30 percent the TV is on all the time.[344] What conversations could you be having with your son, what books could you be reading with him and to him, what activities could you be engaged in together if you cut your TV time in half?

Playing sports together: terrific. You're out there with the neighborhood kids, practicing teamwork and sportsmanship skills, getting the heart rate up, working up a sweat—bravo. *Watching* sports on TV: sure, your eyeballs on the screen drive enormous ad revenues that enrich, say, Michael Vick (the Philadelphia Eagles quarterback signed a $100 million contract, dog cruelty convictions notwithstanding) and Frank McCourt (the reviled multimillionaire Dodgers baseball owner ran his team into bankruptcy), but what's it doing for *you?* What benefit are *you* getting from the experience? What's your son getting out of it? "Let's not forget the companies that usually advertise on televised sporting events—beer, cars—load up on sexual images or masculine stereotypes," Peyton adds.

As with all else, it's a question of balance. In general, when it comes to the TV sports, default to this: turn it off. Most if not all of it. Select the very best games, withdraw from the rest. Or go cold turkey. Your choice. The world awaits you and your son, and you won't find it watching curling or March Madness.

Video Games: Watch the "Dose"

WHAT ABOUT video games, the bane of every modern mom's existence? But also, in some ways, our salvation, because at least our boy is at home in the next room, safe, blowing off a little steam, engaged in a fun activity that's more interactive than TV, right? He has to figure out clues and negotiate around the virtual world—and, well, he just *loves* it so much.

The Xbox, the Wii, Nintendo, smartphone apps—collectively, "gaming." They occupy a special category. Is there a boy in America who's not a gamer? Or who wouldn't play more if his parents let him? Or who isn't playing more than Mom thinks he is? Gaming has taken over male free time, dominating it. Gamers over two years of age (!) spend an average of thirteen hours per week playing computer games. "Extreme gamers"—one in twenty-five players—play forty-eight hours per week.[345]

As with watching sports, this is an activity that skews male. For teens, for example, video game play averages eight hours a week for girls but fourteen hours per week for boys.[346] (That's based on self-reports, which I believe are low. If a pollster asked me, I'd underreport my personal online Scrabble addiction.)

For gamers' brains it's not all bad news, some say, so long as the games are chosen carefully and are played in moderation. Author Steven Johnson says that modern media is making us smarter, and gaming for kids has its brain benefits: "In some ways, what they're doing now with the Thomas trains is what they'll be doing in a few years with their video games: mastering a complex system, learning all the different characters, building an environment, and exploring it together."[347]

Unlike, say, TV watchers, who become inactive and zone out, gamers *are* thinking, making decisions—sometimes quickly, under pressure—expressing themselves, even creating art and music (*Rock Band*) or exercising a bit (*Wii Fit*). So gaming has its upside. Interactivity is better than passivity.

The problem is the "dose." Boys want to play endlessly, and as a busy parent will attest if they're being honest, you look away for just a minute to throw in a load of laundry and answer a few e-mails, and you look back to discover to your horror that your son has been playing sunup to sundown, without having brushed his teeth. As they do, their attention spans also grow shorter and weaker. Gamers also show increased aggressiveness, as many popular games are gory and violent.[348]

I asked a group of twelve-year-old boys how much time they spent playing video games. They immediately worked backward. "I get home from school at four o'clock," one eagerly jumped in, treating this as an easy math problem. "I go to bed at nine. Less than an hour for homework and ten minutes for dinner. So, four hours!" he said, triumphant at having arrived so swiftly at the answer. The other boys agreed, with minor modifications of their arrive-home and go-to-bed times. The formula was the same: *I play every waking minute that an adult isn't making me do something else.* What about on weekends? "About ten hours a day," they all estimated. And they are underestimating, as I happen to know that they all play on their phones on the school bus, at recess and lunch, in the car, and even during class, though they know they aren't supposed to admit that to a nosy adult like me.

Many gamers know they have a problem. Fifteen percent of

kids feel they play too many video games; over half said they sometimes try to stop, unsuccessfully.[349] The problem is the obsession, as nearly any parent of a boy who can't stop for dinner, or a visit with Grandma, or to read a book will tell you. The tears, the drama when the handheld gets taken away: consider them a cry for help from a young addict.

And we can't say the boys self-select, so that perhaps those who choose computer games would have attention problems anyway. Boys randomly selected to play video games over a four-month period did less homework and had lower reading and writing scores than the control group.[350] Because the games are too addictive, too distracting.

As with TV, turn them down to a very limited dose or eliminate them entirely.

––––––––

FOR MANY of us reducing television and video game time is conceivable, but going cold turkey and getting rid of the screens altogether is not. What is life like inside a family with two rambunctious boys and no TV or video games?

Let's return to the Cothran-Bray family. Comfortable couches and a reading chair encircle the living room, with reading lights ready to accommodate readers of all ages. Books lay open-spined on the sofa's arms. A complex, recently completed jigsaw puzzle sits proudly on a low table. Everyone plays with Cera, the black Lab with prematurely grey whiskers, as they answer my questions.

"If you take out the screens, there's a big chunk of time, so what are they going to do?" asks Daddy Peyton. "For one thing, they have to learn to read as early and as fast as possible. My boys love board games. But you can't play a board game if you can't read the instructions. That motivated them when they were two and three. If they became bored with their game, there were always building materials like Legos or K'nex." I can assure you that every time my nephews visited me, I'd awake in the morning to a complex web of Hot Wheels tracks, wooden block towers teetering to the ceiling, strips of colorfully decorated paper draping from ceiling to floor and back again, and other architectural masterpieces. (If you lose the TV, be prepared to accept a bit more chaos in your home. Grin and bear it during the creative years.) "And when they got bored with that, they discovered *Calvin and Hobbes* or dumb joke books."

Children will play spontaneously with what's available, as they always have. On a recent trip to Nepal, one of the world's poorest countries, I saw children everywhere playing outside with bits of twigs, pebbles, or lining up for turns on crudely made enormous swings. From the standpoint of their mental and physical functioning, those impoverished third-world children are engaging in healthier activities—playing with peers, getting some exercise and fresh air, socially interacting, devising creative play with what odds and ends they can find—than American kids, who are plopped in front of a television five hours a day.

And Peyton underplays his sons' astonishing reading ability and range with his comment about cartoon books. Sure, comics and graphic novels do grab Cosmo and Tennessee's attention, but Cosmo talks excitedly about serious books he's read recently, pulling them off the shelf and handing them to me.

"Have you read *The Book Thief?*" he asks. "It's narrated by the spirit of death." His eyes widen, waiting for me to absorb how cool that is. "About a girl in Hitler's Germany who steals books..." and off he goes for five or ten minutes, giving me every plot point, awed. "Or *Bounce?* There are these tribesmen in Kenya, they are amazing runners, but other tribes, just ten miles away aren't, and this book explains why that is..." Cosmo outlines for me why talent is less important than previously believed and how, according to the book he's holding, opportunity and hard work are most of the story. He moves on. "Have you read *Brain Rules?*" His typical torrent of words rapidly follows. "It explains why all these things happen, like the stereotype that boys can't accomplish anything. Though at my school it's true. Seventy percent of the boys in my grade don't even *try*, they're goofing off all the time." He mulls over this disturbing fact, which seems to have dawned on him just as he said it. Returning to the book, he opens it to the table of contents. Excitedly giving me a concise summary of each chapter: "Oh! This one was *really* interesting," he says of the chapter on neurons and brain wiring. He moves his finger down to chapter eleven and stops. "*This* was the best chapter," he says, "about gender differences in our brains. Have you read this?"

C'mon, kid, who do you think you're talking to?

Actually, I hadn't. But I read it that night.

Currently Cosmo's favorites are long, multibook fantasy series like *The Inheritance Cycle*, a wildly popular four-book set (the author, Christopher Paolini, wrote the first draft when he was just fifteen). Urgently, Cosmo reminds his mother of a book he *needs*. "For school?" I ask. "No, I just *need* to read it."

Do his friends read as much as he does? "Actually, I have a friend who reads more. He reads two thousand to three thousand pages a month!" I didn't fact-check as to whether that claim was true or not. What is striking is that these boys one-up each other by comparing pages read monthly—a parent's and teacher's dream.

Audio books have been a key part of all this wordiness and story loving. When they were younger, Ellen recorded herself reading her sons' favorite books, and they'd listen to the stories on headsets in the car or play them over and over while they built castles out of blocks. Today, as adolescents, they still enjoy audio books checked out from the library or exchanged with friends. The boys nearly always have one on while they are doing other projects. Ellen credits listening to books with most of Tennessee's extraordinary vocabulary—at ten, he'll drop "photosynthesis," "realistic fiction," "subservient," "mystical," and "revere" within a few minutes of chattering. Of her younger son, Ellen says, "He's always been my more kinetic boy. He needs to be moving, climbing, twisting. Sitting still with a book has always been a challenge for him." Today Tenny is a gymnast who shows off a dozen quick front- and backflips on the backyard trampoline. "So he'd put on an audio book and listen to it while he was running around. Eventually he'd get tired and then pick up the book itself to finish the story faster."

Not having a television set has another hidden benefit Ellen mentions: her kids aren't bombarded by commercials so "they don't want the stuff!" Ellen reports giddily. Her boys haven't been dragged into the consumer culture. "They don't even know a lot of the junk that's out there," she says. "So we don't have to deal with the begging for stuff we don't want to buy. It's such a treat." Peyton mirrored that. "The real concern for us was the advertising more than the shows themselves."

Peyton and Ellen recognize that their no-TV decision might make their boys social oddballs, so they do allow them to watch a limited number of pre-approved episodes now and then, on Netflix, where there are no commercials. The family watches together and then discusses the shows. They refuse to let the programming isolate their children, and they don't let themselves use it as the crutch most of the rest of us parents do.

How do Cosmo and Tenny feel about their lives? Do they feel they are missing out on something that most of their friends are connected with? Are they outcasts, social misfits? Hardly. They *brag* about their lack of screen time. "We don't have TV, we *read* or *talk to each other*," they say in that adolescent *duh* tone that instantly conveys their belief that their lives are better than yours.

What about computers? What are the rules there? The boys do not own their own computers. They use school PCs, and at home they use the family laptop on a limited basis. There's a computer available in the living room for anyone who wants to use it—and the large screen faces out so that anyone can see what anyone else is looking at any time. "We walk into the boys' bedroom when they're on the laptop, unannounced," Ellen said. "That could happen at any time, and they know that. So far we've never had a problem with them being on an inappropriate site."

But they rarely go off alone to their room with the laptop anyway, Ellen says, highlighting another significant social difference between the Cothran-Brays and the typical family. Many adolescent boys come home, go directly to their room, close the door, and sit in front of a flickering television set and computer screen hour after hour, pried out of their rooms only for necessary events like eating, using the bathroom, or glowering at mom. Cosmo and Tenny "want to be out and about," says Ellen. "The worst possible thing is for them to be sent to their room. They want to be in the living room, where the family action is. They hate to be isolated." It's been this way since birth for Cosmo and Tenny: the fun is where the family is, not where screens beckon.

As I'm leaving, another recently enjoyed book comes to Cosmo's mind. "Oh! *The Old Man and the Sea! So good.* Have you read it?" (I didn't mention that I didn't read Hemingway until high school—and never voluntarily.)

"Oh! Auntie Lisa! Also have you read—"

"Cosmo," I said, "I'm sorry, but I have to go now. How about if you e-mail me a list of your favorite books so that I can recommend them to other boys?"

Again, he was incredulous. "That would take *forever!*" he insisted, annoyed with my insane requests.

He thought another moment, then concluded soberly, "It would be an impossible job."

RULE 5:

BECOME AWARE OF THE DATA PINGING IN AND OUT OF YOUR BOY'S BRAIN

NOW THAT I've advised you to eliminate the competition, I'm also going to get realistic. Our twenty-first-century children spend more time sitting in front of electronic screens than in any other activity besides sleeping. (And some spend *more* time in front of screens than in dreamland.) You should decrease that screen time as much as you can, but you probably can't eliminate all of it. We all know that they'll be shooting aliens on their friend's iTouch on the school bus, watching TV shows on their cell phones, using the school library computer to check in online. Thug culture will stream into their ears. Few are going to go to the Cothran-Bray extreme, and even there, media seeps in.

Parents, know your enemy.

Because no matter how much you try to turn down the volume, it is there. Facebook, Xbox, action films, *World of Warcraft*, hip-hop, text messages, *The Wizards of Waverly Place*, *The Avengers*, ringtones— media bombards your boy from virtually the moment he wakes up in the morning until he closes his eyes at night. Reading books and learning writing skills are critically important for your boys' future, so turning down or turning out television and video games is important. But let's face facts: your kids are going to watch or listen to or play at least some reality shows, feature films, podcasts, radio, YouTube videos, computer games, websites, and apps, either at your home, a friend's house, on his computer or game console, on his tablet, phone, iPod, the sole of his shoe—well, just about. He'll be on Nick.com, Yahoo! Kids, Gchat, Hulu, and other websites you've never heard of. He'll be getting text messaged commercials from Lord knows who. On Facebook and Gmail he'll be getting advertising specially targeted to him, based on the content of his messages and e-mails to his friends.

George Orwell's *1984* has arrived, just a few decades behind schedule. Only it's not big government that's watching us; it's corporate America.

Somehow the world has turned into a place in which young people take in about ten times more media than we did, and we know less and less about it, as the whole media train seems to pull out ahead of us, steaming away, while we're back at the station, bewildered. Our families are increasingly fragmented, and I'm not talking here about single parents. How old school the day seems when Mom, Dad, and the kids used to watch TV or listen to music together. Now everyone has their own devices and headphones, and they watch entire networks built around their age group or interests—alone.

Woe to the parent who doesn't know what messages the kid is absorbing.

The key fact about new media is this: your boy's screen time is not "virtual reality" to him. It is a vital part of his everyday experience, as real as his breakfast cereal and your goodnight kiss. If you ignore it, you are closing your eyes to a major—perhaps *the* major—part of his life.

We've seen how two-thirds of popular rap and hip-hop music teaches your son exactly the opposite of the values you're trying to instill: arrogance, gun love, glorification of rape and murder. At a minimum, if your son is listening to these toxic messages, you need to know.

Kids spend hours and hours on their computers, pretending to do homework while they get sucked into the black hole of Facebook or other social media sites, without their parents having any idea of the messages they are sending and receiving—with sometimes tragic outcomes that reflect thug culture.

To give two particularly sobering examples, in September 2010 eighteen-year-old Rutgers college freshman Tyler Clementi jumped off the George Washington Bridge to his death after a schoolmate posted a surreptitiously recorded video of Tyler with a gay partner on Twitter. The tweet: "I saw him making out with a dude. Yay."

A little over a year later, in December 2011, fifteen-year-old Amanda Cummings threw herself in front of a bus after schoolmates tormented her online. Even after she died, the Facebook bullying of the New York City girl continued. Riffing on her last name, one young man wrote on Amanda's *memorial page*: "Bus was cummin', Bitch was watchin', Oh hurry Amanda, Your bus cummin'." Another added, "I guess she didn't saw it cummin' YEEAAAAH."

Where were the parents of these kids?

I spoke with Amanda's grieving mother on the television show, *Dr. Drew*. This online cruelty before and after her daughter's death deeply affected her: was there anything that could be done to these heartless tormentors? "There ought to be a law," she said. But because of our strong First Amendment protecting free speech, kids and adults in the United States have the legal right to be mean, even to be this callous to the mother of a recently deceased child, I had to tell her. The US Supreme Court recently upheld the rights of lunatic fringe protestors to carry "God Hates Fags" signs at military funerals—one of the more outrageous and disgusting free speech cases ever to come before the high court. "Speech is powerful," Chief Justice John G. Roberts, Jr. wrote for the majority. "It can stir people to action, move them to tears of both joy and sorrow, and—as it did here—inflict great pain." But under the First Amendment, he said, "we cannot react to that pain by punishing the speaker."

Teen suicides are extreme—but all too common—examples of what happens when young people, steeped in thug culture and devoid of parental supervision, mess around online and quickly turn cruel. Bullied kids used to be able to leave school and at least take refuge at home. Today the torment continues around the clock, online.

There is only one solution, the same solution there's always been: parents. The government does not have the right to monitor your kids' private online postings—but you do. Generally, prosecutors can't punish your son for Facebook bullying. But you can. Schools won't check websites to see whether your kid is bullying or being victimized or whether he's posting drunken pictures of himself, blogging about subjects that are contrary to your family's values, dropping the F bomb, or calling girls "sluts" or "whores"—the most common online attacks on girls. But you must. You have the right *and the responsibility* to walk in without prior notice and see what your son is doing online. You should insist upon your son's username and password for every site he visits, especially Facebook, Twitter, and similar chat and social media sites. You have the right and the responsibility to review his browsing history. You have the power and the obligation to use parental controls and filters, such as Net Nanny, Cyber Patrol, OnlineFamily.net, or Safe Eyes.

If your son refuses to give you his usernames and passwords, if he refuses to let you view his Internet-browsing history, you have the right to take away his computer or other devices. A condition of his access to the Internet must always be your ability to watch him there. You would not allow him, as a minor child, to roam the globe on his own. Nor should he be allowed to roam unaccompanied on the World Wide Web until he is an adult.

Many parents feel this would inhibit their child or violate his privacy. But I have covered too many cases of kids who were harassed or verbally attacked or who were victims of online predators to agree with that position. Besides, when you tell your child in advance that you will be monitoring his web use, he's on notice that, so long as he is a minor, he simply will not have online privacy. If he doesn't agree, you have the option of going dark: removing Internet access from his life entirely until he's ready to agree.

Most parents are shocked—*shocked!*—to learn that their kid is an online bully. Or they can't believe that their kid is sending around provocative photos—until it's too late. They had no idea that their child was fragile and posting messages about suicidal intent. Most of the time the evidence was all there, if only a parent had taken the time to look. I can guarantee you that after the next teen tragedy that began online, commentators will wring their hands and say, "Where were the parents?"

Don't let us be talking about you.

Amanda Cumming's grief-stricken mother told me that she didn't know much about computers, so she never monitored her daughter's Facebook page. Her message to parents: *don't make the mistake I did.* If you're not computer savvy, take a class, ask your kid to teach you, or take the computer away. Closing your eyes to your kids' online world is no longer an option. Whether we like it or not, whether we thought we signed up for this particular job or not, careful monitoring of your kids' online life is now required of you.

The same goes for television, movies, and other media he's watching and listening to. Watch shows with him. Listen to his music. We've already seen some of it. If you can't understand the words, Google the song title for the lyrics. Make sure you're sitting down before you start reading them. If you don't understand the slang, crack the code by asking kids about it and doing further online research on sites like UrbanDictionary.com.

Knowledge is power. Know what you're up against.

You must open your eyes and ears to his media consumption to fully understand the constant media feed into his brain so that you can speak up and critically analyze it with him.

Because that's the next step.

RULE 6:

TEACH YOUR BOY TO BE EVER-CRITICAL OF ALL MEDIA

HUMBLE ATTITUDE—CHECK.

College expectations—check.

A focus on reading—check.

TV and video games minimized—check.

Parental awareness of kids' media intake—check.

Next up, you need to instill in your boy a very healthy skepticism toward the media in general. Therefore, you must teach him *how to understand* all this media that's infiltrating his brain. For parents today this is a challenge because most of us didn't grow up with this kind of media onslaught. We can't just pass along our parents' wisdom on the subject because our moms and dads didn't have to do much more than tell us not to sit so close to the TV when we watched the *Cosby Show*. (How quaint their concerns now seem: "It will strain your eyes!" They were right about that, by the way.) You must assume a role your parents didn't have to shoulder: media critic and media literacy instructor.

You can do this.

How do you monitor and talk about media with your son? Give him the facts, show him your own healthy cynicism about what's being offered to you, and discuss, discuss, discuss.

You don't have to re-invent the wheel. The art and science of picking apart popular media is a growing specialty, sometimes taught in high schools and colleges, called media literacy. The Center for Media Literacy has boiled it all down to five key questions, which should be in the back of your mind any time images or sounds are flickering in you and your son's general direction:

1. Who created this message?
2. What techniques are used to attract my attention?
3. How might different people understand this message differently from me?
4. What lifestyles, values, and points of view are represented in or omitted from this message?
5. Why was this message sent?[351]

Let's start with the first and last questions. Who creates the messages pinging their way into your child's brain—and why? The most important item here to understand and teach your child is that unlike his "real" world of home and school, run by caring, trustworthy adults who want the best for him, the media world is controlled by a handful of giant corporations whose only goal is to create profits. Viacom/CBS, Disney, Time Warner, News Corp, and NBC/GE control the big four networks, 80 percent of the primetime television market share, most cable channels, as well as vast holdings in radio, publishing, movie studios, music, Internet, and other sectors.[352] By definition, publicly traded corporations exist to generate revenue for their shareholders. This means that those who run them are legally obligated to work only toward that end. (This is why corporations aren't "people," no matter what the Supreme Court says. People care about things other than money. People have souls.) Even when corporations purport to act in the public interest or, say, donate to charity, that's done to generate "good will" for their companies—that is, to make consumers like them more, improve their reputation, and, thereby, generate more profits.

Media companies harbor no illusions about their objectives. They are straightforward about the fact that they exist solely as money-making machines. Former Disney CEO Michael Eisner once said, "We have no obligation to make history. We have no obligation to make art. We have no obligation to make a statement. To make money is our only objective." "We are here to serve advertisers," the head of CBS once said, "That is our raison d'être."[353]

Explain that to your child, then watch the television show, DVD, website, or computer game together and ask yourselves, *How does this generate money for corporations? What are they trying to sell you? How are they trying to make you feel good about their brands?*

After about age ten, most kids understand that commercials are trying to sell them stuff, but they're less aware of all that sneaky product placement going on during their shows or flashing around on websites. Maybe you're unaware of it too, as it's so ubiquitous. Any time you see a label or hear a brand mentioned, that's not an accident: it's negotiated, bought, and paid for. When a radio DJ mentions a brand, that's a commercial, folks. It's on a celebrity's ball cap? Paid for.

Product placement is now a $25 billion industry, growing annually.[354] Many shows, especially on cable, are hour-long commercials for one company after another, lovingly mentioned by the hosts and contestants. "Our friends at Ford...," begins Ryan Seacrest frequently on *American Idol*. They're not friends. Friends don't have to pay you to say nice things about them. It's a sales job, like those Coke cups the judges drink from, labels always facing forward. Don't fall for it. In our home we shout out "product placement!" anytime we notice one on TV. Some shows generate a lot of yelling.

In your boy's favorite films, product placement has mushroomed to dizzying new levels. Apple products appeared in 30 percent of the thirty-three top films in 2010; Nike, Chevy, and Ford in 24 percent, and Sony, Dell, Land Rover, and Glock (yes, the gun) in 15 percent. In fact, the latest *James Bond* movie will cover one-third of its budget with $45 million in product placement revenue. The *Bond* and *Mission Impossible* franchises consist mainly of product advertising strung together with bits of plot.[355]

This embedded advertising is enormously profitable. The popular-with-kids show *The Apprentice* helped Staples generate a half-million dollars in sales in just two hours. Pontiac sold one thousand Scion cars in forty-one minutes after its appearance on the same show.[356]

You can mention to your son, by the way, that books are the last form of popular media without product placements, which, perhaps, is why the publishing industry is struggling and shrinking.

The second and third media literacy questions—"What techniques are used to attract my attention?" and "How might different people understand this message differently from me?"—are worth regular discussions in your home. All the swooshing, flashing lights, bright colors, and promises of exciting developments "after the break" are designed to keep him watching through the commercials; they are all gimmicks. Start taking note of them. And although *your* boy might not take thug culture messages to heart—or so he claims—consider with him whether some of the vile lyrics we've seen might impact others. Does he see kids swaggering at school, mimicking the clothing, the language (like "gangster" and "thug"), the hypermasculinized behavior of rappers? *Where does he think that comes from? How did the creators of the messages get the audience to endorse them?*

These questions are all great springboards for discussion of your boy's games and shows. Question number four is one of the most important: What values are included and which are omitted from your show/song/website/movie/game? Ask your son what characteristics he'd like to be known for. Honesty? Integrity? Kindness? Intelligence? What qualities does he look for in a friend? Loyalty? Sense of humor? Fair-mindedness?

Then, what values does he see reflected in his favorite music, games, and shows? Often, as we've seen, graphic violence, and cruelty predominate. Two-thirds of seventh- and eighth-grade boys play M-rated violent games like *Grand Theft Auto*, which are supposed to be sold only to "mature" adults.[357] *Grand Theft Auto* is a nonstop blood-and-gore fest, featuring intense violence, strong language, strong sexual content, and drug use. Players can have sex with a hooker and then run her over or shoot her—player's choice![358] Repulsive. These games are everywhere. Only 6 percent of middle schoolers had not played a video game in the prior six months.[359]

Ask your son why the values he surely considers to be important are not reflected in these games or shows. Why are they missing? Is compassion out of style? Is integrity now uncool? Talk to your boy about the real-world consequences of drug use and violence: incarceration, families devastated, injuries, even death. If real life was like his video game, what would happen?

Talk to him about the incarceration and deaths that have befallen popular rappers. They may swagger and talk tough, but many died young. Why are they exalting this lifestyle? If he were a musician, would he?

Popular boys' films have never met a problem that couldn't be solved with assaults and carnage. Is that consistent with your family's values? With yours? What nonviolent methods could have been used to solve the characters' problems?

The more you can foster discussions like these, the more your boy will learn to question what he's being sold. Not only will you help him develop critical thinking skills, but you'll also be reinforcing your own values in the process. Even if he disagrees with your perspective, your words will bounce around in his head long after the conversation is done.

Yes, rich and powerful corporations control our media, but you are still the boss in your house. You are your resident, in-house media authority and critic. And ultimately, you have the power to do the one thing programming aimed at your son never does: respect and engage his mind.

RULE 7:

SUPPORT HIS TEACHER

ONCE YOU'VE made your home an environment that supports reading, thinking, and intellectual curiosity (with a healthy dose of cynicism toward all that media spilling in), it's time to look beyond your home, at the place your boy spends half his day: school. Given the many shortcomings of our failing schools, how best can we shore up his education?

By working with his teachers, not against them. Unwittingly, many parents undermine their children's teachers. This must stop.

"American Teacher of the Year" Ron Clark wrote a CNN.com piece recently that resonated so strongly with teachers and parents that it was the number-two most-shared article of the year on Facebook in 2011, second only to news images of the devastating Japan earthquake.[360] "What Teachers Really Want to Tell Parents" boiled down to this plea: *support us*. Trust us. Don't work against us behind our backs. And don't make excuses for your son unless you want him to grow up jobless and living on your couch at age twenty-five.

I second the motion.

California Charter Teacher of the Year Brad Koepenick, who we saw earlier in this book, has the same message. "What's the hardest part about teaching?" I asked him. "Parents," he said, without missing a beat. I'd just spoken to a few of his students, teenage boys being raised by single moms working two or three jobs. These boys missed their mothers and wished they were around more. Their fathers were largely absent altogether. I thought of them. "Absentee parents, you mean?" I asked. "Oh, no, absentee parents I can deal with," Brad said. "It's the helicopter parents I can't stand. They do nothing but undermine us."

Parents always hovering about, ready to swoop in and rescue their boy at a moment's notice—helicopter parents—are a teacher's worst nightmare: moms who challenge the teacher when the kid gets reprimanded for acting up or dads who march in to demand their child's grade be raised because he's so misunderstood.

Teachers are professionals who spend a lot of time with your boy. They see him in an entirely different environment than you do, which explains why sometimes parents are baffled by a school report that their son is overly sociable in class (*but at home he's so reclusive*) or, alternatively, that he's a holy terror (*at home he mostly sleeps!*—sure, gearing up for the next day's onslaught). In his classroom a wide variety of other kids surround him. He's challenged with various subjects, asked to perform new tasks, expected to learn skills. School stimulates, challenges, annoys, and excites your boy in ways unmatched by your home environment, which is, let's face it, mainly same ol', same ol'. So of course he behaves differently there.

Thus, when your son's teacher tells you he acted up in class, or he smacked Raj or Kevin, or he didn't turn in his homework for a week, or he's mouthing off, *believe it.* As teacher Ron Clark pleads, do not turn to your son and say, "Is this true?" It is true. The teacher just said so. He's not in the business of making up stories about seven-year-olds. What motive would he have to do that? Do not undermine your teacher's authority in the presence of your boy. His respecting the teacher's authority is critical to the teacher's ability to maintain control over your boy and the entire classroom. Teacher and parent should be what we call in the law "allied in interest"—on the same side, working for your boy's healthy development.

Sometimes that can include punishment. If he gets sent to detention, the worst thing a parent can do is storm into the school to demand a reversal of the sentence. You are not a defense attorney (if you are, let your spouse handle the situation). You are a parent, and that means accepting that your son will learn best when he suffers the consequences of his actions. Remove those consequences, and you've deprived him of the lesson.

When a teacher tells you there's a problem with your son, she is sticking her neck out and doing you a favor. She knows parents don't like to hear complaints. She knows she may get push-back. How much easier would it be for her just to give everyone an "A" and turn a blind eye to the slackers and miscreants? Then she'd be popular and well liked. The truly caring teacher takes the rockier path of calling out kids when they deserve it and notifying parents promptly when their kids need correcting. Thank her for providing this service to you. Kids are works in progress; she is helping you see where work remains to be done.

Some children become pint-sized psychologists, offering excuses and justifications for their own bad behavior. *The teacher is mean! I wasn't feeling well! You made me visit Grandma so I didn't have time to do my homework! I can't work in that environment!* They're always the victim—don't fall for it. And don't egg them on by offering up those excuses to the teacher. Instead, help your son succeed by teaching him strategies to behave well and do his work *even if*. *Even if* you aren't 100 percent thrilled with your teacher (which is probably because she is intolerant of his misdeeds), you need to take a deep breath, show respect, and do the assignments. *Even if* you are feeling lousy, you may not use four-letter words at school (hey, where'd he learn those?). *Even if* we have family time, you still need to do your homework. Next time don't wait until the last minute to complete it, and let's communicate better about weekend time so we can both accomplish everything we need to get done, okay?

School is his priority, and his teacher is the expert on how he's doing there. She's the one with the advanced education degree and many hours of continuing education and classroom experience, and she's the adult who personally observes him in the schoolroom all day long. Defer to her judgment.

If you have a genuine issue with your son's teacher, do not discuss a word of it with your son. Your relationship with your kids' teacher should be roughly comparable to that of divorced parents. Though you don't live together, you need to communicate often and amicably, consider yourselves on the same team working together for your kids' success, smoothly hand off your kid one to the other, and never, ever bad-mouth one another in front of your kid. Instead, when a concern arises with your child's teacher, make an appointment to show respect for her time and schedule, go in *without* your child, and discuss it privately as adults. Begin and end the discussion with your appreciation for the time and effort she puts in every day on behalf of your child. (Remember the average of $450 each teacher pays out of her own pocket annually for the benefit of your child's classroom, out of the goodness of her heart. Are you shelling out $450 a year for *her* kids?) If the issue is serious and you get no satisfaction after talking with the teacher, make an appointment and discuss it calmly and privately with the principal. To the greatest extent possible, leave your kid out of it.

Supporting your son's teacher is especially important if he is lucky enough to have a great one. According to a remarkable new Harvard University study that tracked one million children from fourth grade to adulthood, a strong teacher (defined as one better than 84 percent of peers) not only teaches your son a great deal more in the short term, boosting his test scores in the areas taught, but the teacher gives your son some impressive long-lasting benefits. Students from classrooms with great teachers are more likely to attend college, earn higher salaries, live in better neighborhoods, and save more for retirement. They are even less likely to have children as teenagers.[361] One skilled fourth-grade teacher can make that much of a difference in your son's life.

Most of us can tell immediately when our kid is blessed with a teacher like this. He is energetic, creative, fun, yet in control of his classroom at all times. Kids lucky enough to have great teachers come home chattering about school, eager to show off their classwork. They spout off historical facts in carpool and announce they're going to learn some Mandarin over winter break just for fun. When you tell your kid he's going to have to miss a day of school for a family trip, he bursts into tears. And he's right: Mom, Dad, do not let your kid skip a single precious day in this teacher's classroom.

But what if—more likely—your kid lands in an average teacher's classroom or, worse, he suffers from a truly dreadful, bottom-of-the-barrel teacher? If you recognize a serious problem early enough in the school year, ask the principal to move your son to another class. Given how important a teacher is to your son's education, his attitude about school, and his ability to learn and succeed, this is worth doing. If that's not possible and he's stuck in that classroom, give that teacher *even more* support. Mobilize other parents to have a parent volunteer in that classroom as often as possible. The teacher should appreciate the assistance, and he or she will perform better when watched. After school, supplement your child's learning with enrichment programs and tutoring. High school kids can be hired inexpensively to help him with his science homework a few times a week. Your little one will look up to a smart teenager and want to please. In my experience one-on-one focused time in your child's problem areas are a quick boost to his test scores and, more importantly, to his ability to grasp the subject area. Sign your son up for your local library's after-school reading program or museum kids' club, or award him points for extra books read at home weekly, with small prizes he can "buy" with his points.

In short, value every day of your son's education. As we've seen, our kids get far too little to begin with. Cherish days he gets with quality teachers, and supplement days he's enduring with subpar ones. Pack each day with as many tantalizing educational moments as you can while his brain is still developing.

What else does your son's teacher want from you? On one teacher questionnaire, the number-one answer by far was "make sure that kids come to school having had a good nights' sleep." Too many kids stay up late, coming to school the next day sleep deprived and, thus, more excitable, less able to concentrate, and with poor impulse control.[362] I often do speaking events at schools, and I see this every time. As I walked onstage to address a hundred high school kids in San Francisco recently, two of them were slumped asleep in their chairs already—before I'd said a word! I considered teasing them, asking the kids next to them to wake them up. But I remembered how sensitive teenagers can be, and who knows what was going on at home, causing them to be so exhausted at 10 a.m. So I let them be. I imagine teachers everywhere make the same calculation daily when drowsy kids sit before them. Parents, it's your job to make sure they're rested and ready for school each day. They can't learn if they're only semiconscious.

As their classes are jammed with more kids, their facilities crumble, and school days are cut, our teachers are on the front lines, struggling daily with low wages for only one reason: because they care about educating kids. No parent enjoys hearing criticism of her children. But we must listen to our teachers' advice, praise, guidance, and, yes, suggestions for improvement. Leave the helicoptering for the landing strip. Partner with teachers, respect them, and work together as a team for the best interests of your kid. Because in this climate of diminished educational expectations, your son needs all the help he can get.

RULE 8:

TEACH HIM TO RESPECT GIRLS AND WOMEN

THE ODDS of your son tapping you on the shoulder one day and saying, "Hey, Dad, today's the day I'd like you to teach me how to treat girls with respect!" are roughly the same as him developing a passion for Charlotte Bronte novels. But that doesn't mean he doesn't need your guidance in this important area. For some very practical reasons, he does: because thug culture is teaching him exactly the opposite of the attitude toward the other half of the population he needs to survive.

Respecting the female half of the population is no longer simply the matter of human decency it's always been. Yes, being kind to all of God's creatures is a laudable goal, but when it comes to his relations with girls and women, there's a new urgency in teaching our boys how to behave properly. The penalties for crossing the line have become much harsher in the last generation, dipping younger and younger into our population. For your boy, learning to respect females is a critically important life skill that will benefit not only the girls and women he interacts with but also *him*. Immediately.

Oh, he's only a little boy, you say. That's old-school thinking.

Given our new laws and school rules about sexual harassment, it's never too early to start. Boys as young as six have been disciplined for sexual harassment for, say, touching the inside of a fellow first grader's waistband or swatting a little girl on the behind.[363] A nine-year-old was suspended for calling his female teacher either "cute" or "fine"—there's some dispute about which it was.[364] Yes, these cases are ridiculous, but they underscore the severity of many schools' zero-tolerance policies and how boys untaught in the new set of rules can be harshly penalized.

The new campus and workplace policy of zero tolerance for sexism and sexual harassment have caught older boys unaware as well. Frat houses, for example, were until recently the bastion of *Animal House* antics, considered puerile by women, sure, but their boorish behavior was generally just shrugged off as a bunch of dumb, drunk guys blowing off steam. Those days are over. College men are expected to treat women as equals at all times, and when they don't, severe consequences follow. "Any behavior that demeans women is not tolerated by the fraternity," said the Sigma Phi Epsilon fraternity flatly in December 2011, shutting down its University of Vermont chapter after frat members circulated a survey asking, "If you could, who would you like to rape?"[365] Earlier that fall Yale University announced a five-year suspension of the Delta Kappa Epsilon fraternity for its "pro-rape chant," in which pledges yelled, "No means yes, yes means anal!" and "f*king sluts" outside girls' dorm windows. How'd that suspension come about? From vocal, activist, determined women on and off campus: an alumni who garnered five thousand online signatures on Change.org; Yale's feminist magazine, *Broad Recognition*, editorializing and demanding action; and female bloggers, television pundits (like me), and activists nationwide demanding action.[366] The boys' defense in each case? *It was a just a joke! We were just being stupid! We didn't mean it!* That defense didn't help them, and in fact, it no longer is a viable defense for this type of offensive language. It's a new era for women on campus, as zero-tolerance policies are more vigorously enforced than ever before.

We've already seen the shift in power in schools and colleges: girls are outperforming boys, dominating the honor roll, and, often, student government. This new generation of smart, empowered girls does not tolerate offensive words or conduct, and they know how to reach out to prominent women to back them up. You don't want your son to get caught in the crosshairs of women like us.

In the workplace too, consequences for mistreatment of women are often swift and dire. Decades of developments in sexual harassment law and those ever-present sexual harassment training seminars most major companies give mean that women in the workplace no longer tolerate the crude remark, the casual workplace come-on, or the boys-will-be-boys attitude. Your son's female counterparts in school and in his future workplace will be smarter, more confident, more knowledgeable of their rights, and more likely to speak out than ever before. Obnoxious words *will* be reported. Sexist conduct *will* be investigated. And when the company's in doubt, he could easily be fired. No company worth its salt wants the liability of keeping on its payroll a man who already has one strike against him, because if a second woman raises a claim, the company could be liable for punitive damages. So in many cases, especially for young men in entry-level positions, one claim of sexual harassment is enough to get him terminated. In our jobless economy that's not a chance he can take.

Sexual harassment issues aside, your son needs good interpersonal skills in working with women generally. Now that women in their twenties are outperforming and outearning their male counterparts in major cities across the United States, your son is highly likely not only to work alongside women, *but to be supervised and managed by them.* Women now hold 50 percent of managerial positions, and they outnumber men as financial managers, human resource managers, educational administrators, medical and health services managers, accountants and auditors, budget analysts, and property, real estate, and social community service managers, according to the US Department of Labor.[367]

We've seen how thug culture glorifies demeaning and even assaulting women and girls. With those negative messages constantly streaming into his world, what can you do to counteract them to give him a healthy foundation for learning and working with and under females?

Step one: Mom and Dad—or whoever is in your home—must both become active, daily role models for not just teaching respect but also living it. Child psychologist Bruno Bettelheim argues in his book *A Good Enough Parent* that the word "discipline" is rooted in the word "disciple." The best form of "discipline" is for a child to become a disciple—a student or follower—of a beloved parent or other adult, emulating the behavior of the revered and respected guardian. The child identifies with that adult and strives to model his behavior on the admired conduct.[368]

I learned this as a teenager when I was a camp counselor to a brood of eight unruly little girls high up in the Tehachapi mountains of southern California. Often they would ignore my instructions to, say, tidy up their beds, and I thought I had little sway over them. One day I made two long braids in my hair to keep it out of my face (it was the 1970s). The next morning all the little girls, without any discussion, appeared at breakfast with identical braids in their hair. *Well, look at that,* I thought. *Though they may pretend otherwise, those little varmints are watching me. Closely. And copying me.* Once I looked closely I noticed they all put the same amount of syrup on their pancakes as me and claimed to have the same favorite color as I did. Then I noticed my own messy bunk bed. No wonder they never made theirs.

Indeed, children are miniature detectives, carefully watching and recording in their memory banks everything we say and do. Decades from now they'll tell you about an offhanded comment you made, which you had long forgotten, and the profound impact it had on them. And they are tiny Mom and Dad impersonators, trying out your behaviors more than you know.

Nowhere is this truer than when it comes to boys' attitudes about women.

Any man who spends time with boys will have the greatest impact when they "walk the walk." Dads, your son will learn what respect means by observing how you treat other people, especially women. Are you dismissive to his mother? To a waitress? Do you make rude comments about women's bodies in your son's earshot, sizing up who's ugly or fat or hot, even in jest? Do you claim that men are better drivers, that women are too emotional or other outmoded stereotypes? How do you treat your own mother, even if she drives you nuts? Do you chalk up her shortcomings to her gender? How you answer these questions determines the attitudes you are imprinting on your son.

Second, Moms—and this can be even harder—you must *demand respect* for yourself. Not only is the martyr routine not working for you, but it's also sending him a dangerous message about women's roles. Are you picking up after him on a regular basis because it's easier than making him do it himself (it is, granted) and because "it doesn't really matter" (it does)? You are teaching him that women are there to be his servants and to do his dirty work. Teach him how to do dishes properly and to your satisfaction, to wash and dry his own laundry, to sew on a button, to make a few basic meals, and all other stereotypically "female" skills that any grown-up should know. Do you drop everything and cater to him even when he could be taking care of his problem himself? You are teaching him that your time—women's time—is not valuable, that your work and activities are less important than his whims. You may be cleaning up his mess now, but you're setting him up for even bigger messes later.

Third, bring little girls over to play whenever possible. Many children self-segregate by gender, boys playing only with other

boys, and girls with girls. The problem is that we humans naturally become suspicious of those who are absent—those icky,
weird others—and begin to form false generalizations about
them. This is especially true if there's no sister around to set
your son straight. The more female playmates your boy has,
the more he'll become comfortable with them and learn that
girls can be smart or dumb, kind or mean, fun or boring—just
like the boys.

Fourth, condemn disrespectful and stereotypical treatment
of women wherever you encounter it. Point out how few women
exist in his favorite action films, the tiresome woman-who-
trips-and-falls-in-the-chase-scene trope, or the tiny number of
female lead characters in children's books you read together.
Speak out loudly and often against his music's degrading lyrics
about women. In a related context, in my household, when the
song "With a Little Help from My Friends" ("I get high with a
little help from my friends") comes on my playlist, my kids say
in bored unison before I can get a word out, "Yes, Mom, we
know: *by listening to this song you are not advocating drug use.*" Say
it so many times they've committed your parental warnings to
heart! As always, imprint your values on them whenever you
have the chance.

Finally, teach him that respect is *active.* One of my prouder
Mom moments was in a crowded New York City subway when
my teenage son was the only one in the whole darned train
car to jump up and give an elderly woman his seat. *What is
wrong with the rest of you?* I thought. *Didn't your Mamas raise you
to do this?* Opening doors for women is lovely, but even better
is that one young man on every plane who gets up and helps a
woman struggling to load her heavy bag in the overhead compartment. Raise your son to be that guy—the helpful, friendly,
comfortable-with-women guy—and he'll have the edge in his
interactions with females at school, in the workplace, and
throughout his life.

RULE 9:

MAKE COMMUNITY SERVICE A REGULAR PART OF YOUR FAMILY LIFE

THERE ARE lessons that can be learned from books, the classroom, or at home with Mom and Dad, and then there is the wisdom that can only be learned from experience. As parents, we all know that we can tell children hundreds of times not to touch the teapot, but the one time they touch it anyway and burn their fingers, *aha!* Now they get it. Don't blame them—you were the same way as a kid. There is something hardwired in the human psyche that we learn best by *doing*.

Among the best experiences you can give your son to teach him to swagger less, to get him away from the daily media blitzkrieg, to be more compassionate, to count his blessings, to understand more about his neighbors and his planet—in short, to counteract all the thug culture messages—is to make community service a vital part of his life, month in and month out. As our economy sputters, those at the bottom suffer mightily. For example, on any given night over 67,000 veterans are homeless and twice as many experience homelessness during a year. One in four of our children live in poverty.[369] Lending a hand to help a neighbor, alongside your son, brings him out into the real world to see it for himself—and to help.

Community outreach projects vary widely. There's something for every personality and interest: assisting the disabled, playing board games with seniors in your local nursing home, delivering meals to homebound folks, sending CARE packages to service members abroad, ladling out soup for the homeless in myriad food banks around the country. Plant trees, paint over graffiti, build fences, speak English with immigrants, tutor a younger child, collect coats for a winter coat drive. As the economy slumps, service organizations have fewer volunteers and more needy; indeed, some of their former volunteers have switched sides and are now on the receiving end of their services.

Many of us have an odd approach to volunteering and donating to charity: we may do it ourselves, but for some reason unknown to me, we often perform these wonderful activities out of earshot of our children. Why is this? Make it a family affair. You get double credit for time spent with your kids *and* helping others. Your son will see others with his own two eyes and learn about their needs and their humanity. There he will meet people less fortunate than him and experience the emotional surge of making a difference in the lives of others. He will gain the true, earned self-esteem of contributing in a meaningful way to his planet. There is nothing else like it.

Women are out there in their communities lending a hand significantly more than men are. According to the Bureau of Labor Statistics, which tracks American time use, women volunteer at a higher rate than do men across all age groups, educational levels, and other major demographic characteristics.[370] Wherever I go, I see far more women and girls volunteering than men and boys. Whether this is a cause or effect of a less-swaggering gender, I cannot say. But boys have just as much obligation to help those in need as girls do. And they will reap the same lifetime benefits and memories of the good deeds they did. Dads, lead the way and show your boy that contributing to the community is part of what it means to be a man and a citizen.

An easy starting point is your local animal shelter, Humane Society, or other anti-animal cruelty organization. Children naturally love animals, and this compassion for other sentient beings should be encouraged. Your local animal shelter is filled with companion animals in cages, waiting all day for someone to come and speak a kind word to them, scratch them behind the ears, or take them out and train them so they are more adoptable. The stakes are high. A well-mannered dog goes home with a family; a jumper or overly shy animal gets euthanized along with three to four million other dogs and cats annually. Taking your son to the shelter a few times a month to interact with the animals is not only a lot of fun, but he can also feel the satisfaction that he may be saving animals' lives. (Warning: if you don't already have a pet at home when you start this activity, you will—soon. But that's for the best too: children with pets have better social skills, are more emotionally stable, are better able to read nonverbal communication, and even have stronger immune systems.[371])

Or encourage your son to become a member of any other group that regularly does projects to better your community. Your church, synagogue, or other religious group has a list of projects ready and waiting for you and your boy. Jump aboard! If you and he can't find a local organization to address a pressing issue that concerns him, encourage him to start one. Inspire him to become a "social entrepreneur" and organize and speak out about the problems in the world that burn him up. Environmental degradation? Work with him to found a local group that periodically cleans up your local beach or park. Especially at this time of budget cuts, resulting in fewer park rangers and government services, our public spaces can use all the help they can get. Racism? Can he get some friends together to start an organization to raise awareness on the issue, sponsor cross-racial dialogues, or agitate for change?

Bullying? How about making a YouTube video and expressing his feelings on the subject?

Kids are speaking out and effectuating social change every day. Cudahy, California, students Lesly Heredia and Paulina Sanchez got tired of watching their classmates tossing uneaten school lunches into the school cafeteria trash bins every day. Wouldn't donating that perfectly good food to the needy be better? They spent some time to prepare, counting all the wasted edibles in one week. The graph they prepared of those five hundred wasted uneaten food items impressed their principal and even their mayor. Lesly and Paulina then pushed through the new policy: unwanted food gets placed on a common table in the lunchroom. A local church comes by daily to pick it up and serve it to the needy. One hundred entrees, fruits, vegetables, and cartons of milk are reclaimed daily. Success!

Lesly and Paulina are nine years old.[372]

A Texas second grader became disturbed by a newspaper article she read about an injured baby manatee. She made and sold buttons and even wrote a book about the gentle marine animals, raising funds for their protection. Twelve years later Kids Making a Difference is an animal protection organization run by kids, for kids (with adult supervision).[373]

After watching a newscast of a Haitian child crying in post-earthquake rubble, twelve-year-old Blare Gooch thought about how comforting a teddy bear was to him in times of sadness. His teachers allowed him to ask kids, over the school's public address system, to donate stuffed bears, and then local television and radio stations joined in. Blare took his mission to Facebook, where Blare's Bears for Haiti page now boasts of sending over fifty thousand teddy bears to children on the impoverished island.[374]

Each of these projects started with the child's own enthusiasm and ideas, and with just a bit of help from the school or community, others joined in and a cause was born. And the hungry of South Los Angeles, manatees, and Haitian children are the better for it.

Don't forget political activism. As my mother, the indefatigable Gloria Allred, says, "Don't work for charity; work for change." Talk to your son about how these problems arose in the first place. *Why are there so many homeless vets? Or so much animal cruelty? Or suffering people in the third world?* Encourage him to work toward altering the root conditions of the problem. An Internet search can reveal which candidates support your causes. Get involved, take your son to go hear them speak, fact-check their statements, and, if you still like the candidates, help them get elected! Or encourage your son to write to your local representatives or start a petition on Change.org to get your issue noticed.

The mighty oak was once just a little nut with a big idea, as my Dad used to say. We need more little nuts with big ideas. Why not your son?

RULE 10:

TAKE HIM AWAY

*"The world is a book and those who do
not travel read only one page."*

—ST. AUGUSTINE

FINALLY, ONE of the best antidotes to the arrogance of our swagger culture and the ignorance our failing schools engender: take your boy out of his everyday life and into a brand new experience, ideally in a place as different as possible from what he's used to. Travel with him. As they say in *Star Wars*, to a galaxy far, far away.

Because the United States is more geographically isolated than, say, countries in Europe, Americans travel internationally far less than our continental counterparts. Only 30 percent of us have a passport, which is now required for all travel outside our borders. Fifty percent of Americans' international travel is to Mexico or Canada, which makes sense because those are the cheapest international destinations for us, as we can just drive right across our northern or southern borders.[375] But if you troll travel sites, visit off season, fly at odd hours, and/or camp or stay at inexpensive lodges, you can travel to Europe, Asia, Africa, or Australia inexpensively, giving your boy (and yourself) truly life-changing experiences. (If this is just not possible for your budget, stay tuned for close-to-home options.)

Let's get rid of the fear factor right away. Although some Americans don't travel abroad out of safety concerns, many foreign cities and towns have *less* crime than we do—again, our ignorance can get in the way. When I went to Nicaragua a few years ago, several of my friends gasped, "Are you sure there isn't a war going on there?" Nicaragua's civil war ended in 1988. (And its cordillera of active volcanoes is a knockout, its people preposterously friendly, and its prices obscenely low. Definitely go to this Central American gem.) Research the current political and social goings-on in your targeted destination; as in any major city, hold your kids' hands, cross your purse over your body or keep your wallet in a zipped pocket, don't wear flashy jewelry, and don't walk around creepy dark areas alone. Other than that, relax, *do* talk to strangers, try any food that's thoroughly cooked, and take lots of pictures.

Abroad, your son will glean important lessons, small and large, that just cannot be learned at home. Our manner of eating, communicating, worshipping, and interacting with others? That's one way, but it's not the only way. We are but 5 percent of the world's population. The other 95 percent is attached to their spicy (Thailand) or gelatinous (China) entrees, their sultry (Argentina) or high-pitched (India) music, their more conservative (Morocco) or freewheeling (UK) sexual mores. Your assignment: expose your boy to difference. Blow his mind about this world he lives in.

I know from personal experience how coming face to face with folks in other nations can alter one's sense of reality. My fourth-grade teacher's name is forgotten, alas, as are most of the state capitals I once memorized and how to convert pounds to grams, but here are just some of the kooky and profound moments that will always stay with my kids and me.

In Kyoto, Japan, at an elegant restaurant, I pointed out to the waiter that we had no napkins and asked for some. He stammered, "Uh, madame, I am sorry to advise...perhaps you would be willing to go in the restroom and use…uh…toilet paper if necessary?" *What the*—? Then I looked around the restaurant and noticed that no one had napkins. Instead, the neat and tidy Japanese chopsticked small bites directly into their mouths, obviating the need for wiping their faces afterward. Ever since that moment I have seen *us* from *their* point of view: hurried, sloppy eaters shoveling oversized forkfuls into our mouths, then blotting away the drippings that land on our faces. What are we, cave men?

In Tanzania, a country in eastern Africa, as I was climbing Mount Kilimanjaro, I reached into my pack and offered my local guide, a gaunt, wiry man, one of my granola bars I'd brought from the states. He politely (and unconvincingly) said no, as he'd probably been trained to do. "Go ahead," I urged. "I don't really like this flavor." He looked at me quizzically. After he took a bite, I asked him, "do *you* like it?" Again, he seemed baffled, and nodded yes, quickly finishing the bar. It dawned on me: it was food, therefore, he liked it. The entire concept of "liking" sustenance or not was alien to him. After that day, whenever someone tells me that they don't like an item on the menu, I think of this man and our incredible privilege of turning up our nose at food simply because it doesn't suit our taste.

In Kathmandu, Nepal, menstruation is a topic for public discussion. A young American exchange student there told me about how her Nepalese "brothers" would urgently and frequently inquire as to whether she had her period or not. When it came, she was sent to live in another home, with a village woman whose hut had been designated for that purpose. Her host family left her a plate of food on the ground during her time of the month, and anything else—notes, keys—was simply tossed at her feet. Nothing could be handed to her directly. This wasn't done to be cruel, she knew, struggling with this custom. The locals simply didn't want to be "infected" by her "uncleanliness." How can we show respect for their culture if it includes rituals like this, we wondered? As guests in their country yet proponents of equality, what was her proper response to this?

Near Rosarito, Mexico, so that she could dig in her purse for change to buy her prescription, a woman in a drug store line ahead of me, without asking or discussion, casually handed me her baby. She fully expected that I would be happy to lend a hand, and, of course, I did, jiggling the little cutie pie. In America this would never happen, I thought. We'd be afraid of kidnapping. How pleasant and neighborly to assume that your infant would be safe in the arms of the random person in line behind you. What must life be like in this more trusting community?

In Cappadocia, Turkey, my flight arrived late and the last bus to my hotel—or anywhere—had departed. At the sole car rental counter the agent reluctantly informed me that no more cars were available. It was after 9 p.m., and there were no taxis—what could I do? Spend the night in the airport? It was closing too. The rental car agent, understanding my predicament, closed his booth and then insisted on personally driving my companion and me to our hotel, apologizing that we'd have to first drive to his home so that he could update his wife. "But the hotel is an hour and a half away!" we protested. No matter, he said. And drive us he did, refusing offers of money for the three-hour round trip drive he made late that night for two strangers from America. I vowed to up my kindness-to-strangers game henceforth. Living in New York City, no matter how busy I was, I regularly stopped to help confused tourists ever after because of what this man did for me.

Traveling with my two children in China, a mother about my age confided her lifelong yearnings for a second child. Under their "One Child" policy she, like most of her one and a half billion countrymen and women, had been prohibited by law from having additional children. "I always wanted my son to have a sibling," she said wistfully. My kids looked at each other, considering for the first time the luck they had in each other's very existence.

In Tortuguero, Costa Rica, my children, about eight and ten at the time, hiked with a guide and me to sit on a dark, deserted

beach at midnight as we waited for female sea turtles to come
and lay their eggs, just as their predecessors had done in that
very same spot for thousands of years. The guide briefed us
on the exhaustive conservation efforts the Costa Rican government had undertaken to protect this ancient species as he also
educated us about his country's stunning biodiversity; then he
put his finger to his lips. We were expected to sit in silence,
patiently, until the turtles arrived, so as not to scare them or
interfere with their egg-laying ritual. Minutes passed. Ten,
then twenty, then thirty. The children were given blankets for
warmth but no crayons or video monitors or other forms of
entertainment. They were expected to wait, still and silent, for
as long as necessary, in the middle of the night, to show respect
for the reptiles. And they did, learning new levels of patience
they didn't know they had in them. After an hour—the payoff.
Dark and shining, an enormous mama turtle arose from that
ink-black sea, crawled toward us, and deposited her 110 eggs
(we counted) into the hole she carefully dug in the sand right
beside us. Illuminated by the full moon and our guide's turtle-
friendly blood-red flashlight, we experienced a mystical, magic
moment that was well worth the wait. And my kids, sitting on
a log on that Caribbean shore, learned they were capable of
new levels of calm and patience as well as fascination with the
natural world.

Ask any family that's traveled and you'll hear similar stories
of unexpected moments, new ways of looking at the world.
Children make friends across languages and cultures, and they
see how the majority of the world lives: in tiny, modest homes,
huts, shanties, or worse. Yet the world is filled with hospitality,
warmth, and music. Toddlers everywhere giggle at peek-a-boo.
School-age kids are mischievous imps who will always wave
back when you smile and wave to them. As Helen Keller said,
"Although the world is full of suffering, it is also full of the overcoming of it."[376] Let your boy see both sides of that equation.

Of course, the less expensive option of traveling *within* the
United States also provides terrific educational experiences for

your boy. Open your son's eyes to our country's brief but dramatic history: the Revolutionary War, the Civil War, women's suffrage, the civil rights movement. We've seen how breathtakingly ignorant our young people have become about American history. Remedy that by taking him to historical sites that may be in your own backyard or just a short road trip away. At colonial Williamsburg take him to live performances that bring to life eighteenth-century settler America from the vantage point of both slave owner and slave.[377] Visit Independence Hall and Liberty Park in Philadelphia to ponder our founders' conception of liberty and how that has evolved over the last several hundred years.[378] At Antietam National battlefield in Maryland contemplate the bloodiest one-day body count in American history—twenty-three thousand dead—and discuss how future bloodshed can be prevented.[379] New York City's Ellis Island and San Francisco's Angel Island have remarkable exhibits about the experiences of our immigrant ancestors as they arrived for the first time in America.[380] Cincinnati's National Underground Railroad Freedom Center documents the journey of escaping slaves prior to and during the Civil War, and it has the world's first and only permanent museum-quality exhibit about the reality of slavery and human trafficking for millions on our planet today.[381] (While you're in the neighborhood—Ohio—don't miss the Rock 'n' Roll Hall of Fame. Yes, the music of your youth is now of historical interest to your kids. And this may be the most raucous, counterculture good time of a museum on earth.[382])

Our government has preserved over eighty thousand historical sites that sit waiting to inspire you and your family. The National Park Service's National Register of Historical Places breaks them down by geographic area.[383] There is just about one in every county. Most of us have not visited historical sites even in our own backyards. (It took me ten years of living in New York City before I visited the stunning exhibition at Ellis Island, and then I never wanted to leave. Better late than never!)

America has some of the most compelling and innovative museums in the world. A month-long trip to our nation's capital could be consumed with walking through the nineteen museums and galleries that comprise our stunning Smithsonian collection. But while in Washington DC do not, under any circumstances, miss the Newseum, one of my personal favorites, featuring a sobering wall of Pulitzer Prize–winning photographs and a lunch counter from civil rights–era sit-ins amidst its modern, engaging, interactive collection of American news hits and misses through our history. Budding journalists and bloggers, take note. New York's Metropolitan Museum of Art and the Guggenheim dazzle outside (architecture) and in (collections). Your boy's not artsy? Encourage his scientific side, then. I challenge you to take him to New York's Natural History Museum, especially its planetarium, and tell me the astrophysicist show about the birth of stars—thirteen billion years ago—didn't captivate him. While in Manhattan, take him to the Lower East Side's off-the-beaten path Tenement Museum, where he'll go back in time to experience how nineteenth-century working-class immigrants lived.[384]

Wherever you go, never miss the chance to join a guided tour, with a real human being weaving stories and pointing out details you might have overlooked. Set a good example by standing in the front of the group and listening intently to the guide's remarks. Ask an occasional question to demonstrate your intellectual curiosity. Encourage your boy to engage with the tour guide and to pose his own questions or thoughts. Interested visitors make the docent's day. If live guides are unavailable, rent the audio tour. Children enjoy pushing the buttons and wandering aimlessly through an exhibit at their own speed, listening to segments chosen based on their own interest.

Go outside too. Especially if you're a city dweller, broaden your son's horizons, literally, by taking him to big vistas, fresh air, and stunning scenery. Visits to our amazing national parks will spark a new appreciation for the natural world and conservation. (But let him figure that out on his own—just challenge him to climb a mountain or paddle a lake with you.)

Where? A few suggestions. California's rugged, dramatic peaks at Yosemite inspired naturalist John Muir to write, "Nature had gathered her choicest treasures, to draw her lovers into close and confiding communion with her." Allowing your kids to reach adulthood without having sat rimside at sunset at the Grand Canyon is practically criminal. One-third of America can reach it by car in a day, they say, yet the undulating ridges, forested valleys, and gushing streams of Great Smoky Mountains National Park remain gloriously wild. The vast Everglades National Park—1.5 million acres—is a complex web of expansive prairies, mossy forests, mangrove islands, and snaking rivers. Encourage your son's meditative moments as he navigates a canoe through the eerily silent waterways, vigilant for alligators.

Of course, the list is long. Yellowstone, Sequoia, Denali—all spectacular. Arches, Badlands, Big Bend—oh my. Fifty-eight glorious national parks in all, and many states have lovely state parks as well, though some are closing, as we've seen. Visit them while you still can!

Besides the big perks of learning respect for other cultures, forming a better understanding of the world, getting some history and environmental consciousness raising, travel with your son offers other benefits. Really, just about any trip strengthens family bonds. (My kids and I have endless silly inside jokes from our trips.) Freed from the demands of work and school, families on even a weekend trip can focus on the new experience—and on each other. And kids can try on new identities, new roles. Because once away from our homes, we break out of our molds. The picky eater tries an adventurous new salsa in Latin America. Bueno! The kid who was never interested in history is intrigued by the tour guide's stories at Gettysburg and picks up a book on the subject in the gift shop. The boy who never looks away from his iPhone carefully studies maps and gives Mom directions on the drive to the Tubman African American Museum in Macon, Georgia. Suddenly, he gets geography.

Encourage your boy to take his own pictures and keep a journal or blog of his travels. What he chooses to write is up to him: what moved him, what bored him, and why. Have him help choose your destinations and plan the trip and daily activities. My son, a dancer, likes to take a movement class in each new place he visits. Dance: the universal language. I would never have thought of that. Go for it, kid. Figure out a way to explore the local version of his interests: a pickup soccer game, a walk through a school, an afternoon in the local park where he can play with kids his age. Give him a camera to preserve the moments as well as materials to make a photo album or scrapbook after the trip, to remember it always.

In the words of Mark Twain:

> Twenty years from now you will be more disappointed by the things you didn't do than by the ones you did do. So throw off the bowlines, sail away from the safe harbor. Catch the trade winds in your sails. Explore. Dream. Discover.

I would add only: and take your boy along for the ride.

MENTOR A BOY

THROUGHOUT THIS book I've been addressing parents, grandparents, caretakers—anyone who loves and raises boys. But fathers and other men, consider this final plea, addressed mainly to you. Because the data on your specific role in your son's life is so compelling, it deserves its own chapter.

Frankly, it deserves its own library.

We live in an age of the amazing disappearing dad. Through a complex storm of factors, fewer and fewer men are present in their children's lives now than at any time in modern American history. Let's start with fathers who live in the same home as their children. One would think those kids would have the benefit of lots of interaction with Dad—how could they not, living in the same house? Sadly, many fathers who live with their children seem to take the relationship for granted and can't—or won't—make time for their own off-spring. When they inhabit the same house, American fathers spend less than an hour a day with their children.[385] And those dads self-report talking to their kids for only *a few minutes* during that time daily.[386] What's Dad doing? Working a great deal, yes, to be sure; in this tough economy, many wage earners are working long hours or multiple jobs just to make ends meet. But they are also watching TV, which adult men report they do for almost three hours per day.[387] Many young dads spend hours a week on video games. Having grown up with them, they continue gaming into adulthood. Whether due to struggling to make ends meet or trivial distractions or a combination thereof, precious father-son time falls off the day's schedule, day in and day out.

For the millions of children who don't live with their dads, the deprivation is even worse. Four in ten American kids are now being raised by a single mom. For African American kids it's a clear majority: seven in ten children are raised in homes without a father. A significant and rarely discussed reason for this is the large numbers of incarcerated African American men, who have been disproportionately targeted in our War on Drugs, as we've seen earlier in this book. For this and other reasons, in many of these divorced or never-married families fathers have vanished altogether. One in five fathers who live apart from their children say they visit with them more than once a week, and an additional 29 percent see their children at least once a month. But for 21 percent of these fathers, the visits take place just a few times per year. And for 27 percent there are *no visits at all.*[388] If you add together those last two categories, that means that almost half the kids in single-mom households have no real dad to speak of in their lives.

In another study nearly one-third of fathers who do not live with their children say they talk or exchange e-mails with them less than once a month.[389]

Occasional e-mails? Is that what fatherhood has been reduced to?

That's a huge number of children crying out for some adult male attention. As novelist Michael Chabon says, "The handy thing about being a father is that the historic standard is so pitifully low."[390] And this all comes at a time when the ratio of adults-to-children in our youngsters' lives has dropped: fewer extended families living together, fewer teachers in bigger classrooms as budgets are cut, fewer school guidance counselors, librarians, school nurses as we've ever seen. Who are kids supposed to emulate? Thuggish rappers?

It's time to raise the bar, starting right now, because your kids need you *yesterday*. Every developmental stage is critically important: the new beginning of infancy, the curious toddler years, when he comes into his identity in grade school, his awkward preteen stage, his hormonal teenage years. You may tell yourself otherwise, but in your heart you know this is true: *there is no time in your son's childhood when he doesn't need your constant presence.*

Having raised my own kids mainly as a single mom, I bristle at the grim statistics documenting the wounds to children raised in these homes. But here they are, unvarnished. Nearly six in ten children raised in single-mother households are at or below the poverty line, according to the US Census.[391] (This poverty is largely due to the fact that single-mother families are one-income families, the noncustodial parent (usually dad) is delinquent in child support payments,[392] the high rate of unemployment among single moms, and the fact that never-married single moms skew significantly younger than other parents.[393]) Children in single-mother homes have measurably lower academic achievement, more emotional problems, more conduct problems, lower self-esteem, and more problems forming and maintaining social relationships.[394]

The quality of parenting in single-mother homes is worse than in two-parent households. Compared with continuously married parents, single mothers are less emotionally supportive of their children, have fewer rules, dispense harsher discipline, are more inconsistent in dispensing discipline, provide less supervision, and engage in more conflict with their children.[395]

Raising kids alone is hard, especially when struggling with poverty. Single moms are overwhelmed, often working multiple jobs. They need help—your help.

There's been an ugly trend to blame single mothers for many of society's ills. But one hears little outcry against the missing dads, who seem to wind up out of sight, out of mind. In general mothers are the ones who stick around after a breakup (most single moms are in their forties, on their own after a divorce[396]) and *try*. Shouldn't the adult who makes the lunches, dries the tears, goes to the doctors' appointments, shows up for the teacher conferences, does the laundry, and oversees the homework get the *credit*, not the blame? Shouldn't she get our admiration, not attacks? Where is the social condemnation for the parent who disappears—the half of fathers who, after a divorce, lose virtually all contact with their own children?[397]

Asked what the worst part was of their parents' divorce, kids consistently answer: *losing my dad.*[398]

Fathers often complain that divorced mothers make it difficult for them to see their children, so they relinquish control or give up for the sake of family harmony. As an attorney who's handled family law cases, I know how brutally ugly divorces and breakups can be. I have seen both women and men sink to the lowest levels of mudslinging and nastiness. There is plenty of blameworthiness on both sides. But both mom and dad must grasp how tremendously important Dad's continued role in his children's lives can be, force themselves to be amicable, and put aside their differences for the sake of the children. Unless he's abusive or negligent, Dad needs to maintain a continuous presence in his children's lives.

When I got divorced years ago, I told a counselor how upset I was that my ex would take the kids for the day without notifying me where they were going and without filling me in on the details afterward. How dare he! I was their mother!

"You're divorced now," she told me calmly. "You don't get to know that anymore. Do you trust him with the kids?"

I had to admit that I did.

"Have there ever been any health or safety problems when they are with him?"

Uh, no. Never.

"He is their father. He gets to do things his way during his time with the children now. Let it go." I didn't enjoy hearing those words, but they immediately struck a nerve. Yep, I guess that's right.

All exes should heed this advice: let Dad do things his way

during his kid time. Not only is it his right to expect this, but he's also more likely to continue a relationship with the children if he feels supported and respected for his choices during his hours. Not the way you would have done it, Mom? Unless Junior's well-being is threatened, just smile and nod.

And what advantages does your child reap from this Dad time? Even if you don't live with your kids, Dad, your involvement benefits them in school and in their developing lives. In a meta-analysis of sixty-three studies of nonresident fathers and their children, researchers found that children had higher academic achievement and fewer emotional and conduct problems when nonresident fathers were closely involved in their lives.

Case closed.

Re-engaging and reconnecting shows marked improvements in children's hearts and minds.[399] We know it. We don't need any more research. We need dads to man up. You're important. Own it. Please, be there for your kids. It's never too late to make a new start.

———

I'M NOT done.

Men—all men—I have one more request of you, on behalf of today's boys. Be an intentional role model for a boy who needs you. If you are already a father, consider taking another boy under your wing. If you're childless, choose to be a positive presence in a boy's life. Our educational system, the job market, popular culture, and the criminal justice system are failing our sons. But I have met many boys for whom just one caring man—an uncle, a guy in the neighborhood, a dad who'd disappeared but then, after six years, *came back*—made a difference.

THEY. NEED. YOU. If I have convinced you of anything in this book, I hope it has been that.

They need your time, your attention, your guidance, and your values. They need you to demonstrate to them *your* definition of what it is to be a man. That respect is earned not from being the most arrogant criminal on the block but through hard, honest work and treating others with dignity, integrity, and the other values you hold dear.

Boys need role models, men willing to step up to the plate to show them how manhood is done. Because genuine male role models make an enormous difference in kids' lives. In one study boys without male role models in their lives—one in four said they didn't have a single one—were three times as likely to feel disconnected from their peers, significantly less likely to feel happy and confident, and three times as likely to suffer from depression. Many of these boys without male role models reported that they couldn't remember the last time they felt happy or confident and that they had no sense of their identity.[400]

They couldn't remember the last time they'd been happy? We think of childhood as such a halcyon, carefree time. Nostalgically, we sometimes wish we were kids again, without a care in the world. But the reality is that so many boys are lonely and rudderless, and without a man to show them the way, they are flat-out miserable.

As we've seen, the best, most effective form of "discipline" is for a child to become a disciple—a follower—of a beloved parent or other adult, emulating the behavior of the revered guardian. The child identifies with that adult and strives to imitate him.

Gentlemen: pick a boy, any boy, to be your disciple. Superimpose your values over the empty values blasted at him by megacorporations and our thug culture every day. My plea: change the course of a boy's life. All those boys who think reading is for girls? Who are hurtling down a path toward a lifetime of minimum-wage work at best, prison at worst? They need you to be a regular, positive presence in their lives. Today. Yesterday. For a tiny investment of your time, you can change a life and model for a boy what a thinking man says and does.

Yes, I mean you.

Look around. I guarantee you won't have to look far. Boys in your family who are missing an adult male to lead them—step in. How about those unruly neighbor boys—isn't their behavior a cry for guidance? Your coworker's kid? Couldn't he use your companionship?

The sons of single mothers you know await you. There is no more grateful person in the world than a mom struggling to raise a family solo, who you've relieved for the evening or, better yet, every Sunday morning. Make it a regular, continuing get-together. Or make it official and join an organization that's been matching kids with mentors for years, like Big Brothers Big Sisters (formerly "Big Brothers," with its one hundred years of experience), and prepare for one of the most joyful and meaningful relationships of your life. Your church, mosque, or synagogue may have mentorship programs waiting for your help.

Before I get to the specifics on what you need to do with your newly befriended boy, let's knock down the excuses that are already springing to your mind. *No time! No money! I'm not much of a role model—I'm a wild man myself. Still immature. I've made mistakes. I'm still making mistakes. I don't know anything about kids; in fact, they scare me. Can't someone else do it?*

Get over it. The time investment is small. A few hours every other weekend is enough (though a few hours once a week is better).

I know two men who are Big Brothers. Both are busy, successful business owners. Both travel frequently. Neither had any experience mentoring or raising kids when they started. So what? They did it anyway. They, and thousands of others like them, make it work. Both have been present in their lives of their "little brothers" (called "Littles" in the organization) for years, and they rave about the experience.

The money issue is even easier. Organizations like Big Brothers will tell you not to be a "Disneyland Dad"—they specifically tell you *not* to spend much money on the kid. You're there to hang out and give advice, not be Santa Claus. Expensive trips? No. Biking together in your local park? Yes. Buying him

the latest game console? No. Taking a hike together or throwing a ball? Yes. Expensive restaurant meals? No. Going out for
pizza? Sure. Talking about girls? Absolutely! Keep it simple.
And the program regularly holds free events and gives away
tickets to theme parks, concerts, and, especially, ball games to
make it as easy and inexpensive as humanly possible for you to
have a little fun with your Little.

The time and money issues don't amount to much. Big
Brothers requests just two hours every other week. The real
impediment is most men's "who, me?" fear, the one that tells
them some other guy would be a better role model than them.
When it comes time for men to help boys, the swagger suddenly vaporizes.

My friend Eric is and always has been a wild child himself,
as any of his friends who've attended his legendary lingerie
parties or adult-themed scavenger hunts will attest. Prior to his
settling down in his forties with one woman and having two
boys of his own a few years ago, Eric's frequent, extravagant
Malibu beach house parties were legendary in a town known
for sex- and stripper-fueled all-nighters.

Nevertheless, he's been a friend to Matt, his Little, for twenty-
five years, through the Jewish Big Brother program, beginning
when Matt was just five years old and had suffered the death of
his father. Eric had every excuse not to do it, but he gave it a
shot anyway. He says,

> I was definitely *not* the paradigm of a Jewish Big Brother.
> For one, I was more atheist than Jewish (Jewish by cul-
> tural identity, not belief). Also, my lifestyle was, shall we
> say, somewhat edgy. But Matt got a reliable relationship
> that exposed him to my love of movies, scuba diving,
> and even golf. And since his exposure to me was regu-
> lar, he never floated into meaningless rebellion and nor
> did he embrace any of the wilder sides of my lifestyle
> (somewhat to my surprise).

When he began the program, Eric agreed to the one-year commitment asked of him. The promise seemed daunting to him then, as a carefree, different-woman-every-night, young, single guy. But year after year, he stuck with it. Because through his relationship with this fatherless boy, Eric noticed he was growing into himself:

> I am a rule breaker. But I learned it was much easier to rebel against authority and challenge the rules when they are being shoved down your throat, but much tougher to maintain that bent when you are put in charge of creating rules for someone who needs guidance.

Matt's version of their relationship mirrors Eric's description of Eric's immature young adulthood. But Matt didn't care:

> When I met Eric, he was basically a child in his midtwenties (that isn't to say he isn't a child in his early fifties now!). I was a very shy kid, and Eric was a very outgoing adult. We made plans once every week or two, and even though he would show up late most of the time, we would always have a great time.

An inauspicious beginning. But the relationship evolved, and deepened. With his Big Brother there was joy for Matt in sharing Eric's interests, like photography. Matt was delighted:

> Things like taking me to the LA Zoo and letting me use a camera to take pictures and showing enthusiasm for the strangest things were contagious. He introduced me to a world I don't believe I would have seen without him.

Eric is affluent, and he eventually took Matt on vacations abroad. Although Matt enjoyed that tremendously, he remembers warmly the small, "kid" stuff too:

> Eric was also quite educational. He would constantly challenge me when I would say something and not use the proper English (he taught me the meaning of the word "bitch" and the difference between "good" and "well"). He also loved board games, and we would play chess during every meal both in LA and on vacation. He was reliable; even if he was late, he would still be there.

How important was it for Matt to have a guy to hang out with?

> Once every week or two Eric would take me out and do things only guys would do. My mom would never think to buy a bunch of water guns, take me to Roy Rogers park, and have a huge water fight. Sporting events, playing basketball, going to many, many movies that my mom would have never watched—all of these things would have never been possible without Eric and are things that formed me as a person.

Matt waxed on about Eric's role in his life. Eric taught him to respect people who are different, for instance. And Eric came up with his own rules, based on his values, which worked for both of them. One example: Eric had a "mouth." He used colorful language and allowed Matt to say what he liked when it was just the two of them, but he also taught Matt the importance of being appropriate in other social settings.

Matt loves his single mom and credits all her hard work and guidance for making him into the man he is today—a commercial real estate property manager who's getting his MBA at the University of Southern California. Eric attended Matt's wedding recently, and Matt is excitedly looking forward to the birth of his first child. Matt is a friendly, gracious young man who is a pleasure to know. By any measure, Matt is a success story.

He might have turned out all right with just his mom, Matt says, but he brims with gratitude for Eric:

> He has made an enormous impact on my life and has guided me to realize both who I want to be and don't want to be. I always want to continue my relationship with him.

None of this is the least bit surprising. Eighty-six percent of former Littles surveyed agree that their Big instilled values and principles that have guided them through life.[401]

Mentoring a boy isn't just a warm and fuzzy thing to do; it consistently produces measurable results. In a study of Littles compared to similarly situated kids who weren't in the Big Brothers Big Sisters program, researchers found that after just a year and a half in the program, the Littles' lives improved. They were

> 46 percent less likely to begin using illegal drugs (minority Little Brothers were a whopping 70 percent less likely to start using drugs),
> 27 percent less likely to begin using alcohol,
> 52 percent less likely to skip school,
> 37 percent less likely to skip a class, and
> 33 percent less likely to hit someone.[402]

Little Brothers were also more likely to feel competent doing school work and showed improvement in their grade-point averages. Intriguingly, they trusted their parents more (perhaps their single moms became more trustworthy, buttressed with this bit of additional support from the Big and the organization, or perhaps the children could let down their guard around adults as a result of bonding with their Bigs) and had better social relations with their peers (perhaps from the additional socializing time with their Bigs).[403]

The downside? You may have an awkward moment like this one, which another Big Brother described to me:

> My Little would sometimes introduce me to people as his dad. Obviously he told this white lie because he so wanted a father. He was prouder and more confident by having a dad. I considered what to do, but I never had the heart to correct him. I felt that his fantasy of having a dad was far too important to him for me to put the kibosh on it.

This Big Brother describes his friendship with his Little as "one of the most meaningful of my entire life."

Mentoring a boy isn't a job for someone else. It's a job for you. You've read about all the forces buffeting our boys, challenging them, throwing stumbling blocks in their paths. Did you wonder why somebody didn't do something?

You are somebody, and this is what you can do.

———

WHAT WOULD you do with your Little? All the same activities we've seen in this book.

Enthuse about books. My fiancé, Braden, also a Big Brother, finishes each outing with a library or bookstore run. Help your Little browse and choose a book, then ostentatiously choose one for yourself. At the beginning of your next get-together discuss his pick. Good? Not so much? Why? Be honest about yours too—why you couldn't stop reading it, or why you didn't connect with that author. Take him to bookstore readings or book fairs where authors usually speak and answer questions for free. (I am thrilled to see kids at my events, and I call on them first during Q and A.) Light the reading spark in him, fan the flames daily, and watch his grades, his love of learning, and his intellectual curiosity skyrocket.

My mother often quoted Eleanor Roosevelt when I was growing up: "Great minds discuss ideas; average minds discuss events; small minds discuss people." Take him on a hike, and as you scramble up rocks, talk to him about ideas—yours, his, the ideas of others that one or both of you has come across in your reading or community events. Sure, engage him with traditional "boy" talk of sports, cars, and bodily function jokes if the two of you enjoy that, but also get to know him as an individual. What themes in the books you're reading together seem to move him? Why? What bothers him about his world? What would he do to change it? Why are there so many homeless people? Should we bring the troops home? Should mentally challenged kids go to mainstream schools? Does he see or experience racism in his school, his community?

There is more to life than football games. Take him to a documentary film—bonus points for taking him to a foreign film where he is exposed to another culture *and* is required to read (subtitles) for an hour or two. Go to a rally on a political issue that's important to you. Take him with you on volunteer projects, to local historical sites. Teach him to be a media critic. Call him on his attitude if you notice some swagger. Set his college expectations, and sign the two of you up for local college tours. Teach him to respect girls and women as well as people of different ethnicities. Talk frequently about your values. Take him to work with you and explain to him what you do.

In short, get him excited about ideas and show him through your words and deeds that what's going on in his mind is more important to you than how far he can hit a ball or what brand of sneakers he's wearing. Talk to him about *your* male role models. Be the man you want him to grow into. Model for him what a thinking man says and does. And have a hell of a lot of fun in the process, because your Little is going to worm his way into your heart.

You got this.

And if you share with me (and others) how it goes (www. Twitter.com/LisaBloom), we are going to flood you with love.

A FINAL THOUGHT:
THE POWER OF PARENTING

WHEN I was preparing to interview boys for this book, I thought about how to engage them. Who was I, after all? Some random woman off the street, from their point of view, who'd decided to write a book about them. So what? Why would they talk to me at all, much less open up on the topics I was interested in? How would I get past their natural resistance? How would I break the ice?

I asked a school principal about the difference between his male and female charges. "Boys fear saying something sissy or unmasculine," he told me. "Peer pressure is a big factor. They're very sensitive, but they pretend not to be."

Considering adolescents' natural wariness of strange adults and adding to that boys' notorious tough-guy veneers and underlying awkwardness, I figured I had my work cut out for me.

Surprise! I needn't have worried. Because boy after boy was *eager* to talk to me about his life. They readily answered my questions, considering some thoughtfully, and jumping right into others. They opened up about the topics I led with—their favorite books; whether they liked reading and, if so, which books; and their opinions about the media. Boys skipped lunch to keep the conversation going.

In one particularly energetic conversation a group of high school boys all gathered around a table to express offense that Cartoon Network is now running shows with cleavage! *That is so wrong*, they all agreed. *Cartoons should be for kids! What is this?!* I was taken aback by that one. But they insisted that younger boys should be able to watch a kids' network without it being oversexualized and that Cartoon Network should not get away with this outrage.

Who knew *this* would be an issue that ignited them?

When I tentatively broached more serious topics, again concerned I might get cut off, the floodgates opened. Teenage boys told me about being arrested or overcoming drug addiction at age fifteen. With rage in his eyes, a young man told me about the day he learned that his father wasn't his real father. His entire family had betrayed him, he felt. He planned to join the Marines as soon as he graduated from high school in order to get away from all the "liars." Another told me about his father being shot and killed and about going to his funeral. After that he did a lot of cocaine—so much that he's surprised he's still alive. He's off the drugs now, he said, because of poetry. His teacher had turned him on to spoken-word poetry, and it had become a powerful vehicle for him to express his rage.

I just never knew what I was going to discover once I scratched the surface with these boys.

A teacher came and pulled this young man away from our conversation because he had to get to class. I could have talked to him for hours more, and he could have done the same, going off with his teacher reluctantly. "Will you be here later?" he asked, walking off. "No," I had to say. "I won't—sorry."

I began to feel as though I might be the first person in years just to sit and ask them questions about their experiences, opinions, and feelings, the first to really listen to their answers. They were so happy, so grateful that someone was showing an interest in them. And the words came tumbling out.

What's your family life like? I asked one group.

"My parents are always working." This was said with more admiration than blame, and I heard it often. Mainly, it was just a fact. Several high school boys told me that they felt guilty staying in school rather than dropping out to help support their families.

"My mother and sister and I interact only for very limited periods. We are all doing other things."

And often I heard:

"I am home alone most of the time."

I began to feel remorseful that I was only interviewing them for a book and that I wouldn't be returning to continue the conversation on another day, much less give them some of the additional adult attention that they so clearly needed. *Can I adopt all of them?* I thought.

Suppressing my maternal instincts and struggling to maintain some journalistic distance, I asked about swagger culture. Needing no further explanation, they all smiled, lightly punched each other's arms and nodded knowingly, telling me all about the new male code to preen and strut and constantly exude faux confidence. "Gotta keep up the *swagga!*" they laughed. Then, more seriously, "There's social pressure to be the tough guy," they told me. "If you cry, you're done." Silence fell over the group.

I considered that each of them likely contributed to that peer pressure and that they probably discouraged each other from showing emotion. "Well, what would *you* do if a boy was crying?" I asked.

"I would sit and listen to him," one said, quietly. The others nodded agreement.

And that, ultimately, was the answer to the questions I'd come to ask them. At the heart of all of our discussions was this core of yearning from our boys:

Listen to me.

Pay attention to me.

Get to know me.

Spend time with me.

Protect me.

They may not fully understand what they need to be protected from. Their hopes and dreams may not be fully formed. They may not be able to articulate exactly what's missing from their lives. They may not know why they're angry, withdrawn, struggling in school, or tearing up.

But they ache for our attention and guidance—and they blossom under it. Boys lit up talking about a book Mom had given them or a day spent with "Dad." ("He's not really my dad," a skinny fifteen-year-old confided in me, "but he is, you know?" Yes, I do know.) Because the power of parenting is lasting and profound. It is perhaps the most magical gift we humans have: the ability to shape the life of a small, beloved child, to instill lessons that will likely outlast even our own lives.

It's a tough time to be raising a boy. But every moment you spend with him, every book you read together, every time you live your values, show him the world, set high expectations for him, and model for him how a decent adult conducts himself will reap beautiful dividends in his life. The parenting choices we make today will resonate for years—decades—and can lead our children to the bright, secure futures we all want for them. And one day he may sit down with his own children, tell them to turn off the thug messages, and take them volunteering in the church basement.

"Why are we doing this?" his kid may ask.

"Because that's how my parents raised me," he'll say.

And it will all have been worth it.

ACKNOWLEDGMENTS

AS I finish this, my second book, I've discovered something nearly universal about people in publishing: they share my deep, almost inexplicable abiding passion for the written word, and they do it for love. Americans may be reading less, the industry may be in turmoil, and book people may earn pennies compared to what their brainpower would be worth in the corporate world. But people like Laura and Dan and Josephine and Fawn will labor for hours to push me for a more persuasive source cite, to suggest a better word choice, to place a comma differently, or to find just one more cherished title to recommend to boys. All for the love of books.

These are my people.

Without Laura Dail, who understands and shares my passion for unvarnished social commentary, I'd probably still be an author wannabe. Laura has grown from book agent for *Think* to project czar for this book, offering her own insightful edits, overseeing all aspects of the business end of getting this book out and into your hands. Her constant good cheer, keen intelligence and friendship are godsends in my life. Dan Smetanka, my trusted editor, has the unenviable job of telling writers which sections of their beloved work must be cut. Much as I hate to admit it, he's usually right. Dan helped strengthen every bit of the manuscript that became this book, on a short deadline. With her ever-present can-do attitude, Josephine Mariea worked her magic, copy editing every word, polishing up the grammar, punctuation, spelling, and footnotes, also on a very tight time deadline. And I knew that my former Court TV producer and friend Fawn Mendel, mother of two boys and avid book lover herself, would be perfect to help compile the Books Boys Love appendix. Joseph Pittman ably guided us through the final printing and distribution phase. Mark Goldman, Ryan McCormick, and Jessica Hilpert showed great energy and commitment in getting the word out about this book. What a pleasure it was to work with each of these talented, hardworking people.

Nothing inspires me to put it out there like other writers who have the guts to put their name on books that speak uncomfortable truths about powerful institutions. I have never met Michelle Alexander, but I am grateful that she had the courage to write the most powerful book of 2011, *The New Jim Crow: Mass Incarceration in the Age of Colorblindness*. More than any other, this book stirred me to think about what we are doing to our boys and young men. I also was moved in 2011 by Joseph Keon's *Whitewash: The Disturbing Truth About Cow's Milk and Your Health* and Ben H. Bagdikian's *The New Media Monopoly*, also mentioned herein. Authors and independent publishers who give us meticulously documented, unnerving facts notwithstanding giant, well-funded forces aligned against them do us all a valuable service. Buy ten copies of their books and give them to everyone on your holiday list.

Then there's the authors I actually know and hang out with. My vegan sister writers Chloe Coscarelli and Julieanna Hever gave me constant pep talks through endless edits, and sometimes delicious snacks too. My author friends and high school classmates Joe Loya and Lisa Solis-Delong met me for much-needed occasional lunches, to get my bleary-eyed, greasy-haired, sweatpants-sporting self out of the house, into the sunlight, to talk earnest writer talk. Whew! I needed that.

Over thirty thousand other people also keep me company, on Twitter and Facebook, as I daily post my rants and raves, including the germs of ideas for this and future books. I am lucky to have a fired-up cadre of outspoken people accompanying me there, and I appreciate each thought-provoking response, agree or disagree. How lonely it must have been for writers before social media.

And oh, my nearest and dearest. My precious friend Rochelle Schieck listened to me rattle on about boys in America as we trekked the Annapurna Circuit in Nepal, and later read an entire draft of this book on her phone on the New York subway. Now that's devotion. Julie Greer, my bestie, gets me through everything, always has, always will. My mother, Gloria Allred, my daughter, Sarah Bloom, and my son, Sam Wong, have gracefully accepted that part of their lives now includes dropping everything to read my drafts. Given the oversized intellect of this group, I am fortunate to be able to conscript them into service.

Speaking of family, my brother Peyton Bray, my sister-in-law Ellen Cothran-Bray, and my nephews Cosmo and Tennessee Cothran-Bray took a leap of faith, allowing me to interview and write about them, using their real names. Big appreciation and love to them all. (Special note to my brother: did too.)

How do people write without dogs? I have no idea. My rescue pups, Soda and Moxie, silently, patiently kept me company through sixteen–hour days of research and writing, occasionally presenting their sweet faces for petting and dropping chew toys into my lap for play breaks. Without their grounding, I think I'd have disappeared entirely into my computer monitor. *Who's a good dog?*

My fiancé, Braden Pollock, put up with my 24/7 writing style, everything else on hold, for months on end, without complaint and with his trademark nonstop love and complete support. Every writer should be blessed with a partner like this.

Finally, I am deeply indebted to each of the boys who sat with me and opened up about their lives. Their willingness to be candid, to laugh with me, and to go deep and even shed tears, motivated me to write directly to parents about what boys need. I hope this book in some small way repays their honesty and courage. This book is for them.

APPENDIX:
BOOKS BOYS LOVE

OUR WORLD is filled with amazing books for every taste. Our job is to connect our boys to them. He says, "I can't find any good books to read!" Hear this as: "Help me find something to amaze and delight me!" How? Enlist his teacher or his school or city librarian, ask his friends what they have enjoyed, hit up other parents for recommendations. Here are some titles to get you started, a list of tried-and-true books boys love. And if your son hits on something that should be added to this list, share it with other parents and me on Twitter (@LisaBloom). Let the reading begin!

Ages Birth to Two Years

YUMMY YUCKY by Leslie Patricelli. What's more fun than boogers, earwax, and mud pies? Patricelli teaches little ones a valuable lesson—play with mud, but please don't eat it. Spaghetti is yummy, but worms are yucky. Whether they get the message or not, little boys will love the subject matter (even if you don't), the pictures, and the fun in this book. Patricelli has an entire series of books that are also worth checking out.

*How Do Dinosaurs…*series by Jane Yolen. Most boys love

dinosaurs. In Yolen's series kids learn lessons from her dinosaurs. Babies will enjoy the vibrant illustrations, and toddlers will learn how everyday things can be giggle-worthy and exciting.

Mommy Loves by Anne Gutman. Along with the beautiful illustrations, this book has a sweet message that even the youngest of readers can understand. All mommies—whether they are cats, fish, pigs or humans—love their babies. Yes, we do.

Goodnight Moon by Margaret Wise Brown. Still a classic and a crowd pleaser after all these years, it's the perfect bedtime story for infants and toddlers. Having read this to my own kids at least four thousand times, I still know this lovely book by heart, two decades later. It is complete with beautiful illustrations that have stood the test of time. Parents and older siblings, check out a very modern parody, *Goodnight iPad* by Ann Droyd.

On the Day You Were Born by Debra Fraiser. With gorgeous illustrations and a story that will tug at the heartstrings of the adult reader, this book tells the story of the birth of a baby and how the world welcomes him. Adults will ooh and ah while babies goo and gah. I have given this book as a baby shower gift many times.

The Very Hungry Caterpillar, Brown Bear, Little Cloud, all by Eric Carle. Carle fills kids hearts as he fills the caterpillar's tummy in his classic book about eating your veggies. Carle's other books can't miss with appealing illustrations and accessible stories for babies.

Everyone Poops by Taro Gomi. Enter a circle of laughing toddlers and you can almost guarantee the word "poop" is the reason for the giddiness. Don't fight it; turn it into a reason for reading. In *Everyone Poops* toddlers can get a closer look at elephant poop and mice poop—just what they've always wanted!

First Hundred Machines by Roger Priddy. Even from day one there is something about boys and things that go. This large, colorful board book has impressive photos of diggers and loaders, police cars, boats, planes, and more. Little boys will turn the pages on their own as soon as their little fingers figure out how.

Ages Three to Five Years

THE *DINOSAUR VS.* series, including *Dinosaur vs. Bedtime, Dinosaur vs. The Library,* and *Dinosaur vs. The Potty* by Bob Shea. Boys and dinosaurs go together like peanut butter and jelly. In this series nothing can stop this dinosaur. He is able to take on whatever comes his way, and he'll be any boy's hero.

If You Give…A Mouse a Cookie (A Cat a Cupcake, A Pig a Pancake) by Laura Numeroff. This series is a huge hit with little boys, who will laugh at the long, silly chain of cause and effect. Offer a mouse a cookie, and he'll certainly ask for a glass of milk to go with it, and on and on. The pictures in this book make it even more of a pleasure to read.

The Big Book of Trains by DK Publishing. This book is a must for train-obsessed boys. I can't explain why they love them, but again, use it to bring them to a book. *The Big Book of Trains* includes more than fifty color photos of amazing trains that will impress and draw in little train enthusiasts.

Parts by Tedd Arnold. This is definitely a gross-out book for the kind of kid who appreciates that sort of thing. The narrator starts noticing his parts—hair, skin, teeth—are falling off. Plus he's convinced his brain is dripping out of his nose. This is a book boys can really sink their teeth into—as long as those teeth aren't falling out!

The Gas We Pass: The Story of Farts by Shinta Cho. These are the fart jokes for the preschool set. This book actually takes itself a little too seriously, considering the subject matter. But little boys, who—let's face it—all love fart jokes, will be thrilled to get to read about this lovely topic before bed.

Cars Galore by Peter Stein. Stein drives the reader through an array of cars, not just in all shapes and sizes but also with some of the most bizarre cars you will never see on the road. From a rock-and-roll car to a smells-like-a-skunk car, the prose reads like Dr. Seuss and the illustrations like a fifties diner. It's a book that will really start the engine of a little car lover while being something the whole family can enjoy.

Knuffle Bunny series by Mo Williams. A modern-day *Velveteen Rabbit,* this series of three books follows the growth of Trixie and her Knuffle Bunny that she carries with her wherever she goes. In the first book Trixie losses Knuffle Bunny at the laundromat mat but doesn't have the language to tell her daddy. In *Knuffle Bunny Too* Trixie's friend at preschool happens to have the same one-of-a-kind Knuffle Bunny too. The result is a late-night rendezvous for Trixie's daddy when the wrong Knuffle Bunny comes home. The third book, *Knuffle Bunny Free,* shows a more "grown up" Trixie, who leaves Knuffle Bunny on a plane and has to figure out how to get through the days without her sidekick. These books speak to the kid who has his own favorite stuffed animal. Plus, the use of black-and-white photos along with colorful, whimsical illustrations will impress kids and parents alike.

Where the Wild Things Are by Maurice Sendak. Let the wild rumpus start! All boys dream of being king of the Wild Things, and Max actually gets to do it without missing dinner. This classic book hasn't lost its appeal with the preschool set. Max dons his wolf suit and takes a wild ride "in and out of weeks and over a year" to where the Wild Things are. Probably my all-time favorite kid book.

He Came with the Couch by David Slonim. Lint, crumbs of food, cat hair…the usual stuff kids find on their couches. But in this sweet story Sophie finds a muppet-like creature who is much more than just a couch potato. He came with their brand new couch and isn't leaving. Sophie's family finds out their unexpected visitor has a case of "upholsterosis" and proceeds to take him to see the world—doctor's orders. Boys will definitely get a kick out this book and might just hope their next couch comes with a new friend too.

Hi! Fly Guy by Tedd Arnold. *Casablanca* for the preschool set. The first in a series of *Fly Guy* books, marks the beginning of a beautiful friendship. We're introduced to Buzz and his pet Fly Guy, who happens to be a fly. Buzz works to defend his new friend and shows the world that a fly can, in fact, be a pet—a smart pet at that.

True Story of the Three Little Pigs by Jon Scieszka. Of course there is another side of the story! There always is. In this modern version of the classic story the wolf gets a chance to tell the tale from his perspective. Can a bad cold explain it all? Maybe it's the fault of the flimsy houses that the pigs build? Like boys this age, there is an explanation for everything, even when caught in the act.

Trains: A Pop-Up Railroad Book by Robert Crowther. A must-have for a train enthusiast. This book has 3-D trains and pull-tabs along with interesting facts that will excite train lovers everywhere.

Ages Six to Nine Years

CAM JANSEN series by David Adler. Jennifer "Cam" Jansen earned her nickname because of her photographic memory. She uses it to solve mysteries along with her best friend, Eric. Cam closes her eyes and takes a "picture" of the scene and that helps her solve each mystery. Cam Jansen has solved more than thirty cases so far, and there is no sign of her stopping any time soon. These books are a good transition for young readers who are starting to read chapter books.

Encyclopedia Brown series by Donald Sobol. For the budding detective in all boys—this is *Law & Order* for the grade school set. Leroy Brown, aka Encyclopedia Brown, hasn't met a mystery that he can't solve—and his dad is certainly thankful for that. After all, Encyclopedia Brown's dad is the chief of police, and his son has helped him get to the bottom of many a mystery. The fun part about these books is that readers are able to solve the mystery along with Encyclopedia Brown. Answers can be found in the back of the book. This is a classic series that has legions of new fans.

Nate the Great series by Marjorie Weinman Sharmat. Another great young detective series. Nate has been delighting young readers since 1972, working on more than twenty cases. After a breakfast of pancakes, Nate takes to his case—a lost item, or similar situation—always remembering to leave a note for his mom on the refrigerator. As children make their way through the series, new and fun characters are introduced into Nate's world.

Chocolate Fever by Robert Kimmel Smith. This book has stood the test of time because chocolate never goes out of style, especially for kids. Henry loves chocolate too; in fact, it's almost all he ever eats: chocolate milk, chocolate cake—you name it. But what happens when Henry breaks out in chocolate spots? To avoid doctors Henry runs away and has some fun adventures along the way. Kids will read along this delicious tale with the big question in mind: is there a cure for chocolate fever?

The Bailey School Kids series by Marcia T. Jones and Debbie Dadey. In the town of Bailey the kids come face to face with some really strange adults. But upon further investigation some of these adults are actually much more than strange—they are zombies, aliens, vampires, and ghosts.

Freckle Juice by Judy Blume. What could be more fun than mixing up a concoction of the grossest stuff in your refrigerator? That's just what Andrew does in an attempt to sprout freckles. Andrew wants nothing more than to be covered in freckles like his classmate Nicky, so much so that he forks over his allowance for a "freckle juice" recipe from Sharon, a conniving girl in his class. Ending up with a stomachache instead of freckly skin, both Andrew and Nicky learn to love their skin with and without freckles.

Magic Treehouse series by Mary Pope Osborne. Boys will get to go on a different adventure in every book with Jack and his little sister, Annie. Thanks to an amazing discovery—a magic treehouse—Jack and Annie are able to read books that take them to faraway lands and historical sites, complete with pirates, mummies, and more.

Harry Potter series by J. K. Rowling. The worldwide

phenomenon of Harry Potter is really all it's cracked up to be. What kid doesn't dream of going to a school for Wizardry, flying around on a broom, and battling the world's most powerful villain—He Who Must Not Be Named—and coming out on top? Rowling created a character who is so easy to love; despite being one of the world's most famous wizards, Harry is humble. My kids grew up with these, going off for a weekend into their room and reading each one cover to cover.

Diary of a Wimpy Kid by Jeff Kinney. Do boys keep diaries? Diaries, no; journals, yes. Greg keeps a journal with lists of popular kids and other stuff that is important in middle school. Greg doesn't mince words, mind you. He gets straight to the point and will have kids laughing aloud when they read this book. Of course, it doesn't hurt that "boogers," "butts," and "jerk" gets thrown around a lot.

Captain Underpants by Dav Pilkey. The title of this book alone is appealing to boys, especially when it is the school principal who turns into Captain Underpants and dons nothing but underwear and a cape. The two protagonists are George and Harold, the class clowns. They publish their own comic book that they sell on the playground. With characters like Pippy Pee-Pee Poopypants, Dr. Diaper, Wedgie Woman, and the Bionic Boogerboy, it is no wonder this is the kind of book boys will happily pick up and devour.

Bunnicula series by Deborah and James Howe. A bunny named Bunnicula wreaks havoc when he moves into a house with a cat named Chester and a dog called Harold. A tomato sucked dry of all its liquid tips Chester off that Bunnicula might actually be a vampire bunny. Now it's up to the team of Chester and Harold to rid the house of this blood- (or tomato-, as the case may be) sucking creature.

Frindle by Andrew Clements. Nick discovers the power of words—or one specific word to be exact—in this fantasy classroom tale. But Nick never expects when he renames a pen "frindle" that it will catch on like wildfire—not just in his school but also in his town and around the country. Although everyone seems to be on board, his fifth-grade English teacher is none too happy about the situation.

Horrible Harry series by Suzy Kline. Being the best friend of the class prankster can be really fun. The narrator of this series, Doug, knows this all too well. His friend Harry gets into trouble and mischief on a regular basis. Laugh-out-loud funny!

James and the Giant Peach by Roald Dahl. After James's parents tragically die, he is forced to live with his evil aunts. But he is offered an escape inside a gigantic peach, where he befriends six magical insects who accompany him on many adventures. Other Dahl classics not to miss include *Charlie and the Chocolate Factory, Matilda,* and *The BFG*—all clever, zany classics.

Discovery Kids Eyewitness books by various authors. Subjects range from weather to chemistry, dinosaurs, archeology, and all that good stuff that boys go gaga over. Just don't tell them they're educational.

Where the Sidewalk Ends and everything else by Shel Silverstein. "Sarah Cynthia Sylvia Stout would not take the garbage out!" begins one of my all-time favorite poems. Silverstein's poems are worth memorizing, repeating, and flat-out loving.

Ages Ten to Fourteen

MIKE LUPICA Sports Books. These are the perfect books for young sports fans. Lupica has the right balance between sports action and emotional drama. These books are definitely a winner for preteen and teenage boys.

Choose Your Own Adventure series by R. A. Montgomery. Choose wisely, or you could end up dead. What red-blooded teenage boy wouldn't want to take on a challenge like that? The beauty of these books is that there isn't just one ending. Boys will relish the fact that there is danger lurking around every corner when reading books from Montgomery's adventure series.

Getting Away with Murder: The True Story of the Emmitt Till Case by Chris Crowe. History buffs will appreciate this important story, often overlooked in school textbooks. Teenager Emmitt Till was murdered for allegedly whistling at a white woman in Mississippi in the 1950s. Till's killers were acquitted on all charges by an all-white jury, yet they continued to brag about the murder after their cases ended. The story sheds light on the horrific racism that existed in the Jim Crow South and should provoke interesting discussions with your son.

Peter and the Starcatchers by David Barry and Ridley Pearson. Before Tinkerbell there was Molly. This prequel to *Peter Pan* is perfect for boys who like pirates, adventure, magic, secrets, and mystery. Complete with a strange trunk of green "starstuff" that holds the secrets to some of the greatest historical figures of all time, stuff that Peter and Molly have to protect. This is the kind of book that will keep teens reading well into the night.

Artemis Fowl series by Eoin Colfer. Artemis Fowl is a boy genius and a criminal mastermind. He pledges to help his family regain its fortune by stealing gold from the fairies. But this isn't your little sister's fairy collection; these fairies mean business. The *Artemis Fowl* series has often been compared to *Harry Potter* for its mass appeal to young adults.

The Lion, the Witch and the Wardrobe by C. S. Lewis. The enchanting first book in the *Chronicles of Narnia*, this story follows adventures of siblings Peter, Lucy, Edmund, and Susan as they enter into the magic world of Narnia. This classic series has stood the test of time for compelling storytelling and was one of my childhood favorites.

Maximum Ride by James Patterson. *New York Times* best-selling author James Patterson takes a stab at young adult fiction with this fast-moving, sci-fi adventure. Max is one of a group of part-kids, part-birds who were bred as an experiment in a lab. Now the six kids who can fly are on the run from Erasers—part-human, part-wolf—who captured one of their own. This story packs a major punch and can be heavy for some kids. Warning: there is violence and bloodshed in this book.

Stormchaser (book one of the *Alex Rider* series) by Anthony

Horowitz. After Alex Rider's uncle is murdered, he finds out that his uncle was a whole lot more than he ever realized. Alex then takes over his uncle's undercover work, diving into a world of amazing gadgets and secret villains—James Bond for the teen set. Complete with high-speed chases and crash landings, *Stormchaser* will definitely suck in even the most hesitant reader—not just to this book but also the entire series.

The Invention of Hugo Cabret by Brian Selznick. The coolest part about this book is that it tells its story with words and pictures. Twelve-year-old orphan Hugo lives in the walls of a Paris train station. He is set on accomplishing the work of his recently deceased father, work that includes solving the mystery of a robot in a museum.

Septimus Heap series by Angie Sage. A series of seven books that develop the story of Septimus Heap, who is declared dead by a midwife at birth and taken away to start a boy army. The same day the family discovers a newborn in the snow and takes her in. Septimus's existence is revealed in the first novel and his adventures continue in all seven books. This series has also been compared to *Harry Potter* and has mass appeal to teenage boys.

Eragon by Christopher Paolini. When he discovers a dragon egg, Eragon, a young farm boy, learns he is truly a Dragon Rider who must follow his destiny. A deeply engrossing book, this fantasy has more than sixty characters to keep track of. It is still an appealing adventure that leads seamlessly into the next book in the series, encouraging children to keep reading.

Percy Jackson and the Olympians series by Rick Riordan. What happens when a kid discovers he is actually a demigod—the son of Poseidon? It takes him on adventures of epic proportions that span five books. Percy Jackson stops a war between the Gods, battles mythological monsters, accidentally sets off a volcano, and more. The stories have spawned a movie and a video game—stuff that is right up boys' alleys.

Hunger Games by Suzanne Collins. A graphic, often violent adventure about a fight to the death between teenagers. In a dystopian world where the United States has collapsed and a country split into twelve districts has come into being, twenty-six teenagers are selected to participate in an event called the Hunger Games that is to be broadcast on TV—all are forced to watch. When Katniss's younger sister is selected, she volunteers herself instead. Chances of survival are next to none. Warning for parents: this book contains violence and gore.

Hatchet by Gary Paulsen. The page-turning, dramatic story of a boy whose plane crashes in the Canadian wilderness. With only a hatchet and his own wits, will he survive?

The Call of the Wild and *White Fang* by Jack London. These are beloved classics about a kidnapped dog, Yukon gold, a wolf-dog who endures human cruelty before finding kindness. The newer editions feature drawings, photos, and maps to enhance the text.

Ages Fifteen to Eighteen

ENDER GAME by Orson Scott Card. The first in a series of books by Card introduces Ender Wiggins, a genetically bred child genius. After being attacked by aliens twice, the government decides to build an army of children. These child geniuses are trained at Battle School by playing games that teach them how to destroy the aliens if they ever did return. Ender is at the top of his class of geniuses. Not that anyone can possibly put this book down anyway, but don't miss the ending!

Catcher in the Rye by J. D. Salinger. Tell your boy this book is *still* on banned book lists, then read him the opening lines: "If you really want to hear about it, the first thing you'll probably want to know is where I was born and what my lousy childhood was like, and how my parents were occupied and all before they had me, and all that David Copperfield kind of crap, but I don't feel like going into it, if you want to know the truth. In the first place, that stuff bores me, and in the second place, my parents would have about two hemorrhages apiece if I told anything pretty personal about them." A timeless classic, still fresh sixty years after it was written.

Lord of the Rings by J. R. R. Tolkien. Most boys have probably seen the movie already, but any teenager into fantasy should read this series of books by J. R. R Tolkien. They are the *Harry Potter* books before anyone even knew who Voldemort was. My brother read these over and over, and his sons love them too.

Lord of the Flies by William Golding. What happens when a plane of teen boys crashes on an island and they are left to their own devices? Things start off under control, but soon animal instinct takes over, groups form, and it's every boy for himself. This is a suspenseful, psychological thriller that pits boy against boy for food, supremacy, and survival. Warning: gory.

The Princess Bride: S. Morgenstern's Classic Tale of True Love and High Adventure by William Goldman. This story is about "Fencing. Fighting. Torture. Poison. True love. Hate. Revenge. Giants. Hunters. Bad men. Good men. Beautifulest [sic] ladies. Snakes. Spiders. Beasts of all natures and descriptions. Pain. Death. Brave men. Coward men. Strongest men. Chases. Escapes. Lies. Truths. Passions. Miracles." It's a story within a story, as a father reads to his son who is sick in bed. The book spawned a movie that quickly became a cult classic.

Twilight series by Stephanie Meyer. A four-book action saga that follows the story of an awkward girl named Bella who falls in love with a vampire named Edward, befriends a werewolf named Jacob, and somehow manages to put herself in extreme danger on a daily basis. These books have taken over the lives of teenagers everywhere and have been made into hit movies. They are books teens will stay up all night to finish.

Paper Towns by John Green. Quentin has a crush on his next-door neighbor, but when she comes to his window in the middle of the night, he learns that she isn't exactly the girl he has always dreamed of. The two go on an overnight adventure that leads to even more revelations for Quentin. Not your girl-friend's love story.

Gone by Michael Grant. It's the scenario that most kids have always dreamed of: a world with no adults. And it happens in the blink of an eye in *Gone*. Everyone over the age of fourteen dies, but the fun and games end quickly. There are no doctors to take care of sick people; there are no teachers, no parents, no police officers to maintain law and order; war is inevitable—a chilling thriller.

The Maze Runner by James Dashner. Thomas arrives into the middle of an ever-changing maze where sixty other teenage boys are trapped. No one knows why he is there or how he got there. After Thomas gets to the "Glade," the first girl arrives and things become even more complex. Boys will enjoy this action-packed thriller until the end, when all is revealed.

The Dresden Files by Jim Butcher. The life of a private detective isn't easy, especially when fighting werewolves, demons, and vampires, just to name a few. Even though the general public doesn't know it, Harry Dresden is protecting them from all these dark forces. Who wouldn't love a story about a private eye who has to tangle with the supernatural on a daily basis?

Into the Wild by Jon Krakauer. Chris McCandless is a talented young college graduate who literally walked away from his life, his emaciated remains found in an abandoned bus in the Alaskan wilderness in 1992. What happened? Brilliant outdoor writer and mountaineer Jon Krakauer reports. Also by Krakauer, *Into Thin Air*, the riveting story of life and death among a motivated group of mountain climbers on Mount Everest.

The Count of Monte Cristo by Alexandre Dumas. As one online reviewer wrote, "Best. Book. Ever." The plot twists and turns in this book about revenge and vengeance set in the turmoil of nineteenth-century France.

NOTES

1   Lucy Komisar, "How the Food Industry Eats Your
    Kid's Lunch," *New York Times*, December 3, 2011,
    http://www.nytimes.com/2011/12/04/opinion/sunday/
    school-lunches-and-the-food-industry.html?src=recg.

2   "Only 1 of 2 Students Graduate High School in US Cities:
    Study," Breitbart, April 1, 2008, http://www.breitbart.com/
    article.php?id=080401184532.kxjxy7xo.

3   Brian Todd, "46 Million Americans on Food Stamps,"
    CNN, August 6, 2011, http://situationroom.blogs.cnn.
    com/2011/08/06/6-million-americans-on-food-stamps/.

4   Jessica Hopper, "Waiting for Midnight, Hungry Families on
    Food Stamps Give Walmart 'Enormous Spike,'" Rock Center,
    MSNBC, November 28, 2011, http://rockcenter.msnbc.msn.
    com/_news/2011/11/28/9069519-waiting-for-midnight-hungry-
    families-on-food-stamps-give-walmart-enormous-spike.

5   Jason DeParle, Robert Gebeloff, and Sabrina Tavernise,
    "Older, Suburban and Struggling, 'Near Poor' Startle
    the Census," *New York Times*, November 18, 2011,
    http://www.nytimes.com/2011/11/19/us/census-measures-
    those-not-quite-in-poverty-but-struggling.html?hp.

6   Nancy Bean Foster, "Cain in Nashua: 'I'm a Leader, Not a
    Reader,'" *Union Leader*, November 17, 2011, http://www.
    unionleader.com/article/20111117/NEWS0605/711189999.

7   Robert Preidt, "Rap Music Glorifying Drug Use," ABC News,
    April 2, 2008, http://abcnews.go.com/Health/Healthday/

story?id=4569665&page=1#.Tuf-IGMk6so.

8   Eminem, "I'm Shady," Metrolyrics, http://www.metrolyrics. com/im-shady-lyrics-eminem.html. He may be drug-free now, but Eminem has no regrets about his lyrics and their influence on his legions of young fans. "New 'Tolerant' Eminem Supports Gay Marriage," *Us Weekly*, June 17, 2010, http://today.msnbc. msn.com/id/37759634/ns/today-entertainment/t/new-tolerant-eminem-supports-gay-marriage/#.Tzp2–P263g.

9   Lisa Bloom, "How to Talk to Little Girls," *Huffington Post*, June 22, 2011, http://www.huffingtonpost.com/lisa-bloom/ how-to-talk-to-little-gir_b_882510.html.

10   Thomas Jefferson, Letter to George Wythe, in *The Portable Thomas Jefferson*, edited by Merrill D. Peterson (New York: Viking Press, 1975), 399–400.

11   Barack Obama, "Literacy and Education in a 21st-Century Economy," Obama Speeches, June 25, 2005, http:// obamaspeeches.com/024-Literacy-and-Education-in-a-21st-Century-Economy-Obama-Speech.htm.

12   "How Does the United States Stack Up? International Comparison of Academic Achievement," Alliance for Excellent Education, March 2008, http://www.all4ed.org/files/ IntlComp_FactSheet.pdf.

13   Somewhat unfairly, admittedly, Shanghai and Hong Kong, among the most prosperous cities in China, were tested separately rather than with the entire Chinese student population taking the exams.

14   "Statistics about Education in America," Students First, http://www.studentsfirst.org/pages/the-stats.

15   "Detroit's 'Shocking' 47 Percent Illiteracy Rate," *The Week*, May 6, 2011, http://theweek.com/article/index/215055/ detroits-shocking-47-percent-illiteracy-rate.

16   Pierre Thomas, Jack Date, Clayton Sandell, and Theresa Cook, "Living in the Shadows: Illiteracy in America," ABC World News, February 25, 2008, http://abcnews.go.com/WN/LegalCenter/ story?id=4336421&page=1#.T02-JvEgf5Z.

17   Lexington, "The Underworked American," *The Economist*, June

11, 2009, http://www.economist.com/node/13825184.

18   "4-Day School Weeks Gain Popularity Across U.S.," CBS News,
      June 4, 2010, http://www.cbsnews.com/stories/2010/06/04/
      national/main6548010.shtml.

19   "Four-Day School Weeks," National Conference of State
      Legislatures, http://www.ncsl.org/default.aspx?tabid=12934.

20   Jason Song, "L.A. Unified Cuts Most Summer School
      Classes," April 15, 2011, http://latimesblogs.latimes.com/
      lanow/2011/04/district-cuts-summer-school-classes.html.

21   Sam Dillon, "As Budgets Are Trimmed, Time in Class Is
      Shortened," *New York Times*, July 5, 2011, http://www.nytimes.
      com/2011/07/06/education/06time.html.

22   Tamar Lewin, "If Your Kids Are Awake, They're Probably
      Online," *New York Times*, January 20, 2010, http://www.nytimes.
      com/2010/01/20/education/20wired.html.

23   Stephanie Simon, "Public Schools Charge Kids for Basics, Frills,"
      Wall Street Journal, May 25, 2011, http://online.wsj.com/article/
      SB10001424052748703864204576313572363698678.html.

24   Ben H. Bagdikian, *The New Media Monopoly* (Boston: Beacon
      Press, 2004), 20.

25   Peggy Blitz, CEO of the California Dairy Council, quoted in
      Joseph Keon, *Whitewash: The Disturbing Truth about Cow's Milk and
      Your Health* (Gabriola, BC: New Society Publishers, 2010), 12.

26   Keon, *Whitewash*, 12.

27   Simon, "Public Schools Charge Kids for Basics, Frills."

28   David Sapp, "ACLU Sues California over Public School
      Fees for Students," ACLU, September 15, 2010,
      http://www.aclu.org/blog/human-rights-racial-justice/
      aclu-sues-california-over-public-school-fees-students.

29   *Hartzell v. Connell*, 679 P. 2d 35, Cal: Supreme Court 1984.

30   David Nagel, "Teachers Spend $1.3 Billion Out of Pocket
      on Classroom Materials," *The Journal*, July 8, 2010,
      http://thejournal.com/articles/2010/07/08/teachers-spend-
      1.3-billion-out-of-pocket-on-classroom-materials.aspx.

31   "Poverty," US Census Bureau, http://www.census.gov/hhes/
      www/poverty/methods/definitions.html.

32   All three of these examples were accessed at www.donorschoose.
      org in September 2011; however, their posts are no longer
      available for viewing.

33   "What Is Thank-You Punctuality and How Is It
      Calculated?" DonorsChoose.org, http://help.
      donorschoose.org/app/answers/detail/a_id/196/~/
      what-is-thank-you-punctuality-and-how-is-it-calculated%3F.

34   Kayla Webley, "Rick Santorum's Misconceptions on
      Public Education," *Time* Swampland, February 28,
      2012, http://swampland.time.com/2012/02/28/
      rick-santorums-misconceptions-on-public-education/.

35   Ralph Waldo Emerson, *The Complete Works of Ralph Waldo
      Emerson*, vol. 10 (Boston: Houghton Mifflin, 1904), 125.

36   "Music Cues: Adlai Stevenson," NPR, February 5, 2000,
      http://www.npr.org/programs/wesat/000205.stevenson.html.

37   Quoted in Kern Alexander and M. David Alexander, *American
      School Law* (St. Paul, MN: West Publishing, 2005), 59.

38   Komisar, "How the Food Industry Eats Your Kid's Lunch."

39   Teresa Watanabe, "L.A. Schools' Healthful Lunch Menu
      Panned by Students," *Los Angeles Times*, December 17,
      2011, http://articles.latimes.com/2011/dec/17/local/
      la-me-food-lausd-20111218.

40   Daniel Boffey, "Jamie Oliver's Healthy School Dinners Continue
      to Boost Learning, Study Shows," *The Guardian*, April 9,
      2011, http://www.guardian.co.uk/education/2011/apr/10/
      school-dinners-jamie-oliver.

41   Peter Eisler, Blake Morrison, and Anthony DeBarros, "Fast-
      Food Standards for Meat Top Those for School Lunches," *USA
      Today*, December 9, 2009, http://www.usatoday.com/news/
      education/2009-12-08-school-lunch-standards_N.htm.

42   Lindsay Hutton, "What's in That Mystery Meat? School Lunch
      Standards Fall Short," FamilyEducation, http://life.familyeduca-
      tion.com/lunch/school/64977.html#ixzz1k73I5W7Z.

43   National Institute of Building Sciences, "National
      Clearinghouse for Educational Facilities," nibs.org, November
      2011, http://www.nibs.org/client/assets/files/nibs/FactSheets/

NIBS_Factsheet_IRT_NCEF.pdf.

44   Building Educational Success Together (BEST), "PK-12
     Public School Facility Infrastructure Fact Sheet," 21st Century
     School Fund, February 2011, http://www.21csf.org/csf-home/
     Documents/FactSheetPK12PublicSchoolFacilityInfrastructure.
     pdf.

45   Joel Hood, "Old School Buildings Put Pressure on CPS'
     Bottom Line," *Chicago Tribune*, December 25, 2011, http://
     articles.chicagotribune.com/2011-12-25/news/ct-met-cps-facili-
     ties-1225-20111225_1_cps-officials-school-buildings-tim-cawley.

46   Kelly Puente, "Thousands of Public School Buildings Not
     Certified to Withstand Earthquakes," *Daily Breeze*, December 27,
     2011, http://www.dailybreeze.com/news/ci_19628157.

47   See Complete College America, http://www.completecollege.
     org/.

48   Public Agenda, "With Their Whole Lives Ahead of Them:
     Myths and Realities about Why So Many Students Fail to Finish
     College," Public Agenda, http://www.publicagenda.org/files/
     pdf/theirwholelivesaheadofthem.pdf.

49   Sara Lenz, "Current Generation May Be First in U.S. History
     Less Educated Than Its Predecessors," *Deseret News*, February
     12, 2011, http://www.deseretnews.com/article/700109556/
     Current-generation-may-be-first-in-US-history-less-educated-
     than-its-predecessors.html; "Governors Who Get It,"
     Complete College America, September 2011, http://www.
     completecollege.org/docs/Time_Is_the_Enemy_Summary.
     pdf; "Educational Attainment by Degree-Level and Age- Group
     (American Community Survey)," NCHEMS Information Center,
     http://www.higheredinfo.org/dbrowser/?level=nation&mode=
     data&state=0&submeasure=240.

50   "A Family Affair: Intergenerational Social Mobility Across OECD
     Countries," Economic Policy Reforms, 2010, http://www.oecd.
     org/dataoecd/2/7/45002641.pdf.

51   Public Agenda, "With Their Whole Lives Ahead of Them."

52   Ibid.

53   Ibid.

54   Ibid.

55   Karen W. Arenson, "Senate Looking at Endowments as Tuition Rises," *New York Times*, January 25, 2008, http://www.nytimes.com/2008/01/25/education/25endowments.html.

56   "Survey: College Admissions Favor the Wealthy," MSN Money, September 23, 2011, http://money.msn.com/saving-money-tips/post.aspx?post=bf17a804-df7a-4064-8a94-40c6a861d244.

57   Annalyn Censky, "How the Middle Class Became the Underclass," CNN Money, February 16, 2011, http://money.cnn.com/2011/02/16/news/economy/middle_class/index.htm.

58   Valley Should Support Online Textbook Movement," *Mercury News*, December 12, 2011, http://www.mercurynews.com/editorials/ci_19533735.

59   Public Agenda, "With Their Whole Lives Ahead of Them."

60   See the Twenty Million Minds Foundation, http://www.20mm.org/.

61   "Online Textbooks Could Work for California," *Los Angeles Times*, January 9, 2012, http://articles.latimes.com/2012/jan/09/opinion/la-ed-textbook-20120109.

62   Annalyn Censky, "Surging College Costs Price Out Middle Class," CNN Money, June 13, 2011, http://money.cnn.com/2011/06/13/news/economy/college_tuition_middle_class/index.htm.

63   Ibid.

64   For example, Chris Taylor, "Is College Worth It?" Reuters Money, September 15, 2011, http://blogs.reuters.com/reuters-money/2011/09/15/is-college-worth-it/; "Is College Worth It?" Pew Research Center, May 15, 2011, http://www.pewsocialtrends.org/2011/05/15/is-college-worth-it/; "Is College Worth It?" *Time*, http://www.time.com/time/interactive/0,31813,2072670,00.html.

65   Nicholas D. Kristof, "The Boys Have Fallen Behind," *New York Times*, March 27, 2010, http://www.nytimes.com/2010/03/28/opinion/28kristof.html.

66   Peg Tyre, *The Trouble with Boys: A Surprising Report Card on Our Sons, Their Problems at School, and What Parents and Educators Must*

Do (New York: Crown Publishers, 2008).

67 Casey Grove and Kyle Hopkins, "Year in Jail Possible for Mom Guilty of Hot Sauce Punishment," *Anchorage Daily News*, August 24, 2011, http://www.adn.com/2011/08/23/2028617/mom-guilty-of-abuse-year-in-jail.html.

68 Tyre, *The Trouble with Boys*.

69 Ibid.

70 Ibid.

71 Kristof, "The Boys Have Fallen Behind."

72 Tyre, *The Trouble with Boys*.

73 Duff Wilson, "Child's Ordeal Shows Risks of Psychosis Drugs for Young," *New York Times*, September 1, 2010, http://www.nytimes.com/2010/09/02/business/02kids.html.

74 Kelly King Heyworth, "Preschoolers on Meds: Too Much Too Soon?" CNN Health, September 21, 2011, http://www.cnn.com/2011/09/21/health/living-well/preschoolers-on-meds/index.html?hpt=he_c1.

75 Tyre, *The Trouble with Boys*.

76 Leonard Sax, "The Boy Problem: Many Boys Think School Is Stupid and Reading Stinks," *School Library Journal*, September 1, 2007, http://www.schoollibraryjournal.com/article/CA6472910.html.

77 Funny, the word "coed" applies to college women only, a throwback to the days when they were so few and far between that their mere presence on campus rendered a previously men's school "coeducational." Are we reaching the point when men will become the new rare birds in higher education, when they will be the real "coeds"?

78 Dan Abrams, *Man Down: Proof beyond a Reasonable Doubt That Women Are Better Cops, Drivers, Gamblers, Spies, World Leaders, Beer Tasters, Hedge Fund Managers, and Just About Everything Else* (New York: Abrams Image, 2011), Kindle location 650.

79 It's quaint that they're still called "bachelor's degrees," isn't it? Mary Beth Marklein, "College Gender Gap Remains Stable: 57% Women," *USA Today*, January 26, 2010, http://www.usatoday.com/news/education/2010-01-26-genderequity26_ST_N.htm.

80 Abrams, *Man Down*, Kindle location 636.

81 "At present, 33 percent of women between twenty-five and twenty-nine years of age hold a four-year degree compared to 26 percent of men." Tyre, *The Trouble with Boys*, 32.

82 Hanna Rosin, "The End of Men," *The Atlantic*, July/August 2010, http://www.theatlantic.com/magazine/archive/2010/07/the-end-of-men/8135/2/.

83 National Endowment for the Arts, "To Read or Not to Read: A Question of National Consequence," November 2007, http://www.nea.gov/research/toread.pdf.

84 Tyre, *The Trouble with Boys*.

85 Liz Bowie, "Boys Lag Behind Girls in Reading in Every State," *Baltimore Sun*, March 17, 2010, http://weblogs.baltimoresun.com/news/education/blog/2010/03/boys_lag_behind_girls_in_readi.html.

86 Sax, "The Boy Problem."

87 Mark Bauerlein and Sandra Stotsky, "Why Johnny Won't Read," *Washington Post*, January 25, 2005, http://www.washingtonpost.com/wp-dyn/articles/A33956-2005Jan24.html.

88 Sax, "The Boy Problem."

89 "Girls and Boys—The Gender Reading Gap," The Literacy Company, http://www.readfaster.com/articles/the-gender-reading-gap.asp.

90 Eric Weiner, "Why Women Read More Than Men," NPR, September 5, 2007, http://www.npr.org/templates/story/story.php?storyId=14175229.

91 Margot Magowan, "Girls Gone Missing: Kids' Movie Posters in 2011," Reel Girl, July 7, 2011, http://margotmagowan.wordpress.com/2011/07/07/heres-a-visual/.

92 Not his real name.

93 Yes, we do.

94 America's Promise Alliance, "Building a Grad Nation: Progress and Challenge in Ending the High School Dropout Epidemic," November 2010, 16, http://www.americaspromise.org/our-work/grad-nation/building-a-grad-nation.aspx.

95 Robert W. Sweet Jr., "Illiteracy: An Incurable Disease or

Education Malpractice?" The National Right to Read
Foundation, http://www.nrrf.org/essay_Illiteracy.html.

96   Trip Gabriel, "Proficiency of Black Students Is Found
to Be Far Lower Than Expected," *New York Times*,
November 9, 2010, http://www.nytimes.com/2010/11/09/
education/09gap.html.

97   "Black Student College Graduation Rates Inch Higher but a
Large Racial Gap Persists," *Journal of Blacks in Higher Education*,
http://www.jbhe.com/preview/winter07preview.html.

98   Carla Rivera, "Minority Men Falling Behind Academically,
Study Finds," *Los Angeles Times*, June 21, 2011,
http://www.latimes.com/news/nationworld/nation/
la-na-education-men-20110621,0,5809820.story.

99   "More Black, Latinos in Jail Than College Dorms,"
MSNBC, September 27, 2007, http://www.msnbc.
msn.com/id/21001543/ns/us_news-life/t/
more-blacks-latinos-jail-college-dorms/.

100   Erik Eckholm, "Plight Deepens for Black Men, Studies
Warn," *New York Times*, March 20, 2006, http://www.nytimes.
com/2006/03/20/national/20blackmen.html.

101   Analysis of 2000 census data by Steven Raphael of the University
of California, Berkeley, found in Ibid.

102   Michael Barbaro and Fernanda Santos, "Bloomberg to Use Own
Funds in Plan to Aid Minority Youth," *New York Times*, August 3,
2011, http://www.nytimes.com/2011/08/04/nyregion/
new-york-plan-will-aim-to-lift-minority-youth.html.

103   Ibid.

104   Alliance for Excellent Education, "Facts about Kids
and Reading," Global Literacy Campaign,
http://www.scholastic.com/readeveryday/facts.htm.

105   Sam Dillon, "U.S. Students Remain Poor at History, Tests
Show," *New York Times*, June 14, 2011, http://www.nytimes.
com/2011/06/15/education/15history.html.

106   National Assessment of Educational Progress (NAEP),
"National Report Card," National Center for Education
Statistics, http://nces.ed.gov/nationsreportcard/itmrlsx/detail.

aspx?subject=history.

107 Dillon, "U.S. Students Remain Poor at History, Tests Show."

108 James Curran, Shanto Iyengar, Anker Brink Lund, and Inka Salovaara-Morin, "Media System, Public Knowledge and Democracy: A Comparative Study," *European Journal of Communication* 24, no. 5 (March 2000): 5–26, 14, http://eucenter.wisc.edu/Media%20System.pdf.

109 "Public's Priorities for 2010: Economy, Jobs, Terrorism," Pew Research Center, January 25, 2010, http://people-press.org/report/584/policy-priorities-2010.

110 Holly J, "Where Is the National Concern about the Literacy Gender Gap?" Getting Boys to Read, http://www.gettingboystoread.com/content/where-national-concern-about-literacy-gender-gap.

111 "LA Times: Splinter Catholic Group Says Galileo Really Was Wrong—The Earth Is at the Center of the Universe," http://bridgetotomorrow.wordpress.com/2011/08/30/la-times-splinter-catholic-group-says-galileo-really-was-wrong-the-earth-is-at-the-center-of-the-universe/.

112 Andrew Zak Williams, "Rick Perry's True ID: Creationism in the Classroom," *The Guardian*, August 23, 2011, http://www.guardian.co.uk/commentisfree/cifamerica/2011/aug/23/rick-perry-creationism-classroom.

113 Eugenia, "How Do Americans Feel about U.S. Foreign Aid and the Millennium Development Goals?" GlobalWA, August 19, 2010, http://globalwa.org/2010/08/how-do-americans-feel-about-u-s-foreign-aid-and-the-millennium-development-goals/.

114 Haya El Nasser, "World Population Hits 7 Billion," *USA Today*, October 31, 2011, http://www.usatoday.com/news/world/story/2011-10-30/world-population-hits-seven-billion/51007670/1.

115 Thomas Friedman, *Hot, Flat, and Crowded: Why We Need a Green Revolution—And How It Can Renew America* (New York: Picador, 2009), 15.

116 Ibid.

117 "Yemen, Population and Failing States," Population

Institute, http://blog.populationinstitute.org/2009/12/30/
yemen-population-and-failing-states/.

118 Alex Thurston, "Nigeria's Terrorism Problem," *Foreign
     Policy*, August 26, 2011, http://www.foreignpolicy.com/
     articles/2011/08/26/nigerias_terrorism_problem?page=0,1.

119 "Yemen, Population and Failing States," Population Institute.

120 Friedman, *Hot, Flat and Crowded*, 11.

121 Mark John, "Horn of Africa Shows Family Planning Need:
     UN," Reuters, August 2, 2011, http://www.reuters.com/arti-
     cle/2011/08/02/us-africa-family-un-idUSTRE7713UB20110802;
     Justin Gillis and Celia W. Dugger, "U.N. Forecasts 10.1 Billion
     People by Century's End," *New York Times*, May 3, 2011, http://
     www.nytimes.com/2011/05/04/world/04population.html.

122 Guttmacher Institute, "Adding It Up: The Costs and Benefits
     of Investing in Family Planning and Maternal and Newborn
     Health," UNFPA, http://www.unfpa.org/webdav/site/global/
     shared/documents/publications/2009/adding_it_up_report.pdf.

123 Every Democratic president since has rescinded the Global Gag
     rule; every Republican president has reinstated it. "Global Gag
     Rule," Population Action International, http://populationac-
     tion.org/topics/global-gag-rule/.

124 The Obama Administration reinstated the funding in 2009. As
     this book went to press, Congress was once again considering
     cutting it.

125 "World Population," Wikipedia, http://en.wikipedia.org/wiki/
     World_population.

126 Guttmacher Institute, "Adding It Up."

127 SAMSHA News Release, "The Costs of Alcohol and Drug
     Treatment," About.com, December 31, 2008, http://alcoholism.
     about.com/od/pro/a/blsam040527.htm.

128 "How Much Does It Cost to Incarcerate an Inmate?" Legislative
     Analyst's Office, http://www.lao.ca.gov/laoapp/laomenus/
     sections/crim_justice/6_cj_inmatecost.aspx?catid=3.

129 "Income Gap Between Rich, Poor the Widest Ever," CBS News,
     September 28, 2010, http://www.cbsnews.com/2100-201_162-
     6907321.html.

130   Between 1992 and 2007 the four hundred wealthiest Americans
      saw their incomes increase by 392 percent, while their
      tax rates plummeted by 37 percent over the same period.
      Michael Kerr, "Depression in a Recession: Unemployment,
      Wealth Inequality and Suicide," Hive Health Media,
      December 31, 2011, http://www.hivehealthmedia.com/
      depression-recession-unemployment-wealth-inequality-suicide/.

131   Sabrina Tavernise, "Middle-Class Areas Shrink as Income
      Gap Grows, New Report Finds," *New York Times*, November 15,
      2011, http://www.nytimes.com/2011/11/16/us/
      middle-class-areas-shrink-as-income-gap-grows-report-finds.html.

132   Lauren Etter, "Roads to Ruin: Towns Rip Up the Pavement,"
      Wall Street Journal, July 17, 2010, http://online.wsj.com/article/
      SB10001424052748704913304575370950363737746.html.

133   Monica Davey, "Darker Night as Some Cities Turn Off
      the Lights," *New York Times*, December 29, 2011,
      http://www.nytimes.com/2011/12/30/us/
      cities-cost-cuttings-leave-residents-in-the-dark.
      html?pagewanted=1&_r=1&sq=street%20lights&st=cse&scp=1.

134   Jim Carlton, "California Puts Brake on Parks," *Wall Street Journal*,
      June 17, 2011, http://online.wsj.com/article/SB1000142405270
      2304665904576383920255484738.html.

135   Kate Abbey-Lambertz, "Detroit Libraries Closing: Protesters
      Sate Sin-in at Lincoln Branch," *Huffington Post*, December
      21, 2011, http://www.huffingtonpost.com/2011/12/22/
      detroit-libraries-closing-shutdown-occupy-detroit-lincoln-
      monteith_n_1166382.html.

136   Ibid.

137   "12 Libraries Closing, 148 People Laid Off," Fox Charlotte,
      March 18, 2010, http://www.foxcharlotte.com/news/
      top-stories/88458092.html.

138   Lance Hernandez, "Denver Library Proposes Closing 7 to 12
      Branches," 7News, April 21, 2011, http://www.thedenverchan-
      nel.com/news/27624710/detail.html.

139   "Indiana Libraries Closing Doors, Cutting Hours," WishTV8,
      November 5, 2011, http://www.wishtv.com/dpp/news/indiana/

indiana-libraries-closing-doors-cutting-hours.

140 Megan Scudellari, "Library Cuts Threaten Research," *The Scientist*, September 28, 2010, http://classic.the-scientist.com/news/display/57728/.

141 See America's Infrastructure, http://www.infrastructurereport-card.org/.

142 Tom Vanderbilt, "Stop This Train!" *Slate*, May 15, 2009, http://www.slate.com/articles/life/transport/2009/05/stop_this_train.html.

143 Tavernise, "Middle-Class Areas Shrink as Income Gap Grows, New Report Finds."

144 G. William Domhoff, "Wealth, Income, and Power," Who Rules America?, November 2011, http://www2.ucsc.edu/whorulesamerica/power/wealth.html.

145 While Wall Street profits were busy jumping 720 percent between 2007 and 2009, the unemployment rate was climbing, rising 102 percent during the same period.

146 "U.S. 'Misery Index' Rises to Highest Level in Almost Three Decades," *Huffington Post*, October 19, 2011, http://www.huffingtonpost.com/2011/10/19/mistery-index-2011_n_1020765.html.

147 Robert Johnson, "A Gut Wrenching Look Inside Lakewood New Jersey's Homeless 'Tent City,'" *Business Insider*, January 1, 2012, http://www.businessinsider.com/robert-johnson-lakewood-new-jersey-tent-city-2011-12.

148 Kerr, "Depression in a Recession."

149 The Pew Charitable Trusts, "Ups and Downs: Americans' Prospects for Recovery after an Income Loss," Economic Mobility Project, January 2012, http://www.economicmobility.org/assets/pdfs/EMP_Ups_and_Downs_FactSheet.pdf, p. 2.

150 Amy Bingham, "As Americans Get Poorer, Members of Congress Get Richer," ABC News, December 27, 2011, http://abcnews.go.com/blogs/politics/2011/12/as-americans-get-poorer-members-of-congress-get-richer/.

151 David Frum, "Stiglitz and Hayek, Strange Bedfellows," FrumForum, January 2, 2012, http://www.frumforum.com/

stiglitz-and-hayek-strange-bedfellows.

152   Ben Woolsey and Matt Schulz, "Credit Card Statistics, Industry Facts, Debt Statistics," CreditCards.com, http://www.creditcards. com/credit-card-news/credit-card-industry-facts-personal-debt-statistics-1276.php#footnote1.

153   EcoHealth Alliance, "National Survey on Pandemic Awareness and Attitudes," EcoHealthAlliance.org, http://www.ecohealthalliance.org/sup/downloads/ EcoHealth%20Alliance%20Survey.pdf.

154   Tom Pauken, "Men Are Biggest Loser in U.S. Economic Downturn," *American Spectator*, March 7, 2011, http://spectator. org/archives/2011/03/07/men-are-biggest-losers-in-us-e#.

155   Twitter: @SenatorSanders.

156   Louis Uchitelle, "When Factories Vanish, So Can Innovators," *New York Times*, February 12, 2011, http://www.nytimes. com/2011/02/13/business/13every.html.

157   Ibid.

158   Rosin, "The End of Men."

159   "Employment and Unemployment among Youth Summary," Bureau of Labor Statistics, August 24, 2011, http://bls.gov/ news.release/youth.nr0.htm.

160   Rosin, "The End of Men."

161   Ibid.

162   Pauken, "Men Are Biggest Losers in U.S. Economic Downturn."

163   Dennis Cauchon, "More Americans Leaving the Workforce," *USA Today*, April 15, 2011, http://www.usatoday.com/money/ economy/employment/2011-04-13-more-americans-leave-labor-force.htm.

164   John Ydstie, "Why Some Men Earn Less Than They Did 40 Years Ago," NPR, September 17, 2011, http://www.npr.org/2011/09/17/140554967/ median-male-workers-income-lower-than-in-1973.

165   "Recession Hitting Men Harder Than Women," *Kansas City Star*, November 20, 2010, http://www.kansascity. com/2010/11/20/2456352/recession-hitting-men-harder-than. html.

166 Richard Galpin, "Spotlight on Indonesian 'Sweat Shops,'"
BBC News, March 7, 2002, http://news.bbc.co.uk/2/hi/
asia-pacific/1860217.stm.

167 "Youth Unemployment in United States in Line with Arab
Spring Countries," Rortybomb, November 14, 2011,
http://rortybomb.wordpress.com/2011/11/14/youth-unem-
ployment-in-united-states-in-line-with-arab-spring-countries/.

168 Names of Giuseppe and other boys interviewed for this book
have been changed.

169 Bagdikian, *The New Media Monopoly*, 27–28.

170 Brooke Donald, "Facebook Aims to Help Prevent
Suicide," *USA Today*, December 13, 2011, http://
www.usatoday.com/tech/news/story/2011-12-13/
facebook-suicide-prevention/51867032/1.

171 "Wired Kids, Negligent Parents?" *New York Times*, January 28,
2010, http://roomfordebate.blogs.nytimes.com/2010/01/28/
wired-kids-negligent-parents/.

172 Charis E. Kubrin, "Gangstas, Thugs, and Hustlas: Identity and
the Code of the Street in Rap Music," *Social Problems* 52, no. 3
(2005): 360–78, 369, http://www.gwu.edu/~soc/docs/Kubrin_
gangstas.pdf.

173 David Luhrssen, "Crips and Bloods," *Express Milwaukee*, May 14,
2009, http://www.expressmilwaukee.com/blog-3664-crips-and-
bloods.html.

174 Of course, there are artists preaching nonviolence, such as the
Black Eyed Peas, who have even weighed in against this very
gang, with lyrics such as, "What's wrong with the world Mama,
people living like they ain't got no Mamas…. We still
got terrorists here living in the USA, the big CIA, the Bloods
and the Crips and the KKK" ("Where is the Love?").

175 Kubrin, "Gangstas, Thugs, and Hustlas," 369.

176 Cynthia Tucker, "Thug Culture Celebrates the Worst of
Its Behavior," *Appeal Democrat*, May 3, 2008, http://www.
appeal-democrat.com/articles/culture-63509-thug-american.
html#ixzz1hl122MgI.

177 Michael P. Jeffries, *Thug Life: Race, Gender and the Meaning of*

Hip-Hop (Chicago: University of Chicago, 2011),
Kindle location 1884.

178 Malcolm MacMillan, "Top 10: Murdered Rappers," Ask Men,
http://www.askmen.com/top_10/celebrity/
top-10-murdered-rappers_3.html.

179 Laura MacInnis, "U.S. Most Armed Country with
90 Guns Per 100 People," Reuters, August 28, 2007,
http://www.reuters.com/article/2007/08/28/
us-world-firearms-idUSL2834893820070828.

180 "Gun Violence Statistics," Legal Community Against Violence,
http://www.lcav.org/statistics-polling/gun_violence_statistics.
asp.

181 "Section I: Gun Violence in the United States," Office of
Juvenile Justice and Delinquency Prevention, http://www.ojjdp.
gov/pubs/gun_violence/sect01.html.

182 Casey McNerthney, "For Teens, Illegal Guns East to Gen on
Streets," Seattle pi, September 1, 2008, http://www.seattlepi.
com/local/article/For-teens-illegal-guns-easy-to-get-on-
streets-1283875.php#page-1.

183 Kubrin, "Gangstas, Thugs, and Hustlas," 372.

184 "Literacy Issues," Reading Is Fundamental, http://www.rif.org/
us/about/literacy-issues.htm.

185 John L. Mitchell, "Easy Access to Guns Fuels Epidemic of Youth
Violence: Firearms: L.A. Teenagers, Seeking Protection or
Status, Steal Weapons from Home or Buy Them Easily on the
Streets," *Los Angeles Times*, March 29, 1993, http://articles.lat-
imes.com/1993-03-29/news/mn-16520_1_easy-access.

186 To read more, see Jay-Z, "Niggas in Paris," Metrolyrics,
http://www.metrolyrics.com/niggas-in-paris-lyrics-jayz.
html#ixzz1hmk9csHs.

187 Elton John, "Eminem," *Rolling Stone*, http://www.rollingstone.
com/music/lists/100-greatest-artists-of-all-time-19691231/
eminem-19691231.

188 "'Jersey Shore' Vinny Guadagnino Raps about Rape,
Pulls Down Song," *Huffington Post*, November 30,
2011, http://www.huffingtonpost.com/2011/11/30/

jersey-shore-vinny-guadag_n_1121574.html.

189   Zack O'Malley Greenburg, "Jay-Z's $50 Million Music
      Box," *Forbes*, September 22, 2010, http://www.forbes.
      com/sites/zackomalleygreenburg/2010/09/22/
      jay-zs-50-million-music-box/.

190   Jeff Rosenthal, "Jay-Z Reopens 40/40 Club with
      Star-Studded Bash," *Rolling Stone*, January 19,
      2012, http://www.rollingstone.com/music/news/
      jay-z-reopens-40-40-club-with-star-studded-bash-20120119.

191   DMX, "X Is Coming," Lyrics Freak, http://www.lyricsfreak.
      com/d/dmx/x+is+coming_20041248.html.

192   "Report: FBI Hate Crime Statistics Vastly Understate
      Problem," Southern Poverty Law Center, Winter 2005,
      http://www.splcenter.org/get-informed/intelligence-report/
      browse-all-issues/2005/winter/hate-crime.

193   Natalie DiBlasio, "Crimes against LGBT Community Are Up,
      Despite Social Gains," *USA Today*, August 1, 2011, http://www.
      usatoday.com/news/nation/2011-07-31-LGBT-violence-lesbian-
      gay-transgender-bisexual-survey_n.htm.

194   David Derbyshire, "How Rap Music Has Gone from
      Condemning Drug Use to Glorifying It," *Mail* Online, April
      2, 2008, http://www.dailymail.co.uk/news/article-553209/
      How-rap-music-gone-condemning-drug-use-glorifying-it.
      html#ixzz1khxwTH9K. Now a full 69 percent of songs in these
      genres contain positive references to drug use.

195   Wiz Khalifa, "Young, Wild & Free," Metrolyrics, http://
      www.metrolyrics.com/young-wild-free-lyrics-wiz-khalifa.
      html#ixzz1hmltM7p1.

196   Lynette Holloway, "Media; Hip0Hop Sales Pop: Pass the
      Courvoisier and Count the Cash," *New York Times*, September
      2, 2002, http://www.nytimes.com/2002/09/02/business/
      media-hip-hop-sales-pop-pass-the-courvoisier-and-count-the-cash.
      html?pagewanted=all&src=pm.

197   Rea Blakey, "Study Links TV Viewing among Kids
      to Later Violence," CNN Health, March 28, 2002,
      http://articles.cnn.com/2002-03-28/health/kids.

tv.violence_1_effects-of-tv-violence-violent-television-study-links-
tv?_s=PM:HEALTH.

198 Joseph White, "Gilbert Arenas, Javaris Crittenton Drew Guns
     on Each Other over Gambling Debt: Report," *Huffington Post,*
     January 1, 2010, http://www.huffingtonpost.com/2010/01/01/
     arenas-crittenton-guns-ga_n_408978.html.

199 Yossi Feins, "1. Javaris Crittenton with Murder," Bleacher
     Report, December 21, 2011, http://bleacherreport.com/
     articles/992236-2011s-top-5-most-notorious-off-field-incidents/
     page/7.

200 Anna Holmes, "The Disposable Woman," *New York Times,*
     March 3, 2011, http://www.nytimes.com/2011/03/04/
     opinion/04holmes.html?pagewanted=all.

201 Annie Yuan, "Charlie Sheen Tour Sells Out in 18 Minutes,"
     Hollywood Reporter, March 13, 2011, http://www.hollywoodre-
     porter.com/news/charlie-sheen-tour-sells-18-167156.

202 "Kevin Federline," *People,* http://www.people.com/people/
     kevin_federline/0,,,00.html.

203 "Exclusive: Wife Claims Evander Holyfield Hit Her, Files for
     Protective Order," Radar Online, http://www.radaronline.com/
     exclusives/2010/02/exclusive-wife-claims-evander-holyfield-hit-
     her-files-protective-order.

204 Mark Z. Barabak and Victoria Kim, "Schwarzenegger Fathered
     a Child with Longtime Member of Household Staff," *New York
     Times,* May 17, 2011, http://www.latimes.com/news/nation-
     world/nation/la-me-0517-arnold-20110517,0,312678.story.

205 Albert R. Hunt, "A Country of Inmates," *New York Times,*
     November 20, 2011, http://www.nytimes.com/2011/11/21/
     us/21iht-letter21.html?pagewanted=all.

206 "Impact of Music, Music Lyrics, and Music Videos on Children
     and Youth," American Academy of Pediatrics Policy, November
     2009, http://aappolicy.aappublications.org/cgi/content/full/
     pediatrics;124/5/1488.

207 Ibid.

208 "Recruit Yuri Wright Expelled for Tweets,"
     ESPN, January 20, 2012, http://espn.go.com/

college-sports/recruiting/football/story/_/id/7484495/
yuri-wright-twitter-posts-cost-college-scholarship.

209 Michelle Alexander, *The New Jim Crow: Mass Incarceration in the
Age of Colorblindness* (New York: The New Press, 2010), 49.

210 Ibid.

211 Ibid., 52.

212 Ibid., 55.

213 Sarah N. Lynch, "An American Pastime: Smoking Pot,"
Time, July 11, 2008, http://www.time.com/time/health/
article/0,8599,1821697,00.html.

214 Alexander, *The New Jim Crow*, 59.

215 John Hoeffel, "U.S. Decrees That Marijuana Has No Accepted
Medical Use," *Los Angeles Times*, July 9, 2011, http://articles.
latimes.com/2011/jul/09/local/la-me-marijuana-20110709.

216 Alexander, *The New Jim Crow*, 59.

217 "Juvenile Detention," Child Trends Data Bank,
http://www.childtrendsdatabank.org/?q=node/380.

218 Alexander, *The New Jim Crow*, 291.

219 Dorothy E. Roberts, "The Social and Moral Cost of Mass
Incarceration in African American Communities," *Stanford Law
Review* 56, pt. 5 (2003–2004): 1271–1306, 1277.

220 Alexander, *The New Jim Crow*, 86.

221 Justice Policy Institute, Rebecca Ruiz, "Eyes on the Prize,"
American Prospect (January–February 2011): A3.

222 Jill Kathleen Doerner, "Explaining the Gender Gap in
Sentencing Outcomes: An Investigation of Differential
Treatment in U.S. Federal Courts," PhD Dissertation, Graduate
College of Bowling Green, May 2009, http://etd.ohiolink.edu/
view.cgi/Doerner%20Jill.pdf?bgsu1237482038.

223 Ibid.

224 S. Fernando Rodriguez, Theodore R. Curry, and Gang Lee,
"Gender Differences in Criminal Sentencing: Do Effects Vary
across Violent, Property, and Drug Offenses?" *Social Science
Quarterly* 87, no. 2 (June 2006): 318–39, http://digitalcommons.
utep.edu/cgi/viewcontent.cgi?article=1001&context=gang_lee.

225 Jamie Fellner, "Race, Drugs, and Law Enforcement in the

United States," Human Rights Watch, June 19, 2009,
http://www.hrw.org/news/2009/06/19/
race-drugs-and-law-enforcement-united-states.

226   "Targeting Blacks: VI. Origins of Racial Disparities in Prison
       Admissions for Drug Offenses," Human Rights Watch, May 5,
       2008, http://www.hrw.org/node/62236/section/8.

227   Jeannine Stein, "Miley Cyrus Quips about Marijuana: What
       Are Pot's Health Effects?" *Los Angeles Times*, November 28,
       2011, http://articles.latimes.com/2011/nov/28/news/
       la-heb-miley-cyrus-marijuana-health-20111128.

228   Alan Duke, "Lindsay Lohan Gets Jail Time for Probation
       Violations," CNN Entertainment, November 2, 2011,
       http://articles.cnn.com/2011-11-02/entertainment/
       showbiz_lohan-probation-hearing_1_necklace-theft-judge-steph-
       anie-sautner-probation?_s=PM:SHOWBIZ.

229   "Johnny Jolly Get Six-Year Prison Term," ESPN, November
       17, 2011, http://espn.go.com/nfl/story/_/id/7246845/
       green-bay-packers-johnny-jolly-sentenced-6-years-prison.

230   "Targeting Blacks: VI. Origins of Racial Disparities in Prison
       Admissions for Drug Offenses," Human Rights Watch.

231   Alexander, *The New Jim Crow*, 96.

232   Ibid., 115.

233   Ibid., 86.

234   Dorothy E. Roberts, "The Social and Moral Costs of Mass
       Incarceration in African American Communities," *Stanford Law
       Review* 56 (April 2004): 1271–1305, http://blogs.law.columbia.
       edu/4cs/files/2008/11/dorothy20roberts20-20social20and-
       20moral20cost20of20mass20incarceration.pdf, p. 1277.

235   Ibid.

236   Bruce Western and Becky Pettit, "Incarceration & Social
       Inequality," *Dædalus* (Summer 2010): 8–19, 16, http://
       www.mitpressjournals.org/doi/pdf/10.1162/DAED_a_00019.

237   Alexander, *The New Jim Crow*, 139.

238   Ibid., 118.

239   "No Second Chance: Summary," Human Rights Watch, http://
       www.hrw.org/node/11892/section/2.

240 Ibid.

241 Alexander, *The New Jim Crow*, 291.

242 W. D. Johnson, "The Advantages of Hiring Ex-Cons," eHow.com, April 20, 2011, http://www.ehow.com/ info_8261375_advantages-hiring-excons.html.

243 Alexander, *The New Jim Crow*, 151.

244 Roberts, "The Social and Moral Costs of Mass Incarceration in African American Communities"; Hunt, "A Country of Inmates."

245 "No Second Chance: Summary," Human Rights Watch.

246 Hunt, "A Country of Inmates."

247 "Humility Quotes," Finest Quotes.com, http://www.finestquotes.com/select_quote-category-Humility-page-1. htm#ixzz1iQCpAM9P.

248 Ibid.

249 David Brooks, "The Modesty Manifesto," *New York Times*, March 10, 2011, http://www.nytimes.com/2011/03/11/ opinion/11brooks.html.

250 "Humility Quotes," Finest Quotes.

251 A lovely, notable exception: Garrison Keillor, whose homespun and wise books and radio shows routinely extol humility and bring arrogant SOBs down to size.

252 Brooks, "The Modesty Manifesto."

253 Me included, to some extent: Twitter: Twitter.com@LisaBloom; Facebook: Facebook.com/pages/Lisa-Bloom.

254 Katherine St. Asaph, "Trend Timeline: The Decade in Swagger and Mick Jagger," Pop Dust, July 7, 2011, http://popdust.com/2011/07/07/ swagger-mick-jagger-kesha-black-eyed-peas-jonas-brothers/.

255 Brooks, "The Modesty Manifesto."

256 Po Bronson and Ashley Merryman, *NurtureShock: New Thinking about Children* (New York: Twelve, 2009), 12.

257 Mary Bruce, "China Debuts at Top of International Education Rankings," ABC News, December 7, 2010, http://abcnews. go.com/Politics/china-debuts-top-international-education-rankings/story?id=12336108#.T0z-SfEgf5Y.

258   Brooks, "The Modesty Manifesto."

259   Robert Preidt, "Confidence Helps Boost Teenage
       Girls' Math Skills," ABC News, January 12, 2010,
       http://abcnews.go.com/Health/Healthday/
       confidence-helps-boost-teenage-girls-math-skills/
       story?id=9534390.

260   "International Men of Immodesty," *Medical News Today*, April 20,
       2009, http://www.medicalnewstoday.com/releases/146698.php.

261   "Do Toddlers Pick Up Gender Roles During Play?" PhysOrg,
       June 10, 2010, http://www.physorg.com/news195389420.html.

262   Susan Donaldson James, "Baby Storm Raised Genderless
       Is Bad Experiment, Say Experts," ABC News, May 26,
       2011, http://abcnews.go.com/Health/baby-storm-
       raised-genderless-gender-dangerous-experiment-child/
       story?id=13693760.

263   "Male Modesty Not Appreciated by Female or Male Interviewers,
       Study Suggests," *ScienceDaily*, July 29, 2010, http://www.science-
       daily.com/releases/2010/07/100729122330.htm.

264   Joe Loya, http://www.joeloya.com/.

265   "Overconfident Students Score Lower in Math, UB Researcher
       Says," University at Buffalo, December 28, 2010, http://www.
       buffalo.edu/news/12126.

266   Bronson and Merryman, *NurtureShock*, 10.

267   Stephanie Rosenbloom, "Ambition + Desire = Trouble," *New York
       Times*, June 17, 2011, http://www.nytimes.com/2011/06/19/
       fashion/scholars-discuss-weiners-behavior.html?src=recg.

268   Andy Green, "The 7 Most Horrifying 'Jackass' Injuries," MTV,
       http://clutch.mtv.com/2011/05/24/worst-jackass-injuries/.

269   Steve Jefferson, "TV Show Blamed for Anderson Death," WTHR,
       December 17, 2009, http://www.wthr.com/story/1052153/tv-
       show-blamed-for-anderson-death?clienttype=printable
       (death of thirteen-year-old boy); Harold Kruger, "Driver Free
       in Marysville Stunt Death," *Appeal Democrat*, June 2, 2005,
       http://www.appeal-democrat.com/news/king-15310-mcgrath-
       merry.html (death of a sixteen-year-old girl); "'Jackass' Movie
       Copycat Lands in Hospital," MSNBC, March 8, 2007,

http://www.msnbc.msn.com/id/17515065/ns/us_news-weird_ news/t/jackass-movie-copycat-lands-hospital/ (third-degree burns to hands and genitals); Emily Farache, "Another 'Jackass' Copycat," E Online, April 24, 2001, http://www.eonline.com/ news/another_jackass_copycat/41509 (broken leg).

270 "Ryan Dunn," Wikipedia, http://en.wikipedia.org/wiki/ Ryan_Dunn.

271 "Roger Ebert's Ryan Dunn Death 'Jackass' Tweet Provokes Criticism, Debate," *Huffington Post*, June 20, 2011, http://www. huffingtonpost.com/2011/06/20/roger-eberts-ryan-dunn-death-jackass_n_880950.html#s295271&title=SteveO.

272 "Are Men Better Drivers Than Women?" insurance.com, January 9, 2009, http://www.insurance.com/auto-insurance/safety/ are-men-better-drivers-than-women.aspx.

273 Seth Borenstein, "Women Drivers? They're Safer than Men," MSNBC, January 20, 2007, http://www.msnbc.msn. com/id/16698153/ns/technology_and_science-science/t/ women-drivers-theyre-safer-men/.

274 Jeff Sommer, "How Men's Overconfidence Hurts Them as Investors," *New York Times*, March 13, 2010, http://www.nytimes. com/2010/03/14/business/14mark.html.

275 Ibid.

276 Robert Sanders, "Girls' and Boys' Math Performance Now Equal," *UC Berkeley News*, July 24, 2008, http://berkeley.edu/ news/media/releases/2008/07/24_math.shtml.

277 Bronson and Merryman, *NurtureShock*, 10–27.

278 David Brooks, "The Wrong Inequality," *New York Times*, October 31, 2011, http://www.nytimes.com/2011/11/01/opinion/ brooks-the-wrong-incquality.html.

279 "Census Bureau Reports Nearly 6 in 10 Advanced Degree Holders Age 25–29 Are Women," US Census Bureau, April 20, 2010, http://www.census.gov/newsroom/releases/archives/ education/cb10-55.html.

280 Catherine Rampell, "College-Educated Workers Gaining Jobs, High School Grads Losing Them," *New York Times*, January 9, 2012, http://cconomix.blogs.nytimes.com/2012/01/09/

college-educated-workers-gaining-jobs-high-school-grads-losing-them/.

281 Julie Mack, "What's the Value of a College Degree? Turns Out Education Improves Everything from Health to Marriage," MLive, January 23, 2012, http://www.mlive.com/education/index.ssf/2012/01/value_of_higher_education_exte.html.

282 See Complete College America, http://www.completecollege.org/.

283 Dominic Rushe, "Apple Pips Exxon as World's Biggest Company," *The Guardian*, August 9, 2011, http://www.guardian.co.uk/business/2011/aug/09/apple-pips-exxon-as-worlds-biggest-company.

284 Thomas L. Friedman, "Made in the World," *New York Times*, January 28, 2012, http://www.nytimes.com/2012/01/29/opinion/sunday/friedman-made-in-the-world.html?src=recg.

285 Charles Duhigg and David Barboza, "In China, Human Costs Are Built into an iPad," *New York Times*, January 25, 2012, http://www.nytimes.com/2012/01/26/business/ieconomy-apples-ipad-and-the-human-costs-for-workers-in-china.html?src=me&ref=business.

286 Charles Duhigg and Keith Bradsher, "How the U.S. Lost Out on iPhone Work," *New York Times*, January 21, 2012, http://www.nytimes.com/2012/01/22/business/apple-america-and-a-squeezed-middle-class.html?pagewanted=all.

287 Organisation for Economic Co-Operation and Development, "The Knowledge-Based Economy," OECD, 1996, http://www.oecd.org/dataoecd/51/8/1913021.pdf.

288 "What It Costs to Go to College," College Board, http://www.collegeboard.com/student/pay/add-it-up/4494.html.

289 "Aid per Undergraduate Student," CollegeBoard, http://trends.collegeboard.org/student_aid/report_findings/indicator/Aid_Per_Undergraduate_Student.

290 Sara Lipka, "Two-Thirds of Students Get Financial Aid, Federal Report Says," *The Chronicle*, April 14, 2009, http://chronicle.com/article/Two-Thirds-of-Students-Get/42736.

291 Blake Ellis, "Average Student Loan Debt Tops $25,000,"

CNN Money, November 3, 2011, http://money.cnn.
com/2011/11/03/pf/student_loan_debt/index.htm.

292   Complete College America, "Time Is the Enemy: The Surprising
       Truth about Why Today's College Students Aren't Graduating…
       And What Needs to Change," Complete College, September
       2011, http://www.completecollege.org/docs/Time_Is_the_
       Enemy_Summary.pdf.

293   Wesley Yang, "Paper Tigers," *New York Magazine*, May 8, 2011,
       http://nymag.com/news/features/asian-americans-2011-5/.

294   Soo Kim Abboud and Jane Kim, "How Do Asian
       Students Get to the Top of the Class?" Great Schools,
       http://www.greatschools.org/parenting/teaching-values/
       481-parenting-students-to-the-top.gs.

295   Yang, "Paper Tigers"; Karen R. Humes, Nicholas A. Jones, and
       Roberto R. Ramirez, "Overview of Race and Hispanic Origin,"
       US Department of Commerce, March 2011, http://www.census.
       gov/prod/cen2010/briefs/c2010br-02.pdf.

296   "Table 74. Religious Composition of R.S. Population: 2007,"
       US Census, http://www.census.gov/compendia/statab/2009/
       tables/09s0074.pdf; "Hillel's Top 10 Jewish Schools," Hillel,
       February 16, 2006, http://www.hillel.org/about/news/2006/
       feb/20060216_top.htm.

297   John Rogers, "Moshe Kai Cavalin, 14-Year-Old Boy Genius,
       Writes Book Revealing Life in College at Age 8," *Huffington
       Post*, September 15, 2012, http://www.huffingtonpost.
       com/2012/02/15/boy-geniuss-book-reveals-_n_1278639.html.

298   Joseph Berger, "In East Harlem, 'Keep Out' Signs Apply to
       Renters," *New York Times*, October 30, 2011, http://www.nytimes.
       com/2011/10/31/nyrcgion/east-harlem-landlords-keep-apart-
       ments-sealed-up.html?pagewanted=all.

299   Caralee J. Adams, "Elementary Students Encouraged to
       Set College Goals," *Education Week*, December 7, 2010,
       http://www.edweek.org/ew/articles/2010/12/08/14colleges_
       ep.h30.html?tkn=YTZFEFJT1QMrFHPDHTXghp3gZmNE2E8So
       ciE&cmp=clp-edweek.

300   Since instituting the new collegiate approach, the 525-student

Los Pen has gone from being the lowest-performing school in the 33,000-student Poway Unified School District to one of the top schools in California and a recipient of the National Blue Ribbon School Award.

301   Franklin Crawford, "10th Anniversary of the Great Cornell Pumpkin Prank, and We Still Don't Know Whodunit," *Chronicle Online*, October 31, 2007, http://www.news.cornell.edu/stories/Oct07/pumpkin.anniversary.html.

302   Jenna Beck, "The Top Five College Science Pranks," Hypercube, November 20, 2007, http://www.bu.edu/phpbin/news-cms/news/?dept=1127&id=47783&template=228.

303   Complete College America, "Time Is the Enemy."

304   Yet we continue to cut prison educational programs. That's a shame because the research establishes that the more schooling an inmate gets behind bars—GED, even college education—the less likely he is to re-offend. This is true independent of employment; that is, even if the more educated offender fails to get a job upon release, the education itself seems to have a "normalizing" effect on him. Nevertheless, budget-strapped California reserved some of its deepest budget cuts for prison rehabilitation and education programs recently. Michael Rothfeld, "As Rehab Programs Are Cut, Prisons Do Less to Keep Inmates from Returning," *Los Angeles Times*, October 17, 2009, http://articles.latimes.com/2009/oct/17/local/me-rehab17.

305   "USA Must Halt Life without Parole Sentences for Children," Amnesty International, November 30, 2011, http://www.amnesty.org/en/news/usa-must-halt-life-without-parole-sentences-children-2011-11-30.

306   Christy Visher, Sara Debus, and Jennifer Yahner, "Employment after Prison: A Longitudinal Study of Releasees in Three States," Urban Institute, October 2008, http://www.urban.org/UploadedPDF/411778_employment_after_prison.pdf.

307   "Literacy Statistics," Begin to Read, http://www.begintoread.com/research/literacystatistics.html.

308   Steve Cohen, "A $5 Children's Book vs. a $47,000 Jail Cell—Choose One," *Forbes*, December 25, 2010, http://www.forbes.

com/sites/stevecohen/2010/12/25/a-5-childrens-book-vs-a-47000-jail-cell-choose-one/.

309   "National Endowment for the Arts Announces New Reading Study," National Endowment for the Arts, November 19, 2007, http://www.nea.gov/news/news07/TRNR.html.

310   John A. Sellers, "Scholastic Report: Kids Still Read for Fun—Teens, Less So," *Publishers Weekly,* June 11, 2008, http://www.publishersweekly.com/pw/by-topic/childrens/childrens-book-news/article/3251-scholastic-report-kids-still-read-for-fun–teens-less-so-.html.

311   Ibid.

312   More on this in my first book, *Think,* including a Recommended Reading list to make you smart.

313   "Quotes by Karl Kraus," All Poetry, http://allpoetry.com/quote/by/Karl%20Kraus.

314   Sellers, "Scholastic Report."

315   For tips on how to squeeze significantly more reading into your life, see my first book, *Think.*

316   "My Dad Is Number One Role Model (...but David Beckham Is a Good Substitute), Say Boys of Today," *Mail* Online, January 12, 2011, http://www.dailymail.co.uk/news/article-1346343/Dads-popular-David-Beckham-role-models-boys.html.

317   "Teens List Parents as Their Top Role Models," Junior Achievement, May 8, 2003, http://www.ja.org/about/releases/about_newsitem122.asp.

318   Tyre, *The Trouble with Boys.*

319   Sellers, "Scholastic Report."

320   "What Kindergarten Teacher Wish Parents Knew," *Parents,* http://www.scholastic.com/resources/article/what-kindergarten-teachers-wish-parents-knew.

321   Sellers, "Scholastic Report."

322   My brother, Peyton Bray, and I shared the same father, different mothers. Technically we are half-siblings, but I love him with my whole heart, so I never refer to him that way.

323   Alana Semuels, "Television Viewing at All-Time High," *Los Angeles Times,* February 24, 2009, http://articles.latimes.

com/2009/feb/24/business/fi-tvwatching24.

324   Amy Chozick, "Summer TV's Top Target: Boys," *Wall Street Journal*, July 13, 2011, http://online.wsj.com/article/SB1000142 405270230381210457644179059762646.html.

325   Janice D'Arcy, "Infants and Toddlers Spending Twice as Much Time with TV, DVDs as They Are with Books, New Report Says," *Washington Post*, October 25, 2011, http://www.washingtonpost.com/blogs/on-parenting/post/infants-and-toddlers-spending-twice-as-much-time-with-tv-and-dvds-as-they-are-with-books-new-report-says/2011/10/25/gIQAaRyYEM_blog.html.

326   Benedict Carey, "Parents Urged Again to Limit TV for Youngest," *New York Times*, October 18, 2011, http://www.nytimes.com/2011/10/19/health/19babies.html.

327   "Fast-Paced, Fantastical Television Shows May Compromise Learning, Behavior of Young Children" *ScienceDaily*, September 12, 2011, http://www.sciencedaily.com/releases/2011/09/110912075658.htm.

328   Lynn Herrmann, "Study: Too Much Media Dumbs Down Children," *Digital Journal*, May 4, 2010, http://digitaljournal.com/article/291548.

329   "Popular TV Shows Teach Children Fame Is Most Important Value, Psychologists Report; Being Kind to Others Fell Dramatically in Importance Over 10 Years," *ScienceDaily*, July 12, 2011, http://www.sciencedaily.com/releases/2011/07/110712094237.htm.

330   Ibid.

331   Ibid.

332   "Meaner than Fiction: Reality TV High on Aggression, Study Shows," *ScienceDaily*, May 21, 2010, http://www.sciencedaily.com/releases/2010/05/100521191235.htm.

333   "Parents Should Limit Young Children's Exposure to Background TV," *ScienceDaily*, July 15, 2008, http://www.sciencedaily.com/releases/2008/07/080715071452.htm.

334   "Turn Off TV to Teach Toddlers New Words," *ScienceDaily*, June 27, 2007, http://www.sciencedaily.com/releases/

2007/06/070627221722.htm.

335 "Children Under Three Can't Learn Action Words From TV—Unless an Adult Helps," *ScienceDaily*, September 15, 2009, http://www.sciencedaily.com/releases/2009/09/090915100947. htm.

336 "TV Food Advertising Increases Children's Preference for Unhealthy Foods, Study Finds," *ScienceDaily*, June 30, 2011, http://www.sciencedaily.com/releases/2011/06/110630112640.htm.

337 Chozick, "Summer TV's Top Target: Boys."

338 "TV Food Advertisements Increase Obese Children's Appetite by 134 Percent," *ScienceDaily*, April 24, 2007, http://www.sciencedaily.com/releases/2007/04/070424130951.htm.

339 "Too Much TV Linked to Future Fast-food Intake," *ScienceDaily*, January 29, 2009, http://www.sciencedaily.com/releases/2009/01/090129213436.htm.

340 National Endowment for the Arts, "To Read or Not to Read."

341 "Longest Time Spent Watching Sports TV—Jeff Miller Sets World Record," World Records Academy, January 8, 2010, http://www.worldrecordsacademy.org/society/longest_time_spent_watching_sports_TV_Jeff_Miller_sets_world_record_101493.htm.

342 "Table 1. Time Spent in Primary Activities (1) and Percent of the Civilian Population Engaging in Each Activity, Averages Per Day by Sex, 2010 Annual Averages," Bureau of Labor Statistics, June 22, 2011, http://www.bls.gov/news.release/atus.t01.htm.

343 Anna Salleh, "TV Shortens Life by 22 Minutes Per Hour," ABC News, August 16, 2011, http://www.abc.net.au/news/2011-08-16/television-shortens-lifespan/2841190.

344 Jenna Bryner, "TV Causes Learning Lag in Infants," Live Science, June 1, 2009, http://www.livescience.com/5480-tv-learning-lag-infants.html.

345 Eddie Makuch, "Time Spent Gaming on the Rise," Gamespot, May 27, 2010, http://www.gamespot.com/news/6264092/time-spent-gaming-on-the-rise-npd.

346 "Video Game Addiction," Wikipedia, http://en.wikipedia.org/wiki/Video_game_addiction (citing a Harris poll).

347 Steven Johnson, *Everything Bad is Good for You.*

348 Tyre, *The Trouble with Boys.*

349 Ibid.

350 Robert Weis and Brittany C. Cerankosky, "Effects of Video-Game Ownership on Young Boys' Academic and Behavioral Functioning," *Psychological Science* (February 18, 2010), http://pss.sagepub.com/content/early/2010/02/17/0956797610362670.abstract.

351 Center for Media Literacy, http://www.medialit.org/.

352 Anup Shah, "Media Conglomerates, Mergers, Concentration of Ownership," Global Issues, January 2, 2009, http://www.globalissues.org/article/159/media-conglomerates-mergers-concentration-of-ownership.

353 Ibid.

354 "Infographic: The Growing Product Placement Industry," Marketing Tech Blog, http://www.marketingtechblog.com/product-placement-infographic/.

355 Ibid.

356 Ibid.

357 Sreeraman, "M-Rated Violent Video Games Most Popular among Young Teens," Med India, July 3, 2007, http://www.medindia.net/news/Mrated-Violent-Video-Games-Most-Popular-Among-Young-Teens-22999-1.htm.

358 Tracy Clark-Flory, "Grand Theft Misogyny," *Salon*, May 3, 2008, http://www.salon.com/2008/05/03/gta_2/.

359 Sreeraman, "M-Rated Violent Video Games Most Popular among Young Teens."

360 Ron Clark, "What Teachers Really Want to Tell Parents," CNN Living, September 6, 2011, http://www.cnn.com/2011/09/06/living/teachers-want-to-tell-parents/index.html?iref=allsearch.

361 Raj Chetty, John N. Friedman, and Jonah E. Rockoff, "The Long-Term Impacts of Teachers: Teacher Value-Added and Student Outcomes in Adulthood," Executive Summary of National Bureau of Economic Research Working Paper no. 17699, December 2011, http://obs.rc.fas.harvard.edu/chetty/

va_exec_summ.pdf.

362   Valerie Strauss, "The Surprising Thing Teacher Want from
       Parents—Willingham," *Washington Post*, August 30, 2010, http://
       voices.washingtonpost.com/answer-sheet/daniel-willingham/
       how-can-parents-help-teachers.html.

363   Maria Papadopoulos, "Sexual Harassment Settlement for
       Brockton Boy Costs City $180K," *Enterprise News*, February 12,
       2010, http://www.enterprisenews.com/answerbook/brockton/
       x1328936162/Brockton-reaches-settlement-with-family-in-sexual-
       harassment-case; Juju Chang, "First-Grader Labeled a Sexual
       Harasser," ABC *Good Morning America*, April 4, 2008, http://
       abcnews.go.com/GMA/AsSeenOnGMA/story?id=4585388#.
       Tw44Y29ST5Y.

364   "School Says 9-Year-Old Sexually Harassed Teacher,"
       News- Record, December 6, 2011,
       http://www.news-record.com/ content/2011/12/06/
       article/school_says_9_year_old_sexually_harassed_teacher.

365   Devin Karambelas and Lauren Drasler,
       "Ralliers Respond to Fraternity Rape Survey,"
       Vermont Cynic, http://www.vermontcynic.com/mobile/news/
       ralliers-respond-to-fraternity-rape-survey-1.2682888.

366   Alex DiBranco, "Victory! Yale Disciplines DKE Frat for Pro-Rape
       Chant," Change.org, May 18, 2011, http://news.change.org/
       stories/victory-yale-disciplines-dke-frat-for-pro-rape-chant.

367   Ginka Toegel, "Disappointing Statistics, Positive Outlook,"
       Forbes, February 18, 2011, http://www.forbes.com/2011/02/18/
       women-business-management-forbes-woman-leadership-corpo-
       rate-boards.html.

368   Bruno Bettelheim, *A Good Enough Parent: A Book on Child-Rearing*
       (New York: Knopf, 1987), 98.

369   See Volunteers of American, http://www.voa.org/.

370   "Volunteering in the United States, 2010," Bureau of Labor
       Statistics, January 26, 2011, http://www.bls.gov/news.release/
       volun.nr0.htm.

371   Meghan Vivo, "The Human-Animal Bond," *To Your Health*, no. 2

(February 2008), http://www.toyourhealth.com/mpacms/tyh/article.php?id=999.

372   Matt Stevens, "Two Fourth-Graders Find a Way to Share School's Food," *Los Angeles Times*, December 27, 2011, http://www.latimes.com/news/local/la-me-school-food-drive-20111227,0,3420581.story.

373   Ibid.

374   "Blare's Bears for Haiti," Facebook, www.facebook.com/pages/Blares-Bears-for-Haiti.

375   Natalie Avon, "Why More Americans Don't Travel Abroad," CNN Travel, February 4, 2011, http://articles.cnn.com/2011-02-04/travel/americans.travel.domestically_1_western-hemisphere-travel-initiative-passports-tourism-industries?_s=PM:TRAVEL.

376   "Helen Keller Quotes," Brainy Quote, http://www.brainyquote.com/quotes/authors/h/helen_keller.html#ixzz1jg0UIJKE.

377   Colonial Williamsburg, www.history.org.

378   "Independence," National Park Service, http://www.nps.gov/inde/index.htm.

379   "Antietam," National Park Service, http://www.nps.gov/anti/index.htm.

380   Ellis Island, http://www.ellisisland.org/; Angel Island, http://www.aiisf.org/visit.

381   National Underground Railroad Freedom Center, http://www.freedomcenter.org/.

382   Rock & Roll Hall of Fame, http://rockhall.com/visit-the-museum/learn/.

383   "National Register of Historic Places," National Park Service, http://www.nps.gov/history/nr/.

384   Tenement Museum, http://www.tenement.org/.

385   Mary Batten, "The Psychology of Fatherhood," *Time*, June 7, 2007, http://www.time.com/time/magazine/article/0,9171,1630551,00.html.

386   "Table 9. Time Spent Caring for Household Children under 18 by Sex of Adult (1) and Age of Youngest Child by Day of Week, Average for the Combined Years 2006–10," Bureau of Labor Statistics, http://www.bls.gov/news.release/atus.t09.htm.

387 "Table 1. Time Spent in Primary Activities (1) and Percent of the Civilian Population Engaging in Each Activity, Averages Per Day by Sex, 2010 Annual Averages," Bureau of Labor Statistics.

388 Nsenga Burton, "72 Percent of African-American Children Born to Unwed Mothers," The Root, November 9, 2010, http://www.theroot.com/buzz/72-percent-african-american-children-born-unwed-mothers.

389 Matt Allen, "Study Shows Kids Need More Parenting Time with Their Divorced Dads," Dads Divorce, June 20, 2011, http://www.dadsdivorce.com/articles/study-shows-kids-need-more-parenting-time-with-their-divorced-dads.html (quoting Pew Research Center Analysis).

390 "Michael Chabon: On What 'Manhood' Means," NPR Books, June 25, 2010, http://www.npr.org/templates/story/story.php?storyId=128087770.

391 "Census Brief: Children with Single Parents—How They Fare," US Department of Commerce, September 1997, http://www.census.gov/prod/3/97pubs/cb-9701.pdf.

392 "Child Support Statistics and Trends," FindLaw, http://family.findlaw.com/child-support/support-basics/support-stats.html.

393 "Census Brief: Children with Single Parents—How They Fare," US Department of Commerce.

394 Paul R. Amato, "The Impact of Family Formation Change on the Cognitive, Social, and Emotional Well-Being of the Next Generation," *Future of Children* 15, no. 2 (Fall 2005), http://futureofchildren.org/publications/journals/article/index.xml?journalid=37&articleid=107&sectionid=692.

395 Ibid.

396 "Child Support Statistics and Trends," FindLaw.

397 Amato, "The Impact of Family Formation Change on the Cognitive, Social, and Emotional Well-Being of the Next Generation."

398 Ibid.

399 Ibid.

400 "The Prince's Trust Macquarie Youth Index," Macquarie Group Foundation, http://www.princes-trust.org.uk/pdf/

Youth_Index_jan2011.pdf.

401 "Our Impact on Juvenile Justice," Big Brothers Big Sisters,
     http://www.bbbs.org/site/c.9iILI3NGKhK6F/b.7721459/
     k.38AF/Our_impact_on_juvenile_justice.htm.

402 Ibid.

403 Ibid.